M000248930

VOYAGES TO
Windward

Revisions to Paperback Edition

Some of the changes on the coast since *Voyages to Windward* was published in 2005 have been noted in the text; others are listed below.

BARKLEY SOUND, BAMFIELD. The coaster *Lady Rose* has been retired. The coaster *Frances Barkley* now plies Barkley Sound on its own.

BARKLEY SOUND, MARBLE COVE. New float homes in this scenic cove restrict anchoring. To see the cove's sea life and interesting geology, tie up at the nearby Port Alberni Yacht Club outstation and take your dinghy over.

BARKLEY SOUND, UCLUELET. Although the bakery I described no longer exists, the Co-op Grocery now has its own bakery. With expansions and updates, the Co-op no longer reminds me of a 1950s grocery store.

CLAYOQUOT SOUND, ADVENTURE COVE. Float houses with multiple anchor lines and abandoned aquaculture frames on the beach at this historic cove make anchoring here and going ashore a challenge, but the historic site is still visible.

CLAYOQUOT SOUND, QUAIT BAY. The Clayoquot Wilderness Resort closed its floating hotel here in 2006. You can still hike the boardwalk to the lake; just check in with the caretaker. Around the corner from Quait Bay, Catherine King and Wayne Adams have expanded their floating complex. They enjoy meeting readers of *Voyages to Windward*.

ESPERANZA INLET, TAHSIS. I was too pessimistic about the future of Tahsis and the Westview Marina. The Marina thrives, its docks chock-a-block with sports fishing and cruising boats. The hardware and small grocery store in downtown Tahsis are still in business. The mall south of town, however, is almost empty.

ESPERANZA INLET, ZEBALLOS. The historic Zeballos Hotel, famous for the ghost of Sussie Woo, burned down in 2008. A new hotel, the Post and Beam Lodge, was built in its place. There's no word of what happened to the ghost.

KYUQUOT SOUND, CACHALOT. The mystery of who is the sculptor of the whale statue at this former whaling center is solved: it's Wayne Adams of Quait Bay.

KYUQUOT SOUND, WALTER'S COVE. Miss Charlie the seal died and the restaurant named for her closed. Coffee and wifi are available at the Kyuquot Inn in the former school house. On Thursday evening, the Inn serves dinner to tourists from the *Uchuck III*, and to boaters when there is space.

CHECLESET BAY, COLUMBIA COVE. Due to silting in the anchorage, this cove is no longer safe for riding out a southerly gale as we did in 2001.

Things that have stayed the same on the west coast of Vancouver Island: brisk sailing winds, spectacular scenery, deserted anchorages, intriguing history and friendly people. And the best way to get there is still by sailing to windward.

VOYAGES TO Windward

Sailing Adventures on Vancouver Island's West Coast

Elsie Hulsizer

H A R B O U R   P U B L I S H I N G

Copyright © 2005 Elsie Hulsizer
First print on demand edition 2015

All rights reserved. No part of this publication may be reproduced, stored in a retrieval system or transmitted, in any form or by any means, without prior permission of the publisher or, in the case of photocopying or other reprographic copying, a licence from Access Copyright, the Canadian Copyright Licensing Agency, 1 Yonge Street, Suite 1900, Toronto, Ontario M5E 1E5, www.accesscopyright.ca, 1-800-893-5777, info@accesscopyright.ca.

Harbour Publishing Co. Ltd.
P.O. Box 219, Madeira Park, BC V0N 2H0
www.harbourpublishing.com

Cover and page design by Martin Nichols
Back cover author photo by Ineke de Lange

Harbour Publishing acknowledges the support of the Canada Council for the Arts, which last year invested $157 million to bring the arts to Canadians throughout the country. We also gratefully acknowledge financial support from the Government of Canada through the Canada Book Fund and from the Province of British Columbia through the BC Arts Council and the Book Publishing Tax Credit.

Library and Archives Canada Cataloguing in Publication

Hulsizer, Elsie, 1946–

Voyages to windward : sailing adventures on Vancouver Island's west coast / Elsie Hulsizer.

Includes bibliographical references and index.
ISBN 978-1-55017-366-6 (cloth)
ISBN 978-1-55017-686-5 (print on demand)

1. Hulsizer, Elsie, 1946– —Travel—British Columbia—Vancouver Island. 2. Sailing—British Columbia—Vancouver Island. 3. Pacific Coast (B.C.)—Description and travel. I. Title.

GV815.H84 2005   910'.9164'33   C2005-903202-2

Acknowledgements

Numerous friends in both Seattle and on Vancouver Island helped me write this book. Thanks to my instructors and classmates at the Photographic Center Northwest. Claire Garoutte first gave me the idea for this book, then encouraged me each step of the way. Carla Fraga taught me to photograph in colour. Rebecca Brown and Richard Lewis showed me that I could be both a photographer and writer.

I would especially like to thank Roberta Cruger and my fellow writers in Roberta's Creative Alchemy writing program for their suggestions, support and inspiration as I progressed through the long process of becoming a writer.

Others who helped include Robert Hale, who gave me important, if painful, criticisms and Carol Hulsizer who helped me through the proposal stage.

The generosity of the residents of the west coast of Vancouver Island never ceased to amaze me. Thanks especially to Babe Gunn, Wayne Adams, Catherine King, Dianne Ignace, Else Klevjer, and the Devaults—Bob, Dan, Fyffe, Evan, and Janine—for sharing their lives and their knowledge of the west coast.

Finally, I want to thank my husband Steve Hulsizer, without whose sailing skills, mechanical abilities and determination to sail to windward, this book would not have been possible.

Table of Contents

Prologue

When I was seven years old, my parents moved us to a house on Three Tree Point on the shores of Puget Sound. I still remember my first day there—the glint of sunlight on the water and my first smell of seaweed on the beach. That afternoon I stood on the sand in my bathing suit facing a sturdy little girl with short blonde hair and the improbable name of "Pooh." Pooh handed me a bulky orange life jacket and said, "We have to wear these life jackets. It doesn't matter if you don't know how to swim. You'll just float. It's fun."

I looked at the bulky life jacket and then at the water where strands of pale green seaweed floated on the surface. When Pooh had come to my doorstep shortly after we arrived to invite me to go swimming, I had thought it sounded like fun. Now I wasn't so sure. I climbed into the orange life jacket and tied the canvas ribbons in front. Then I stepped gingerly into the water, my city-bred feet feeling every pebble and barnacle. Seaweed entwined itself around my ankles. While I stood back, Pooh ran in ahead of me, jumping in the water with a "whoop!"

Pooh was a year younger than I and I wasn't about to let a mere baby show me up. I waded into the water up to my armpits, gasping as the cold water crept into my swimsuit. I lost my footing and felt myself adrift. My arms flailed against the water and my feet frantically searched for the bottom. Then I realized I was floating—my feet were off the bottom but I was okay. I started to dog paddle as my father had taught me in the community pool. Pooh was right, it was fun.

In a few weeks I was running barefoot across the pebble beach, swimming without a life jacket, digging clams at low tide and fishing for rockfish and flounder from Pooh's rowboat. Several years later, my father built an 18-foot plywood sailboat and on summer weekends my parents would take the family sailing across the Sound. We visited the lighthouse on Maury Island, picked blackberries along the uninhabited beaches and searched for sand dollars on the tidal flats. Sometimes we'd take longer sails, and when we did my parents would always insist on starting our trips by sailing to windward. That way we'd have an easy ride home downwind.

I grew up believing that summers were for sailing and exploring the shore and that it was always better to go to windward first.

Introduction

Maamałni

In the summer we become *Maamałni,* "those whose houses float about on the water." The Nuu-chah-nulth, the First People of the west coast of Vancouver Island in British Columbia, coined this term for the first European explorers to arrive there by sailing ships. Nuu-chah-nulths still use *Maamałni* today to refer to white men. It's a fitting name for cruising sailors like us, for like those first Maamałni, our boat is our house. And although this coast is no longer uncharted and unknown, we still go as explorers to a foreign land.

My husband Steve and I made our first trip to the west coast of Vancouver Island in 1980. Just two years before, we had completed a year-long sailing voyage from Boston to Seattle in our Chesapeake 32 sloop, *Velella.* That trip had been a homecoming for me, a dream fulfilled for Steve and a taste of adventure for both of us. It started us looking for something more exciting than the standard Seattle sailing vacations to the San Juan Islands in Washington State.

Sailing friends recommended Barkley Sound on the west coast of Vancouver Island. The wind blows strong there every afternoon, they told us, and we would find real wilderness—old-growth forests, fallen totem poles in the forests and deserted anchorages. Although we had sailed by the west coast of Vancouver Island on our way to Seattle two years before, a fog bank had hidden the coast from view. And despite having grown up in Puget Sound, I had a vague idea that Vancouver Island ended somewhere just beyond the entrance to the Strait of Juan de Fuca. So, when we purchased a chart of Vancouver Island, I was surprised to see that the island stretches more than 200 miles from the

Sailing to windward. A freshening breeze calls for reefing the mainsail.

mouth of the Strait of Juan de Fuca in the south to Cape Scott in the north. About three-quarters of the way up the coast, the Brooks Peninsula sticks out into the Pacific Ocean, forming a natural barrier to northbound travel. The area between the Strait and Brooks Peninsula became our cruising ground. In that stretch of coast are four sounds, several major inlets, countless islands, bays and coves and stretches of unprotected coast. Barkley Sound is only the first of five major cruising areas. The others, which all rival it in beauty and adventure, are Clayoquot Sound, Nootka Sound, Esperanza Inlet, Kyuquot Sound and Checleset Bay.

There was just one problem: the winds would be against us. The prevailing summer winds blow from the northwest down the coast of Vancouver Island and into the Strait of Juan de Fuca. I dreaded sailing to windward. I knew it meant spray in my face, living at an angle, bracing myself to keep from falling downhill and cooking with pots sliding off the stove. But I also knew we could do it; our boat was capable and so were we. We could endure the lurches and bounces and salt-encrusted faces because we would be in good anchorages every night.

We survived that first trip and returned 17 times, all but once to windward. We made four trips in *Velella*, and 14 in our Annapolis 44 sloop, *Osprey*. Most sailors who go beyond Barkley Sound usually do so by circumnavigating Vancouver Island—motoring north up the east coast through the protected inside passage and sailing south with the prevailing northwest winds on the exposed west coast. But in a two- or three-week vacation, we didn't have time to circumnavigate; we had to sail to windward all the way—out the Strait of Juan de Fuca, into the Pacific Ocean and north up the coast. We discovered that in a two-week vacation we can get as far as Hot Springs Cove at the north end of Clayoquot Sound; it's actually closer to Seattle than Desolation Sound, a common cruising destination on the inside of Vancouver Island. In a three-week vacation we can easily get as far as Esperanza Inlet. If we push we can reach Checleset Bay, just south of the Brooks Peninsula.

To the people who ask why we don't circumnavigate Vancouver Island we say, "Why take all that time to go around when we can get to the best part sooner by sailing to windward?" On our trips to the west coast, we have found brisk sailing winds, spectacular scenery, quiet anchorages, intriguing history and interesting people. We like to spend as much time as possible there.

In the early days of our explorations, we intended our trips to be a refuge from urban life—from deadlines, pollution and change. The first chink in that notion came with our first view of a west coast clear-cut: roads slashed across brown hillsides; landslides choked salmon streams. Our notion of the region as wilderness changed. In researching Vancouver Island's history for this book, I learned that clear-cuts and declining salmon runs were part of a pattern. The history of the west coast of the Island is one of voyagers, not settlers. It's the history of the exploitation to near destruction of one resource after another: sea otters, seals, halibut, pilchards and now salmon and trees.

Will the pattern end with the forests and the salmon? A new culture is growing on the west coast of Vancouver Island—based around managing for abundance instead of harvesting for short-term profit. Changes like those add to the coast's interest for us and keep us going back.

This book is about voyaging to windward, about travelling the difficult route. It's about our summer voyages to the west coast of Vancouver Island and the voyagers who went before us. I like to think we can learn from them. The book is also the story of our discovery of the real Vancouver Island, not the wilderness we first imagined but a living, changing coast connected to the rest of the world. To discover that we had to sail to windward.

The Voyage Out

Here in the Strait of Juan de Fuca, geography and weather can conspire to create some of the roughest waters on the coast. These conditions drive many sailors into the protected waters of the inside passage. Secretly, I hoped for calms, but I knew that Steve hoped for wind. But we were willing to endure anything because the Strait was the shortest and most direct way to what we considered the best cruising ground on the coast.

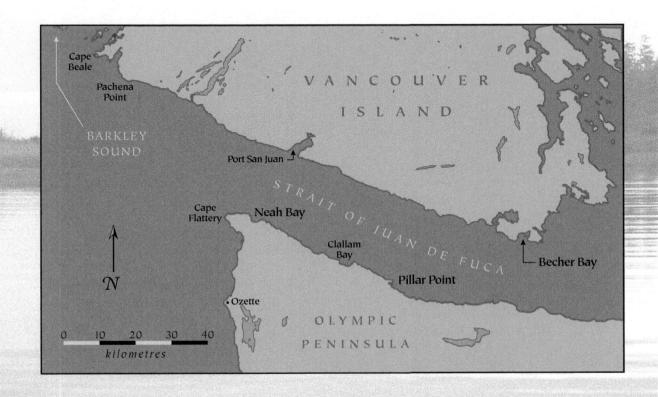

The Strait of Juan de Fuca

Taking the Risk

JUAN DE FUCA STRAIT …is liable to all those sudden vicissitudes of weather common to high northern latitudes; and in few parts of the world is the caution and vigilance of the navigator more called into action than in entering it.

—*Vancouver Island Pilot*, Great Britain Hydrographic Office, 1864

Morning sun bounced across the water, throwing the lighthouse and the windswept trees on Point Wilson, at the entrance to the Strait of Juan de Fuca, into relief. I could feel the tug of ocean swells on the boat as the confines of Puget Sound gave way to the broad open spaces of the Strait.

We had left our moorage in Seattle's Shilshole Bay Marina at 3:30 that morning to catch the ebb tide at its beginning. The water had been calm under a starlit sky and *Osprey* had made good time under power. Now the current was nearing its max, gathering speed and sweeping us north ever faster. I didn't know what awaited us beyond Point Wilson and that made me anxious. This was our fifth trip out the Strait, in 1987, and I knew we could expect just about any condition except having the wind with us. The calms might continue to give us an easy ride to our anchorage at Pillar Point or the westerlies could blow up to gales, bringing with them thick fog. Secretly, I hoped for calms, but I knew that Steve hoped for wind. He likes to sail.

We might face strong winds and fog later in our trip, of course, but here in the Strait, geography and weather can conspire to create some of the roughest waters on the coast. Mountains line both sides of the 120-mile Strait and funnel the wind east or west. In the right conditions during the summer the Pacific High offshore pushes strong westerlies through the Strait while low pressure inland from thermal heating pulls the westerlies ashore even faster, creating gale-force winds. And with ocean air can come fog.

West wind blowing against outgoing tides creates short, steep seas—guaranteed to toss a small sailboat about. But the alternative, leaving with an incoming tide, would be worse. A six-knot sailboat fighting a three-knot current and 25 knots or more of wind is a sure loser. These conditions drive many sailors into the protected waters of the inside passage. But we were willing to endure them because the Strait was the shortest and most direct way to what we considered the best cruising ground on the coast. And after all, this was what we had been preparing for during the last hectic weeks: the need to be ready for anything the sea threw at us.

Through the binoculars Steve scanned the water beyond the point. Far ahead dark water signalled a change.

"Wind. Let's get the sails up."

Changing the jib. A trip out the Strait of Juan de Fuca can produce just about any weather—except a following wind.

My hopes for an easy ride shattered, I went forward to raise the mainsail. By the time I had undone the ties and cranked the sail up the mast, the wind was sending it shaking. Waves broke around the boat every which way. The bow plunged into a trough, then rose on a crest, sending water rushing to the stern. Seconds later another wave lifted the stern and water rushed back to the bow. With the boat riding like a hobby horse and the deck looking like a washtub, I abandoned the idea of raising the jib. Instead, I crawled back to the cockpit, hanging on to handrail and lifelines to keep from being thrown overboard. We were in a tide rip.

For the next 15 minutes, Steve struggled with the wheel to keep us on course while I hung onto the dodger. The strong spring ebb swept us past Point Wilson, into the open Strait. There, the rip ended as abruptly as it had started. The waves eased, the wind diminished. We raised sail and headed northwest.

Not all entrances into the Strait are so traumatic, only those when strong outgoing tide meets strong incoming wind. Sometimes the entrance is easy and the rest of the trip is hard. One grey morning in 1991, we passed Point Wilson in a 15-knot breeze, riding easily through rips that were only beginning to build. Steve's sister Ann and her husband Bryan were with us for their first trip to the west coast of Vancouver Island. Steve was enjoying the opportunity to teach two novices the fine points of sailing.

"We're even going to get some sunshine," Steve said, pointing ahead at a patch of blue sky.

I watched the blue patch grow and race down the Strait toward us, pushing the clouds away as it came. It was moving much too fast to be an innocent sun break. *Osprey* heeled sharply in a rising wind. As the waves built, spray flew over the bow and we plunged into the short, steep waves. In the next hour, we reefed the main, changed the jib, then reefed the main again. Ann, whose only previous sailing experience had been on quiet little Menemsha Pond on Martha's Vineyard, volunteered to change the jib. In life jacket and harness she stood on the bow hanging onto the forestay while sheets of cold water poured over her.

But of all the conditions we have experienced in the Strait, the scariest is fog. And of all the times in fog the scariest was in 1992, when we were almost run over by a

Steering the boat in the Strait of Juan de Fuca.

tug. We entered a fog bank off Bush Point, a few miles south of Point Wilson. Four hours later we were still sailing in a cold damp world of white, listening anxiously for the warning blasts of ships' foghorns and peering sightless at the white wall ahead of us. Mist fogged my glasses. My eyes ached from the effort of peering into the fog. From *Osprey*'s spreaders our foghorn blasted a warning every two minutes.

Our loran gave us our position but not that of container ships, oil tankers, tugboats and fishboats. To learn where they were we listened to the VHF radio, tuned to the Vessel Traffic Service (VTS) on channel 5A. Near buoy "PA" off Port Angeles, we heard the long deep blast of the *Exxon New Orleans*. We knew its identity only because of the radio. The horns we did not hear worried us even more. We knew that the *Ocean Victor*, a tug with tow, was near us—but where? We listened anxiously but heard only the *Exxon New Orleans* moving away. Finally, Steve called VTS on our radio. As a small boat we weren't part of the Vessel Traffic System, but we could call and talk to the Coast Guard in Seattle who operate it.

The *Ocean Victor* was close to our position, the Coast Guard told us and advised us to call on 5A so they could hear our conversation. The *Ocean Victor* answered Steve's call promptly. "I see you on my radar," the skipper said. "You're 400 yards off my beam and heading for my tow. I hear your horn. I'll blow mine now."

A few seconds later we heard the sharp blast of a tug's horn just ahead of us, closer than any ship should be in fog. I scrambled for the jib sheets as Steve yelled, "helm's a lee!" *Osprey* swung through the wind and away from the tug and tow. What would have happened if we hadn't monitored VTS and known that the tug was near? Would the tugboat skipper have blown his foghorn without our call, or would he have watched on his radar as we collided with his barge or ran between the barge and its tow? Years later, the memory of that experience still terrifies me.

In 1994 we installed radar on *Osprey*. Now we can see ships and tugs in the fog on the radar screen. Still, we always keep our VHF radio tuned to the VTS channel when in the Strait.

Early explorers once hoped that the Strait of Juan de Fuca was the legendary Northwest Passage, or Strait of Anián, rumoured to run between the North Atlantic and the North Pacific. From the 15th century until the time of James Cook, finding the Northwest Passage was the chief ambition of many a seaman. Riches and a fast passage home awaited the man who found it.

The idea that the Strait of Anián might be near the latitude of what we now know as the Strait of Juan de Fuca surfaced in 1625 when an English clergyman, Samuel Purchas, published *Hakluytus Posthumus, or Purchas his Pilgrimes: contayning a history of the World, in Sea Voyages and Land Travells by Englishmen and Others*. Purchas told the story of an Englishman, Michael Lok, who had met a Greek named Juan de Fuca in Venice in 1596. Juan de Fuca, who was also called Apostolos Valerianos, claimed to have been a pilot for the Spaniards in the New World and to have been sent north in 1592 by the Viceroy of Mexico to discover the Strait of Anián. Between 47 and 48 degrees north

latitude he found a broad inlet marked at its entrance by "a great Hedland or Iland, with an exceedingly high Pinacle or spired rocke, like a piller thereoupon." He followed this inlet inland for 20 days and came out into the North Sea.

Although numerous historians have searched in Spain and Mexico for evidence that Juan de Fuca actually sailed for the Spanish, no official trace of his voyage has ever been found. Here in the northwest, a gaggle of professional and amateur historians have squared off on whether or not Fuca discovered the Strait or even existed. Edmond Meany, in his 1907 edited version of Captain George Vancouver's journal concluded the story was a sham. Twenty-six years later Henry Raup Wagner came to the same conclusion. The latitude, he noted, was not correct.

On the other side, J.T. Walbran, writing in 1909, cited the spired rock near Cape Flattery, called De Fuca's pillar, as proof Fuca had seen the Strait. More recently, in 1991, Don Marshall methodically countered every argument of the anti-Fucans. Marshall argued that one degree of latitude error was minor for the age in which Fuca sailed, that the records of Fuca's voyage could have been lost and that Fuca could have mistaken Queen Charlotte Sound for the North Sea. He cited scientific opinion that between 1400 and 1800 AD the North Pacific experienced a mini-ice age. Fuca could have seen ice floes and assumed he was in the North Sea. Because he turned around and went back the way he came, he would never have known his mistake.

When I read of Juan de Fuca telling his story to Lok and Lok in turn telling the story to Purchas, I remembered the game I played as a Campfire Girl, called "gossip." A group of girls would sit in a circle close together. One girl would whisper a story to the girl on her left. That girl would then whisper the story to the girl on *her* left, and so on around the circle. When the story reached its originator, she invariably burst into laughter—her story had changed so much.

I can imagine the details of Juan de Fuca's story changing with each telling—the strait widened, the journey lengthened, the temperature dropped, the latitude changed.

Fog may explain why some of the early explorers missed the Strait of Juan de Fuca. The first to miss it was the Spanish pilot Juan Perez in the *Santiago* in 1774. Sailing from

A fog bank in the Strait of Juan de Fuca. Fog may explain why some of the early explorers did not see the Strait of Juan de Fuca.

Estevan Point toward California, Perez sighted two land masses to the east but failed to recognize the Strait. Four years later, Captain James Cook passed close enough to describe and name Cape Flattery without seeing any hint of the Strait. In his journal he referred to the Strait as the "pretended Strait of Juan de Fuca," and said of it, "nor is there the least probability that ever such thing existed."

The first *documented* sighting of the Strait of Juan de Fuca was by the fur trader Captain Charles Barkley of England in the *Imperial Eagle* in 1787. Barkley's wife, Frances, who accompanied him, wrote in her diary:

> ...to the great astonishment of Capt. Barkley and his officers, a large opening presented itself, extending miles to the eastward with no land in sight in that direction.
>
> The entrance appeared to be about four leagues in width, and remained about that width as far as the eye could see. Capt. Barkley at once recognized it as the long lost strait of Juan de Fuca, which Captain Cook had so emphatically stated did not exist.

The *Imperial Eagle* did not enter the Strait—Captain Barkley was a fur trader not an explorer. The honour of being the first European to enter the Strait fell to the Spaniard Manuel Quimper in the *Princesa Real* in 1790. Only 43 feet long on the keel the *Princesa Real* was 16 feet on the beam and carried a crew of 40. Of her sailing ability, Quimper wrote that she "made no headway to windward."

The *Princesa Real* entered the Strait heading east on June 10. After stopping at Sooke Bay and Royal Roads to erect wooden crosses and claim the land for their King, the ship reached its easternmost anchorage off Dungeness Spit on July 8. Natives wearing English, Portuguese and Chinese coins for earrings came out to greet them. The *Princesa Real* left Dungeness heading west on July 17. When the wind was favourable, they sailed. When the wind was calm, they towed the ship with the longboat. When winds or current were contrary, they anchored. It took the *Princesa* seven days to reach Neah Bay, a distance of only 60 miles.

One of the *Princesa*'s anchorages, Pillar Point, 26 miles east of Port Angeles on the American side, is our favourite anchorage when going out the Strait. Anchorages are scarce in the Strait of Juan de Fuca; we tried almost all of them before settling on Pillar Point as our favourite. On our first trip, we went first to Victoria to clear customs, then to Port San Juan (on the Vancouver Island side). Victoria was fun but going there added a day to our trip. And at Port San Juan, ocean swells kept us awake most of the night. On our second trip, 1981, we stopped at Port Angeles the first night, Neah Bay the second, checking into Canadian customs at Ucluelet on the third day. That route cut a day off the outbound trip and gave us two good nights' sleep, but put us into Port Angeles by early afternoon. An afternoon in a port so close to home didn't make sense. In 1983, on our third trip, we took friends as crew and sailed straight through to Ucluelet, dispensing with anchoring all together. That trip convinced us we needed to find a way to shorten our trip without having to sail all night.

We first heard of Pillar Point as an anchorage in 1978. We were on the last leg of our trip from Boston to Seattle via Hawaii and had stopped in Neah Bay on our way into Puget Sound. Eight hundred miles out of Hawaii the flexible rubber coupling that joined *Velella*'s engine to the propeller shaft broke, turning our engine into nothing more than a giant battery charger. We had read in the *US Coast Pilot* that in the days before auxiliary engines sailing vessels often took a week or more to sail the Strait so we weren't looking forward to the remaining sail to Seattle.

While we were waiting for the wind to come up, we met a Canadian couple in a steel boat named *Pinocchio*. We noticed the boat because it was painted red with a cartoon Pinocchio on its stern. The owners told us they were heading for Mexico. They were sitting in Neah Bay waiting for a north wind and suffering from bad colds—and from cold feet over their first ocean sail. They wanted to hear about our trip, which was ending as theirs was beginning, so they invited us aboard.

We told our hosts about our concerns about sailing in the Strait without an engine. They got out the chart of the Strait of Juan de Fuca and pointed to Clallam Bay, Pillar Point, Port Angeles and Dungeness Spit.

"There are anchorages on the US side. They aren't great but you can use them."

We didn't stop at Pillar Point that year, choosing Clallam Bay instead. Pillar Point is completely open to the east and we assumed it was an emergency anchorage only. What we didn't realize is that although Pillar Point is an open roadstead, it's actually more protected than Clallam Bay. The curve of the land forms a hook that stops the swells coming in from the ocean and massive rock pillars climb straight up at the water's edge to block the wind.

By 1984, on our fourth trip to the west coast of Vancouver Island, we had spent enough time in the Strait, and had listened to enough weather

A sandstone pillar marks the entrance to the anchorage behind Pillar Point.

forecasts for the area, to know that the chance of an east wind in the Strait in the summer is just about nil. So when we motored for a whole day out the Strait in a flat calm and heard on the weather radio that only light westerlies were expected that night, we decided it was a good year to try Pillar Point. We approached the anchorage carefully, keeping a close watch on the depth sounder. A tidal flat extends out from the mouth of the Pysht River and kelp beds line the shore to the east, leaving only a narrow band for anchoring. We finally chose an anchorage off the mouth of the river. From there we could look up the Pysht River to the valley beyond and across to the sandstone pillars, standing like ramparts guarding the anchorage. The scenery awed us.

We returned a year later, when the westerlies howling down the Strait were kicking up a steep sea. We beat to windward all day, tacking back and forth across the Strait and slamming into the waves. Then the tide turned, setting current as well as wind against us. I was nervous about approaching Pillar Point in those seas, but I didn't want to stay out in the Strait either. We sailed in, ready to turn fast and make a quick retreat. But when we rounded the point, the wind slackened and the swells diminished. When I awoke the next morning after a good sleep, I knew we were onto a good thing.

Since then we have anchored there seven times. We have learned that the best spot to anchor is tucked in close to the pillars away from the river, in 20 to 25 feet of water. A gentle swell comes into the anchorage and when the wind dies the boat rolls to the swells. We talk about putting out a stern anchor but never have; we know the swells will

Dungeness Spit with Olympic Mountains in background. Mountains line both sides of the 120-mile Strait and funnel the wind east or west.

die at night. Eagles and ospreys nest among the trees on the pillars and dive for fish at our bow. At sunset, the pillars stand out against a pink sky. Pillar Point is so rugged and wild and the pillars so spectacular that when we anchor there I feel as if our adventure has already started, even if we are still in our home state.

Several summers after seeing *Pinocchio* in Neah Bay, we were surprised to see the boat tied up in front of the Empress Hotel in Victoria. We were even more surprised when the owners told us, "After you left we cruised slowly home, bought a camper and became land cruisers." I could understand being afraid to go cruising, but I couldn't understand not going anyway—not taking the risk. For that was how I felt about anchoring at Pillar Point.

Neah Bay

Wimps Go up the Inside

Three long canoes pulled away from the shore and headed toward us, propelled by a blur of flailing arms and paddles. In seconds the canoes passed so close we could see muscles bulging and hear voices chanting.

We had come to Neah Bay in 2001 to see the annual Makah Days canoe races, but we hadn't expected to be in the middle of the racecourse. That morning we had watched the race committee set out buoys near our boat. We had expected them to ask us to leave, but they had barely glanced our way. Our boat and several others anchored nearby were just part of the racecourse—obstacles with front-row seats. For the next several hours we watched as canoes from all over the Northwest raced by, bearing names like *Rainbow*, *Sweet Daddy* and *Autumn Song*. With a stamina that could only come from hours of practice, the paddlers fairly flew around the bay.

Few cruising sailors would consider Neah Bay a desirable cruising destination. Most view it as only a stopover on the way to Barkley Sound or Mexico, a port to spend as little time in as possible. Until earlier that year, I would have agreed. But here we were on our second visit of the year.

As a high school and college student I had passed through Neah Bay on my way to Makah Bay on the Washington coast to explore tide pools and collect sea creatures.

Native paddlers from British Columbia and Washington State compete in canoe races during Makah Days at Neah Bay.

Morning fog swirls around Seal Rock outside Neah Bay.

I remember dilapidated houses, unpaved streets and a general air of despondency. The small town depressed me so much that if I ever needed to stop myself from laughing at an inappropriate time, I would think of it. The few times Steve and I had anchored here on our way north, the view of crumbling piers and clear-cut hills had discouraged us from going ashore.

Then, in 1999 the Makah Tribe became famous for killing a whale. While reading about that event in *A Whale Hunt* by Robert Sullivan, I realized that the Makah and their neighbours—not Captain Cook, not George Vancouver, not even Juan de Fuca—were the Northwest's first voyagers to windward.

Sullivan's book inspired me to read more about the Makah. I learned that they share a common language and common culture with the Nuu-chah-nulth, the people of the west coast of Vancouver Island—also called the Nootka or West Coast People. I took a more careful look at a map of the territory of the Nuu-chah-nulth and suddenly felt a kinship with both the Makah and Nuu-chah-nulth. Their territory almost exactly matches our cruising territory—from the mouth of the Strait of Juan de Fuca to the Brooks Peninsula, three-quarters of the way up the west coast of Vancouver Island.

More than 24 bands of the Nuu-chah-nulth nation once lived in this area. Their names read like entries in our logbook: Ucluelet, Clayoquot, Ahousaht, Hesquiat, Nuchatlaht, Kyuquot, Checleset, and more.

The Makah often crossed the Strait of Juan de Fuca and journeyed north up the coast of Vancouver Island to attend weddings and potlatches. In trade, the Makah were intermediaries between the Chinook tribes to the south and their Nuu-chah-nulth relatives to the north, trading canoes, sea otter skins and dried halibut up and down the coast. Wearing conical hats to shield their faces from wind and sun and chanting special paddling songs, they travelled in ocean-going canoes 35 feet or more in length.

Our first visit earlier that summer had been to see the Makah Cultural and Research Center. I had wanted to see the canoes they had used for these long ocean trips. To get to the museum we had anchored near the centre of the town and dinghied ashore, tying up to a clean concrete float at the new Makah Marina. Two black canoes with reddish interiors were tied up alongside the main dock and we stopped to look at them, wondering if these were the ocean-going canoes we had come to see.

As we left the dock, we walked past gleaming office and restroom buildings. On our right as we walked east out of town we passed a new grocery store surrounded by a giant parking lot. Beyond the store we saw a sign advertising Native carvings and took a side trip into a neighbourhood of recently built houses. We found the store a few blocks inland in one of the houses. Carved masks and brightly coloured prints lined the walls. A display case with a collection of abalone-shell necklaces caught my eye. As we left with our purchases—a necklace and T-shirt—I thought that this wasn't exactly the dilapidated village I remembered.

The museum is in a modern wooden building in a grassy field just outside of town. Most of its artifacts came from an archeological dig at Ozette, south of Neah Bay, where several hundred years ago a mudslide destroyed a Makah village, preserving houses and everything in them under tons of grey ooze. The unearthing of artifacts from Ozette— baskets, tools, clothing and artwork—gave the Makah a new pride in their heritage and a new interest in traditional crafts like canoe making. The exhibit, only a small portion of the artifacts collected from that site, is an impressive collection, thoughtfully arranged. We spent most of the afternoon touring it.

The canoes were on the floor in the centre of the museum. There were small one-person and two-person canoes used for clamming and fishing and larger canoes, labelled as sealing and whaling canoes. (There were none labelled "racing canoes," which are longer than the clamming and fishing canoes with less freeboard than the sealing and whaling canoes.) The sealing and whaling canoes looked new with freshly painted black hulls and reddish interiors, very much like the two we had seen at the marina. Their pointed bows reared above the floor, ending in what looked like a dog's head with prominent ears. There were no signs saying, "don't touch" so I ran my hand over their smoothly chiselled hulls. I could just barely feel the seam where the bow joined the hull.

The Makah Cultural and Research Center is the main landside attraction for boats visiting Neah Bay.

A rock breakwater protects the newly constructed Makah Marina.

Canoes were so central to the life of the Makah and the Nuu-chah-nulth and the process of making them so arduous that the canoes' owners sometimes kept them in their houses as heirlooms. To cut down a cedar tree for a canoe the Makah would surround it with slaves, each chipping away like beavers with stone hatchets and mussel shells. Once the tree fell, carvers would rough out the ends and dig a portion of the inside out with adzes. Next they would turn the canoe over and shape the bottom, finally turning it back to finish the inside. Sometimes it would take carvers months to complete a canoe, chipping away piece by piece, the adzes thumping on the hollow tree as on a drum, the sound deepening as the cedar thinned.

The anthropologist Philip Drucker noted that the graceful and practical lines of the Nootka canoe made it one of the finest sea-going vessels made by primitive people. Some maritime historians believe that the flowing curves from forefoot to prow and the bold sheer of the Nootka canoe bow inspired the American clipper ships whose bow lines were nearly identical. The Makah canoes had sterns slightly taller than those of the Nuu-chah-nulth canoes, which were more appropriate for ocean-going canoes.

Shortly after seeing their first European ships, the Makah and Nuu-chah-nulth added cedar-bark sails to their canoes. Early missionaries who relied on the canoes and their owners for transportation told of glorious rides in these sailing canoes, sails and paddles propelling them up and down mountainous seas in races reminiscent of yachting.

When they paddled, the canoeists got down on their knees, sat back on their heels, and grasped the paddle with both hands—one hand on top of the paddle and the other in the middle. At each stroke the hand on the top of the paddle pushed forward while the hand on the middle pulled the blade backward through the water in a double-action movement. In this way canoeists could easily go 40 miles in a day.

None of the canoes in the museum claimed to be ocean voyagers, so I went over to the front desk to ask a young woman with pale skin, light brown hair and the round face of a Makah if the museum had any such canoes. She explained that the whaling and sealing canoes were the same as ocean-voyaging canoes. The Makah just equipped them differently. The canoes in the museum, she assured us, were not just replicas; Makah had made them with tools and techniques passed down through generations.

I asked her if the Makah had any stories about crossing the Strait and going up the coast in the ocean. She looked indignant. "They were just going to visit relatives, why would they have stories? Do you have stories about visiting your grandmother on Thanksgiving?" I didn't say so, but I thought that if I had to travel to my grandmother in an open canoe across the ocean, I probably would have stories.

I asked her about the trip tribal members took to Bella Bella for a gathering of tribes in 1993. Her eyes lit up. "We went up the outside," she said, making a motion with her hand to show the canoes going up the coast of Vancouver Island. "Those other tribes were wimps. They went up the inside."

Robert Sullivan described that voyage. The Coast Guard had wanted the Makah to take the inside route with the other tribes, but the Makah insisted on their traditional route. In their canoe, the *Hummingbird*, the Makah travelled 340 miles upwind through rough seas to Bella Bella, north of Vancouver Island. Along the way they stopped at the villages of the Nuu-chah-nulth where their hosts carried *Hummingbird* up the beach on their shoulders and celebrated the arrival of the Makah with food and dance. Tribal members who took the voyage describe it as a turning point for the tribe in their struggle to reclaim pride in their heritage.

We left the museum and walked back to town along the bay. A fog bank was creeping into the Strait from the ocean and a foghorn sounded its insistent and mournful warning. I thought about being in a canoe out in the Strait in the fog with only the direction of the ripples on the water to steer by and felt a new appreciation for the Makah. We thought we were adventurous by sailing up the coast to windward instead of taking the easier route up the inside and back down the outside. But with our radar, compass, Global Positioning System and auxiliary engine, we were the wimps compared to the Makah.

The early Makah did have one advantage for ocean travel that no modern gear can provide: time. They took the time to read the weather, judging it by the sounds the waves make on the shore or by the patterns of clouds on the mountains. With no boss back home to count the days, they waited for the right conditions of weather and currents before venturing to sea. I wish we could do the same. Tomorrow we would head north.

Crossing To Barkley Sound

Courage by Example

In 1997, as we left the Strait of Juan de Fuca for the open Pacific, we could see the horizon far ahead to the west—a sharp thin line where grey skies met greyer seas. Across the grey seas three container ships marched in formation, giants turned into bathtub boats on the big ocean. To the north the dark mountains of Vancouver Island hovered above grey clouds. I looked behind to see the cutter *Caprice*, with our friends Karen and Charlie and their two children aboard, wallowing in the swells. The sight of the boat's mast describing a wide arc in the sky brought home our own boat's motion and I held on to the dodger for support.

I've always felt nervous approaching the open ocean from the Strait and that day the dark skies and rough seas increased my anxiety. The crossing to Barkley Sound is never fun; it's something to be endured to get to the Sound's quiet coves and scenic islands. The seas are always sloppy, the wind fluky, the visibility reduced in fog and mist. The passage's only saving grace is its short distance—only 38 miles from Cape Flattery at the mouth of the Strait of Juan de Fuca to Cape Beale at the entrance to Barkley Sound. I know that no matter how bad the crossing, we'll be in Bamfield by nightfall. This crossing highlights the difference between my attitude and Steve's toward sailing: he hopes for wind; I hope for calm and a quick passage.

A crossing to Barkley Sound from Neah Bay or a trip out the Strait from Victoria is the first experience in ocean sailing for many boats from Puget Sound or British Columbia.

History would say my anxiety was well founded. The Washington coast and the west coast of Vancouver Island were once known as the Graveyard of the Pacific. More than 40 ships came to grief on the 40 miles between Port San Juan and Barkley Sound on Vancouver Island's southwest coast—one shipwreck for every mile. A few examples: the American barque *Ocean Bird*, left Puget Sound March 19, 1864, with a load of lumber and capsized off Cape Flattery in a ferocious storm; the Schooner *Eliza*, last reported off Cape Flattery on January 25, 1864, was found upside down off Port San Juan in March; the schooner *Elsie*, of special interest to me because I share her name, wrecked at the entrance to Ucluelet Harbour in 1870. And then there is the West Coast's *Titanic*: the American steamer *Valencia*, which ran aground at Pachena Point in January 1906. Her demise caused an international scandal and put the Canadian government's indifference to safety on trial. One hundred seventeen of the 154 passengers and crew died only 30 yards from shore—in full view of rescuers helpless to save them in the fierce surf.

Such is the history of the coast we were approaching. As we entered the open water, the wind increased. The seas, freed from the constraints of the land, came at us from several directions at once, jerking the boat every which way. Karen's voice came across the radio. Their daughter, Kari, was seasick; they were turning back. They would wait for better weather before crossing. I watched their boat grow smaller in the distance and felt alone. Were we making a mistake to continue?

Steve's thoughts had been going in the opposite direction. "At last, we've got some wind," he told me, exulting at the same waves that worried me. "We'll finally get to sail to Barkley Sound." In all of our previous crossings we had not yet had enough wind to sail all the way.

Under full main and 120 jib, *Osprey* was rail down and pounding into the seas. I huddled in the upwind corner of the cockpit, clinging to the dodger's steel frame and bracing my feet against the cabin door. Steve, his orange slicker shiny from spray, clung to the wheel, while *Osprey* lurched through the waves.

In some years the wind is so light we have to motor all the way from the Strait of Juan de Fuca to Barkley Sound.

Waves reared up in front of us, monsters out of proportion to the wind that caused them. Suddenly Steve yelled, "Look out!" I ducked even further under the dodger as a massive wave crashed over the bow, swept across the dodger and poured into the cockpit. The boat shuddered, slowed and pushed ahead. The next wave picked the boat up, giving us a brief view of a field of mountainous seas before dropping us with a crash into the trough of the following wave. The *Osprey,* all 11 tons of her—a boat that seemed so solid in Puget Sound—was bouncing on the waves like a cork. The outgoing tide racing to meet incoming westerly winds forced the waves higher and steeper as they met shallower water. Wind, current and swells were conspiring against our small boat.

My friend Ruth once told me how she gave herself courage in bad weather when she and her partner Lawrence crossed to Hawaii in their 35-foot ketch, *Calypso*. She would say to herself, "Dolores did it, Elsie did it, Randy did it, I can do it"—reciting the names of all the women she knew who had sailed to or from Hawaii.

On these short crossings I give myself courage by thinking of other crossings that I survived and telling myself it will soon be over. But if I want to think of other women who have sailed this coast, I think of Frances Barkley, wife of Captain Charles Barkley and the first white woman to sail to the northwest coast.

Beth Hill tells Frances's story in *The Remarkable World of Frances Barkley: 1769–1845*. Frances Hornby Trevor Barkley was a 17-year-old bride in 1786 when she set out on the first of two voyages to the northwest coast, voyages that took her twice around the world.

The Barkleys' adventure began in Ostend, Belgium where Frances and Charles met and married and where Captain Barkley outfitted the British ship *Loudon*. British law required British ships to pay expensive licence fees to the British East India Company and the South Seas Company in order to trade in China and the Northwest. By outfitting the ship out of the country, giving her an Austrian flag and renaming her the *Imperial Eagle,* the owners hoped to avoid the licence fees.

The *Imperial Eagle* left Ostend on November 24, 1786. On December 10, Frances experienced her first storm at sea. The ship hove to in "strong gales and heavy squalls" while massive waves swept chickens and geese off the deck. After a long passage and a stop in Brazil, they rounded Cape Horn in March in snow and sleet, and arrived in Nootka Sound in June 1787. Frances wrote in her diary that, "the day previously to making the land a dreadful storm from the southeast having been encountered."

In Nootka Sound Captain Barkley and his men did a brisk trade with the Natives for sea otter furs. The *Imperial Eagle* next sailed south, to Clayoquot Sound, where Captain Barkley traded for still more furs and then to Barkley Sound, which he named after himself. Continuing south the *Imperial Eagle* passed the mouth of the Strait of Juan de Fuca and Captain Barkley became the first European explorer to document the Strait's existence.

Barkley's trade on the northwest coast brought the ship's owners $30,000 at market in Macao. From Macao the *Imperial Eagle* sailed to Mauritius where Frances gave birth to her first child and Captain Barkley lost his command. News of the $30,000 profit had caught the attention of officials of the East India Company. To avoid trouble the owners of the *Imperial Eagle* sold the ship and broke their contract with Captain Barkley. Stranded without a ship, Charles and Frances took passage west to England around the Cape of Good Hope, completing Frances's first circumnavigation.

Frances's adventures weren't over. In England Charles took command of the ship *Princess Frederica* and, with Frances and son William aboard, returned to Calcutta where Charles had been born. On this trip, Frances gave birth to a daughter while rounding Cape Horn in a gale.

Frances never recorded her feelings about either the sea or her adventures. But the reminiscences she wrote late in life give one clue. In Calcutta Charles's brother convinced him to leave the lucrative country trade he had planned to establish in order to command the brig *Halcyon*. Frances insisted on going with him along with their two children. She wrote, "I made up my mind to brave every danger rather than separate, thereby at any rate securing his peace of Mind, as well as my own."

She was to need all the determination and courage she could muster. In the Sooloo Islands their daughter Patty died of a violent colic; in Kamchatka the Russian bureaucracy hindered their trade; off Cape Edgecumbe, Alaska, the ship encountered seas so immense that Charles noted in his log the night had been "awful beyond description." War broke out between England and France and in Mauritius French officials seized *Halcyon* and took Charles and Frances as prisoners of war. When they were finally released without their ship, they took passage to the United States. There, Charles used the last of his capital to buy a ship and a cargo of cotton, only to lose both on arrival in England— stolen by *Amphion*'s American sailing master.

Osprey tied next to the steamer the *Frances Barkley* at the Bamfield Public Dock. Boats coming from US waters must now go to Ucluelet to check in.

Despite these tragedies Frances remained a lively, if sometimes sharply critical, observer of the places and people she saw. In Kamchatka she noted that the water was so transparent that the shadows of the surrounding objects, particularly of the volcano in the distance, had a very imposing effect. In Alaska, where she was the first white woman to visit, she commented on the Native women and their labrets, the wooden disks they wore in their mouths, saying, "How any rational creature could invent such an inconvenient machine, I am at a loss to guess."

Few who have not travelled to Barkley Sound know of Frances and Charles Barkley. John Meares, one of the ship's owners, who acquired Barkley's charts and log from the *Imperial Eagle*, got much of the credit for Barkley's discoveries.

I didn't need to find courage by thinking of Frances Barkley for long. An hour after we left the Strait, the wind died. Wind and seas had been only a temporary phenomenon caused by a tide rip. Now the boat rolled in sloppy seas. I went forward to drop the jib, hanging onto handrails and shrouds to stay on the heaving deck. For the next four hours the engine beat a steady thrum.

A close reading of the record of shipwrecks shows most of them happened in the winter when strong winds blow from the southwest or southeast and the Davidson Current sweeps up the coast toward Vancouver Island. Weather statistics show that 53 percent of the time in July the wind in the open ocean off the west coast of Vancouver Island is less than 10 knots. Only six percent of the time does the wind blow more than 20 knots. When it does blow, it blows almost exclusively from the northwest. The difficulty in the summer is more the struggle to get to the west coast against adverse winds or calms than in being shipwrecked on it. Our logbook bears this out. We have never been able to make a whole crossing under sail. The passage I have described was one of the worst we have ever made.

The westerlies came in the afternoon, clearing the skies and sending gusts across the blue water. We raised sail again and beat north, passing the Pachena lighthouse, which was built in response to the wreck of the *Valencia*. With its white buildings and red roofs, the lighthouse looked cheerful against green forest and blue sky. And it helps make our crossing safer.

In the distance we could see the formidable bulk of Cape Beale guarding the entrance to Barkley Sound. Captain Barkley named this cape for John Beale, the *Imperial Eagle*'s purser. John Meares, who had Barkley's log, conveniently renamed it for Daniel Beale, his business associate. We tacked toward it, staying well offshore to avoid the surrounding rocks. The seas can be so rough here, and the rocks so low and treacherous that a boat can come up on the rocks without warning. To make sure we stay far enough offshore, Steve had entered a waypoint in our GPS to tell us when to turn. As we approached the Cape, I went below to watch on the GPS. I could see the numbers go down—0.3 miles, 0.2. 0.1, then finally through zero and up again. We were past. I yelled up to Steve, "Okay! We're past! We can turn."

As we rounded Cape Beale, the wind came behind us, pushing us into Trevor Channel, named for Frances Hornby Trevor Barkley. In the distance beyond the islands we could see the open waters of Imperial Eagle Channel and beyond, Loudoun Channel.

Barkley Sound spread out before us with its forested archipelagos, its rocky shores and its sparkling blue water. The farther in the Sound we sailed, the quieter the water became and the warmer the air. Off came our foul-weather gear, then our sweaters. I sat on the coach roof watching the rocky cliffs slide by and enjoying the sun on my face. When Bamfield Inlet opened up to our starboard, we drifted in on the last of the wind and dropped our sails off the public dock. In front of us was the coastal steamer *Frances Barkley* unloading passengers.

I looked around at the red and white Coast Guard Station, at the pleasant town with its old houses and its boardwalk and at the eagles soaring over the inlet, and thought, "It was worth sailing to windward to get here."

Barkley Sound

Barkley Sound spread out before us with its forested archipelagos, its rocky shores and its sparkling blue water. The farther in the Sound we sailed, the quieter the water became and the warmer the air. Off came our foul-weather gear, then our sweaters. The afternoon wind pushed us up the inlet towards real wilderness—old-growth forests, fallen totem poles and deserted anchorages.

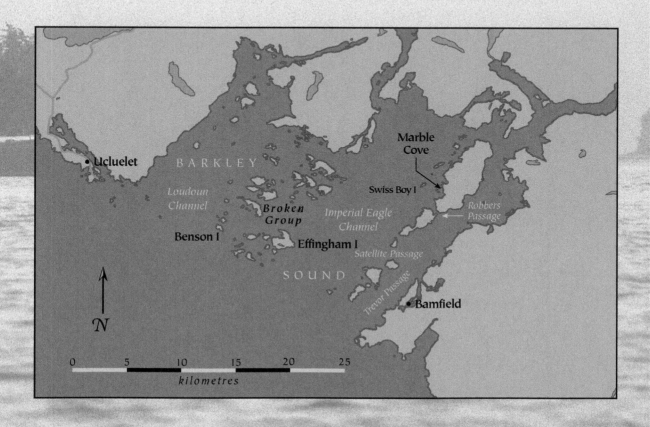

BARKLEY

SOUND

• Ucluelet

Loudoun
Channel

Broken
Group

Benson I

Effingham I

Marble
Cove

Swiss Boy I

Imperial Eagle
Channel

Robbers
Passage

Satellite Passage

Trevor Passage

• Bamfield

N

0   5   10   15   20   25

kilometres

Bamfield

Carving Like Crazy

We stood on the boardwalk in West Bamfield and peered through knotholes in the locked door of the old red net loft turned sculpture studio. Among the shadowy stone shapes of seals, fish, birds and human torsos a sleek, long-necked bird about 10 inches tall caught our attention. It had the elegance of a cormorant stretching its long neck.

We had arrived in Bamfield Inlet in 1992 in mid-afternoon after a near-record crossing under power from Neah Bay. After going through customs and anchoring in the basin at the head of the bay, we had spent the rest of the afternoon criss-crossing the inlet in our dinghy. We bought fishing licences in West Bamfield, groceries in East Bamfield, block ice in West Bamfield. Our goal was to get the shopping done and get out into the islands as soon as possible. We had left the tourist items until the end and had arrived at the sculpture studio to find it closed for the day.

"Let's come back tomorrow," I suggested to Steve.

Many visitors to Bamfield prefer to arrive by the coastal steamers *Lady Rose* and *Frances Barkley* rather than brave the logging road from Port Alberni.

But there wasn't time. The Netloft wouldn't open until noon the next day and we wanted to leave first thing in the morning.

"We'll stop on the way back south," said Steve.

We returned two and a half weeks later. As we sailed into the inlet, the first thing we saw was the coastal steamer *Lady Rose* tied to the public dock in front of the Bamfield Inn. A crowd of tourists was pouring off the boat and down the gangplank. We knew they would be swarming into the Netloft so instead of taking the dinghy all the way into town we tied it up at the public pier in West Bamfield near the anchorage and walked back into town on the boardwalk, waiting for the tourists to leave before entering the Netloft.

Bamfield is really two towns—West Bamfield and East Bamfield—divided by a narrow waterway. Of the two, I prefer West Bamfield: it's a pedestrian-friendly, boat-friendly, car-*un*friendly place. No roads lead to West Bamfield; the few cars there come by barge across the inlet from East Bamfield—and they're relegated to a rough dirt road at the back of the town. The coastal steamers the *Lady Rose* and the *Frances Barkley* still make stops at West Bamfield, bringing tourists, groceries, building materials and residents, and taking away the garbage. Schoolchildren wait for the school *boat*, not the school *bus*.

East Bamfield, on the other hand, has moved a bit closer to the modern world. Boats are still important in East Bamfield but it's now possible to drive there on gravel logging roads. Cars, trucks and boat trailers crowd the road to the dock. East Bamfield has all the modern conveniences: a grocery store just a bit larger than West Bamfield's General Store, a restaurant, a pub, a hardware store and a school. It also has a church and a clinic, both with docks for West Bamfield residents.

But West Bamfield has the best attraction of the inlet: the boardwalk. Stretching along the waterfront for almost half a mile, it provides a meeting place, an exercise area and a centre of commerce for the town. Today it provided strolling grounds for tourists. That the boardwalk was an accident only makes it more intriguing. In 1945 a load of lumber arrived in Bamfield by mistake. Rather than send it back or let it go to waste, Charlie Wickham, the road foreman, decided to put it to good use. Once built, the boardwalk became a public asset. It is now maintained by the Ministry of Transportation.

The first part of the boardwalk goes through a collection of small tourist cabins. I noticed with amusement a group of tourists sitting in a garden in front of a shingled

Opposite: Bamfield's history as the western terminus of the Pacific leg of the "All-Red [cable telegraph] Route" between England and Australia give it a more gracious appearance than many small towns on the coast.

The Netloft on West Bamfield's boardwalk. With no automobile access, development in West Bamfield has focused on the board-walk, which stretches for almost half a mile along the waterfront.

house. A sign above them proclaimed, "Paradise by the Sea." Beyond the tourist cabins the boardwalk passed several solid-looking houses, one of them with laundry waving from a line. Next the boardwalk jogged ashore and entered a short stretch of forest, cool and dark from the shade of fine big cedar and spruce trees. I blinked as we emerged back into the sunshine and saw the entrance of Bamfield Inlet with the open waters of Barkley Sound ahead of us. The boardwalk meandered along the shore again, past the Netloft with its crowd of tourists and into the centre of town. Here was the post office, the general store, the Bamfield Inn with its pub, the Coast Guard Station, and the steamship dock. On the pier we joined a crowd of onlookers watching the crew of the *Lady Rose* unload a pallet of building blocks. The captain, a youngish-looking man, was operating the controls as if he considered his job to be performer as well as sea captain.

When the last pallet of groceries had been unloaded, the last garbage bin put on the deck and the last tourist had waved goodbye, we had the town almost to ourselves.

The Netloft provided gallery area for Babe Gunn's sculptures, many of which repre-sent northwest themes.

We found the Netloft deserted except for the sculptor, Babe Gunn, who was busy sorting through papers at her desk. We wandered among the sculptures in the open-raftered shed, examining the carvings. Babe, a solidly built woman in her fifties with grey curly hair and a comfortable laugh, put aside her paperwork and showed us around. "I use almost all native stone," she told us. "My husband and I get it on the logging roads."

Babe is the sort of resourceful, multi-talented person I associate with the west coast of Vancouver Island. Left alone with three young children, she struggled to earn a living. She started her working life as Canada's first woman Fisheries Guardian, checking boats and people for gear and licences.

When the politics of her job got to be too much, she quit to become a fishing guide. To hear Babe talk it's clear that two events saved her life. The first was meeting her second husband, Arlen, with whom she raised their combined family of six children. The second was discovering carving at the age of 44. Babe told us that before she started carving she thought she was crazy because she had so much energy. But when she carved she could spend 12 hours a day at it and no one would think her crazy. With power tools and stone she created art.

The long-necked bird we had admired on our earlier trip was gone, flown away to the home of a tourist with different priorities than ours. There were other carvings, but once we had seen the long-necked bird, nothing else would do. We asked Babe if she had any others like it. She didn't but she could carve another, similar but not identical. She would send it to us and if we didn't like it, we could return it, no questions asked.

I left the Netloft feeling inspired. I was surprised that the afternoon was almost over; the time with Babe Gunn had gone quickly. There was just time to buy ice cream cones at the general store and eat them as we strolled back to the dinghy. I stopped next to one of the planter boxes and watched a bright yellow and green boat labelled "Pirate's Water Taxi" make its way across the inlet. "Wouldn't it be nice to live here?" I asked Steve. "Yes, but there aren't too many jobs. How would we earn our living?" I had to agree that it really wouldn't be practical, but I liked to imagine myself strolling the boardwalk every afternoon and living in one of the old houses.

The handsome houses and gracious appearance of Bamfield owe their existence to the fact that Bamfield was once more important to the rest of Canada than it is now. In 1902 Bamfield became the western terminus of the Pacific leg of the "All-Red [cable telegraph] Route" between England and Australia. ("Red" refers to the colour mapmakers once used to show the British Empire.) The installation, in East Bamfield, consisted of a powerhouse, offices, bungalows for married men and a hotel-like residence for bachelors.

It was a more formal and elegant time. R. Bruce Scott, who chronicled the station life during that time in his book, *Bamfield Years: Recollections*, tells of men in tuxedos and women in long formal dresses wearing oilskins when going to parties by boat. The ocean liners *Princess Maquinna* and *Princess Norah* stopped here going both north and south. The highlight of the trip for the tourists was always a tour of the telegraph station.

A salmon carved from tangerine alabaster.

But the cost of operating the station in such a remote location never appealed to the Canadian government. In 1959 they laid an additional cable from Bamfield to Port Alberni and built a new station at the new terminus. Bamfield operators sent their last cable to Australia and closed the door behind them, and Bamfield became a sleepy fishing town. Six years later a telephone cable replaced the telegraph cable and the era of the telegraph ended.

With commercial fishing almost gone, tourism, education and training are now the main year-round businesses in Bamfield. Backpackers arrive from walking the West Coast Trail, whose terminus is just a short distance away. Sport fishermen come for the salmon. College students from five universities come to study at the Bamfield Marine Sciences Centre in the old telegraph building. And Coast Guardsmen from all over Canada come to train in the bright red inflatable boats of the Rigid Hull Inflatable Operator Training (RHIOT) School.

Tourism, the Bamfield Marine Sciences Centre, and the Coast Guard's Rigid Hull Inflatable Operator Training (RHIOT) School are the main industries in Bamfield.

We left Bamfield for Seattle the next morning. When the big cardboard box arrived at our house in November, we opened it with anticipation. We pushed aside the newspapers and lifted out the carving with a sigh of relief. It wasn't the bird we remembered, but she had caught the elegance of a long-necked bird in simple grey granite.

That purchase was the beginning of a long friendship with Babe, carried out in our short visits every summer. And it was the beginning of our realization that the best part of the coast is the people. For Babe was only the first of many friends we would make.

In 1999 Babe Gunn sold her Bamfield home and stopped spending her summers there. For a few years the Netloft operated as an artist's cooperative—selling paintings, photographs, crafts and Babe Gunn's sculptures. It closed in 2004. But Babe Gunn's sculptures still grace the town—a mermaid in front of the store, giant clams at the tourist centre, and others.

Marble Cove

Islands in Fog are Closer than They Appear

The fog closed in around us the moment we left Bamfield Inlet, like a door shutting off the land. We were alone in a silent grey world. Calm water reflected grey fog so perfectly that we could barely tell where the water ended and the air began. The slow deep hoot of a foghorn broke the silence. A minute later a Canadian Navy ship loomed, then disappeared, its grey-green hull merging with the mist.

In this thick fog, we were leery of finding the narrow rock-strewn entrance to Robbers Passage, the shorter route to our destination, Marble Cove. We decided to go the long way around—through Satellite Passage and up Imperial Eagle Channel, following the coasts of Sandford, Fleming and Tsartus Islands.

This was our first trip north in *Osprey* and the first time we had a loran on board for navigation. (This was 1987, before GPS.) The fog gave us a good opportunity to use it.

The course for Satellite Passage was marked on the chart—292 magnetic. I steered while Steve plotted our course up the island chain. I kept my eyes glued to the compass needle, turning the wheel the instant our course wandered from 291 or 293. Although the passage was wide, rocks lined either side. The dim outlines of Helby Island and Wizard Islet surfaced in the fog, then disappeared behind us. When our loran showed

Although it's located more than eight miles inside Barkley Sound, Marble Cove has the rugged scenery normally seen on ocean coastlines.

we were out far enough, we turned to the northeast. The spectre of Adamson Rocks off Fleming Island worried us so I steered to leave them comfortably to starboard.

Before we expected it, a dark shape took form in the fog ahead. We assumed it was Fry Island at the entrance to Marble Cove and kept on going. But suddenly rocky cliffs broke through the fog above us, so close we could see the needles on the trees. With my heart beating in fright I jammed the throttle down to dead slow, then shifted into reverse, just in time to keep us off the rocks. I had forgotten that islands in the fog are closer than they appear. In the broad open spaces of Imperial Eagle Channel we had drifted offshore farther than we intended. We had mistaken Swiss Boy Island, farther out to sea, for Fry.

In 1859 the American brig *Swiss Boy*, outward bound from Port Orchard to San Francisco with a load of lumber, sprang a leak and sailed into Barkley Sound to make repairs. Somewhere near here, perhaps off Swiss Boy Island itself, they beached the brig to make repairs. Suddenly, several hundred warlike Huu-ay-ahts swarmed on board, stripped *Swiss Boy* of her rigging, toppled the mainmast into the water and seized the ship's crew, robbing them of their clothes and other personal possessions. After three days the Huu-ay-aht released the crew into the care of the schooner *Morning Star* bound for Victoria. In Victoria the captain of the *Swiss Boy* filed a complaint with the Governor, asking for restitution for a ruined ship and damaged cargo. The *Victoria Gazette* screamed "piracy" and the corvette *Satellite*, with 21 guns, steamed out of Victoria Harbour heading for the scene of the crime.

The *Satellite*'s skipper, Captain Prevost, held an inquiry on board the shipwrecked vessel. A large number of Huu-ay-aht attended, expecting to be praised for seizing a foreign vessel intruding in King George's waters; they were surprised when their sub-chief, George, was arrested and taken to Victoria. But in Victoria Captain Prevost reported that the damage was minimal and the brig so rotten it should never have put to sea. A wood sample bored from the bow had turned to powder in his hand. Public opinion changed rapidly and George was released, his actions deemed to be a misunderstanding by King George's new allies.

As the fog cleared we could see Fry Island and Tsartus Island off to our right. In a few minutes we were anchored in picturesque Marble Cove. We looked around at the sun shining on the rocks of Tsartus Island and we felt a little foolish. Fog clears first on the

Rising sea level following the last glaciation sculpted Marble Cove

land, and had we gone down Trevor Channel instead of Imperial Eagle, we might have been able to navigate Robbers Passage without difficulty.

It's possible to take a dinghy through this tunnel at high tide.

Marble Cove is inside Barkley Sound but has the rugged scenery I expect in more open ocean coastlines: stacks, tunnels, caves and rust-coloured rocks. These fantastic shapes and colours owe their existence to volcanic rocks and glaciation. Glaciers once extended out of Barkley Sound onto the continental shelf, and when they melted, the land rose. The rising sea sculpted this cove by whittling away at the volcanic rocks grain by grain until only the harder rock remained.

The geology makes the area fun to explore and that afternoon we took the dinghy along the shoreline. On Tsartus Island a tunnel leads through a rocky promontory toward Robbers Passage on the east. It is just wide enough for our dinghy. Positioning the dinghy at the opening we waited until we saw a wave building and felt the tug of the water on the dinghy's hull. Then Steve gunned the engine and steered into the tunnel. As we rushed through, I caught glimpses of starfish below and heard a clang as the outboard grated briefly against the bottom.

What I like best about Marble Cove is the sea life. Biologists call regions such as Barkley Sound "protected outer coasts." The combination of fertile ocean water, good circulation, and protection from the worst of the ocean waves makes great tide-pooling.

The next morning at low tide we set out in the dinghy again. We first approached Fry Island where the waves had eroded the soft rocks into Swiss cheese, creating natural burrows for all kinds of strange creatures. Tendrils of red and brown algae draped the rocks and trailed down into the water. I lifted up the algae to reveal purple sponges, small orange corals and leathery bat stars. Colonies of tunicates, primitive sac-like creatures of indeterminate colour, hung from rocky shelves like squishy stalactites. I could smell the pungent odour of iodine and salt of low tide. From every rock came the clicking and rustling of thousands of small animals breathing.

The semi-protected waters of Barkley Sound make for good tide-pooling.

From Fry Island we motored to a sandy beach on Tsartus Island and got out to explore the nearby rocks. Great piles of purple and orange starfish festooned the rocks and mussels grew so thick their shiny dark shells looked like black carpet. Red-beaked oystercatchers prowled among the mussels.

When I was a child growing up on the shores of Puget Sound, I loved to explore the beach at low tide. I could walk barefoot for miles, feeling the warm sand between my toes and stopping to investigate a multi-armed starfish or the smooth shell of a moon snail. When I studied oceanography in college I imagined a life spent studying these creatures, hours spent on the beach. But now I use my scientific training in a job for Seattle's sewer agency, concerning myself with parts per million of cadmium, zinc and copper and the price companies should pay for our services. It's related in a way—the sewers protect Puget Sound—but the connection seems distant in my daily life at work. To explore these tide pools is to reconnect myself to the sea.

One of the best books about sea life on Pacific beaches is *Between Pacific Tides,* written by Jack Calvin and Ed Ricketts. Ricketts is famous as the model for "Doc" in John Steinbeck's *Cannery Row.* In 1945 he travelled to Barkley Sound on the steamer *Princess Maquinna.* He too noticed carpets of mussels. In a journal, a sort of long letter to Steinbeck, he described his experiences. His words on the west coast of Vancouver Island are the best description of the coast that I know: "I don't know why more discerning people don't come up here…. I would read and eat and sleep and watch those Indians, wonderful restful time, and go out in the rain and wind and see that fantastic coastline go by. I get a curious feeling that's a combination of fear of the sea and of seasickness and cold, and liking of the sea and its animals and loving that lovely difficult west coast."

Effingham Island

Christians Eat Alone

I felt the rise and fall of the swells the moment we left Satellite Passage and entered Imperial Eagle Channel, the wide swath of open water in the middle of Barkley Sound. It caught me by surprise. In Trevor Channel the seas were so calm that I had forgotten that Barkley Sound is quite an open sound. A sill, a shallow area at the Sound's mouth, dampens the worst of the seas, but still lets in long rolling swells.

Across Imperial Eagle Channel at the very outer edge of the Sound we could see our destination: Effingham Island, one of many islands in the Broken Group. I've always assumed the name "Broken Group" refers to the incredible number of rocks and small islands that make up this archipelago. On the chart it looks like someone threw down a delicate piece of china to see it shatter into thousands of rocks, reefs, islets and islands.

As we approached the islands, I peered under the jib trying to tell one from another. Was that little one Wiebe Island? Or the slightly larger Dempster Island? The whole area looked like a maze and it would have been easy to get confused—easy and disastrous:

Rocks in front of the village of Huumuuwa. Natives selected village sites for their resources and their views of approaching enemy canoes rather than for protected anchorages.

The anchorage at Effingham Island is one of the most popular stops in the Broken Group for recreational boats.

mistaking one island for another could put us on the rocks. That's an advantage to heading for Effingham Island—it's just prominent enough to recognize easily.

Leaving the jagged brown rocks of Village Reef to starboard, we tacked into Coaster Channel, rounded Effingham light and drifted into Effingham Bay—our sails spread wide in the dying breeze. Just beyond a small island in the centre of the bay, we dropped the anchor.

We had anchored almost exactly where Captain Charles Barkley in the *Imperial Eagle* anchored in 1787 when he first discovered Barkley Sound. Frances Barkley wrote in her diary, "We anchored in a snug harbor in the island, of which my husband made a plan…. The anchorage was near a large village, and therefore we named the island Village Island." John Meares followed Barkley a year later in the ship *Felice Adventure*, using Barkley's drawing as a guide. He named the anchorage Port Effingham and wrote in his journal, "The port is sufficiently capacious to contain an hundred sail of ships—and so fortunately sheltered as to secure them from any storm." The names Village Island and Port Effingham both made it into history, but in 1905 the Geographic Board of Canada renamed the island Effingham Island and the anchorage Effingham Bay.

The small collection of 10 boats, sailboats and powerboats at anchor in Effingham Bay was far from the 100 Meares had envisioned, but still a crowded anchorage by Barkley Sound standards. It's a popular anchorage—one of the best in a southeasterly blow. But that day the sky was blue and the air as balmy as it ever gets in Barkley Sound. From our deck we watched one of *Osprey*'s sister ships, the *Haida*, sail into the anchorage to tie alongside *Osprey*. There are so few Annapolis 44s that watching one under sail was a treat—a chance to see what our boat, or one almost like her, looked like under sail. I was not disappointed: *Haida*'s graceful sheer and long overhangs were a pretty sight.

We had been about to leave Bamfield earlier that afternoon when we saw the *Haida* tied to the town dock. My first reaction was to think, "that boat looks familiar." Then with a start, I realized it looked familiar not only because I had seen it before, but also because it looked like *Osprey*.

We first met Larry and Lori, *Haida*'s owners, in Port Orchard in Puget Sound where they own a house and where Larry finished out *Haida* from a bare hull. I liked them both immediately—Larry for his good-natured laugh and Lori for the way she made me feel she was intensely interested in everything I said. And then of course we had something in common: the same taste in boats.

Another thing we had in common: Larry and Lori were two of the few people we have met who sail the west coast of Vancouver Island like we do—out the Strait and up and down the outside. But then, like us they have a good boat for going to windward.

Larry and Lori were heading south; we were on our way north. We had many things to talk about, and that evening we stayed out in the *Haida*'s large cockpit, sharing a potluck dinner, looking at charts, talking about the places they had visited and the places we hoped to visit on our trip. As we talked the sun set over the islands to the northwest, turning the water red and silhouetting the anchored boats against a red sky. I thought this was a great way to start a vacation—watching a sunset with friends.

In the morning, *Haida* sailed for Puget Sound and Steve and I went off to explore Effingham Island. The village reported by Barkley had been on the east side of the island, facing the open water of Imperial Eagle Channel. It was no longer there but we had an old chart, based on a 1931 survey, that showed a trail across the island and a row of dots labelled "Indian Village." More recent charts omit the village and the trail.

At first we couldn't find the trail. We stumbled through mud, ducking under salmonberry bushes, following others' footprints until finally we came upon a worn path of soft pine needles. We had come ashore on the north side of a small promontory while the trail started from the south side. The trail led uphill across the island through old-growth cedar and spruce. Once we were away from the shore, the undergrowth cleared and walking became easier among the old-growth trees. The ground was covered with swordtail ferns, all neatly trimmed by deer feeding on the new growth.

On the other side of the island we climbed down a rocky ravine and onto a cobble beach. Waves crashed on rocks offshore and crows cawed from the trees. We walked south to a circular sandy beach fringed by a grove of young spruce trees, ducked under some low overhanging branches and walked onto a meadow of small rolling hills. At one spot someone had peeled back the moss and grass to reveal clamshells and bits of burned wood—evidence that we were walking on a midden, an ancient garbage dump.

This village, called Huumuuwa (pronounced "O-mo-o"), was one of as many as 15 separate village sites in the Broken Group Islands. Smallpox, tuberculosis, venereal disease and warfare among the villagers reduced their numbers so greatly that each group could no longer live on its own. The residents of Huumuuwa joined with the Tseshaht of Benson Island who in turned joined with other groups to form the modern Tseshaht band. Some experts believe that before amalgamation each band occupied

The view from the anchorage at Effingham Island includes the sun setting over Mt. Ozzard.

one village site year-round. Afterwards, the newly amalgamated bands moved with the season according to the resources each site offered. Huumuuwa became the Tseshaht summer site. Eventually, the Tseshaht stopped migrating and settled permanently on the banks of the Somass River near Port Alberni. They are still there today.

In the summer of 1896, when Huumuuwa was still a summer village, the Presbyterian missionary Melvin Swartout visited there from Ucluelet with his family and friends, travelling in two sailing canoes. In a fictionalized account Swartout described the village as "a single row of old fashioned lodges, built along the shore just above the high water mark. Behind, for a few yards, the ground was covered with a dense growth of salal, marking the extent of the ancient clearing. Beyond the salal was the forest."

Swartout's party found the villagers preparing for a potlatch—the traditional northwest Native ceremony of dances, feasting and gift giving. Swartout held a service and afterwards the chief came to talk to him. He was troubled by the conversion of one of his friends on the east side of Vancouver Island, and he told Swartout:

"Missionary, we are glad to have you with us....Your medicine is good; your schools are good; and we are pleased to have our children learn the English language …. But, Missionary, we do not understand what a 'Christian' is …. A Christian is a man who never eats with his friends, he always sits down alone with his wife to eat …. He never gives a potlatch …. Missionary, I do not want you to try to make Christians of my people."

Clamshells and bits of burned wood tell us that this mossy area is a midden, an ancient garbage dump.

In 1885 the Indian Act of Canada outlawed masked dances, public giving and other elements of the potlatch. Missionaries, including Swartout, wanted Natives to give up their ways for those of the white man. They considered gift giving to be especially bad. They were shocked to see Natives work and save for years only to give it all away in a day. But to the Natives how much they gave away, not how much they accumulated, gave them status. Potlatches remained illegal until 1951. But in the summer and on holidays the Tseshaht band would make the long trip to Effingham Island, which they still called Village Island, to have potlatches and feasts. Because of its isolated location at the mouth of Barkley Sound, white men rarely came here and the celebrants were safe from the police.

Only the midden remained of the busy village that had once been here. We walked across its mossy carpet and tried to imagine the longhouses, the canoes on the beach, the piles of clamshells, the cries of children and the beat of drums. Then we returned to *Osprey*. That night, we ate dinner by ourselves.

Before we went to bed, Steve went out on deck to look at the stars. I heard him call, telling me urgently to come out and see. I dropped the book I was reading and ran up the companionway steps. Steve pointed to the water, where I saw a sudden flash of green. The flash moved around the boat, first off our bow, then our stern. We heard a splash, then a snort. A sea lion was feeding in the water of Effingham harbour.

Benson Island

Follow That Whale!

Tendrils of fog streamed through the channel between Benson and Clarke Islands, leaving behind streaks of cotton in the trees. I was glad *Osprey* was safely anchored and that we were in the dinghy heading for Benson Island rather than sailing through the fog in the middle of Barkley Sound.

We landed the dinghy on a pebble beach and walked through a grove of spruce trees onto a grassy field. Several small deer the size of golden retrievers browsed on the grass. I had to blink to get perspective because the deer were so small and so perfectly proportioned that for a minute I thought we were looking at larger deer on a larger meadow. They were black-tailed deer, a small subspecies of mule deer whose size adjusts to the size of their home. On very small islands, like Benson Island, they can be quite small.

We walked across the field until we came to a smooth mound running parallel to the beach. From the scattering of clamshells and scraps of burned wood peeking out of a covering of moss, we could tell that the mound was a midden that marked the ancestral home of the Tseshaht band of the Nuu-chah-nulth nation. The Tseshaht lived on this island for generations before joining with other bands and moving to Alberni Inlet. Anthropologists refer to middens like this one as "shell middens," after the dominant type of refuse found in their depths. But the variety of things thrown into these garbage dumps goes way beyond clamshells. It includes fish bones—halibut, salmon, dogfish, ling cod, greenling, pilchard, eulachon and rockfish; seabird bones—

Sailboats in the rocky channel between Benson and Clark Islands.

Pocket beaches on Benson Island make it a popular campground for sport fishermen and kayakers.

loons, ducks, grebes, cormorants, gulls and albatross; and mammal bones—deer, seals, sea lions, sea otters and seven kinds of whale. To the bones, shells and blackened remains of endless campfires, the Tseshaht added worn and broken household objects: baskets, mats, mussel-shell knives, fishhooks, harpoons, grinding stones and ceremonial masks. Thus, the detritus of an entire civilization piled up, year after year, generation after generation. The middens are testimony to the wealth of these small islands and of the sea around them. When the first Europeans arrived, the west coast of Vancouver Island and its surrounding ocean fed 25,000 Nuu-chah-nulth people.

On the far side of the midden we found a well-used trail and followed it up a hill. Huckleberry plants with small shiny leaves and dark bluish-red berries lined the trail. Native women once picked from these bushes while their men fished for halibut and cod or hunted seal and whale. The day before, we had found similar huckleberries on Jaques Island and in the space of an hour had picked almost a quart. They were too tart to eat plain so I had made a pie with them. I wondered what the Native women did without sugar.

That day we didn't linger at the berries, but kept hiking uphill. At first the trail was easy—wide and carpeted with soft pine needles. Then we came to a gully. To cross it we had to hang on to branches of salmonberry while inching our way across a log made slippery by mist. I don't like heights and might have turned back if Steve hadn't urged me on. From the gully we crawled through a tunnel of salal, dark and dank with dew. As dewdrops fell on our heads, our feet squished through soft black mud. We came out of the tunnel at the top of a bluff on the ocean side of the island as sunlight broke through the fog. Offshore we could see Sail Rock emerging from the mist. Near the rock, spouts of mist shot into the air, then drifted away only to rise again somewhere else. A whale was feeding in the offshore waters.

We clambered down the steep bluff to the beach, hanging on to tree roots to keep from sliding. We could hear repeated loud "whumps" and saw jets of spray flying into the air from the rocks to our left. Waves rushing into a cave were pushing air ahead of them, compressing it as the cave narrowed. When the waves receded, the air rushed out with a boom, shooting spray into the air in imitation of the whales.

Members of the Tseshaht band were great whalers. They called this island Ts'isha'. Thanks to the efforts of two anthropologists, Edward Sapir and Morris Swadesh, who interviewed band members when the band moved to Alberni Inlet in the early 1900s, we know more about the Tseshaht and their legends then any other Nuu-chah-nulth band.

The Tseshaht told a story of a great flood. When the flood came, the band was feasting on a whale that the chief, Tlatla'qukw'ap, had caught. The chief, his brother, their wives, children and slaves escaped the flood in large canoes tied together. They took four big boxes of provisions, including the dorsal fin of the whale they had been eating. As they drifted they heard someone singing in one of the boxes. It was the whale fin. The chief joined in and soon everyone in the canoes was singing. The flood was so high that the mountains were underwater. Finally the Tseshaht came to a land of tall mountains that were still dry where they stayed for a long time. When the water started to recede, the chief donned his whale-hunting clothes and the Tseshaht got in their canoes to follow the sinking water. They saw a whale blow and paddled toward it, following it all the way home to Ts'isha'.

The history of Benson Island didn't end with the Tseshaht. One summer when we were poking around in an art gallery in Tofino, I found a pamphlet about Benson Island, written by Jean Buck Walbank. According to Walbank, John Webb Benson from the state of Maine purchased Benson Island for $33, a dollar an acre, in 1893. Benson cleared almost three acres of land for a meadow and near the beach on the eastern side he built a hotel, called Barclay House, as a summer resort for people who liked to fish

Sail Rock is visible from the bluff on the west side of Benson Island.

Waves rushing into a cave on the west side of Benson Island form a "blowhole."

Halibut. Barkley Sound is a popular destination for recreational fishermen.

and hunt. (Barkley was misspelled on the chart as "Barclay" for many years until restored to Barkley by the Geographic Board of Canada in 1904.)

Benson died and his wife sold the island to a mariner named Jens Petersen who in turn sold it to Alfred Henry Clarke in 1919. Clarke, a judge in Calgary who could only spend two months a year on the island, hired Elizabeth and Delmont Buck as caretakers. Like Benson, the Bucks were from Maine. Delmont loved going out in his boat. His favourite expression was the nonsensical, "Which would you rather do or go fishing?" Elizabeth's favourite expression was, "We'll do the best we can." The Bucks occupied a part of the hotel and converted one of the rooms into a schoolroom for their four children. Elizabeth organized parties for the young men from the telegraph cable station in Bamfield. They had bonfires on the beach and the young people sang and talked, rolling up the rugs in the hotel and dancing late into the night. I can imagine the music drifting across the quiet water and the bonfire an isolated bright spot in the dark night.

The Bucks left the island in 1922, worried about living so far from civilization. During prohibition smugglers used the hotel as a haven and left each other messages on the blackboard in the schoolroom.

Judge Clarke died and when his heirs failed to pay the taxes due, the government sold the island at auction to Kyle Kendall for $50.49. Kendall then sold it in 1962 for $10,000 to the marine architect William Garden of Seattle. Garden cleared fields and trails and built a small summer home. In 1975 the Crown reclaimed the land for the Pacific Rim National Park, for $95,000.

We didn't see any sign of the hotel, although we did see a foundation of a small cabin that might have been Garden's summer home. But compared to the long occupation of the Tseshaht, the hotel was just a blip in history.

On the beach next to our dinghy two sport fishermen were cleaning several large halibut. While Steve talked fishing holes and lures with them, I looked longingly at the halibut. I was getting awfully tired of the rockfish we had been eating almost every night. Then I remembered the huckleberry pie on *Osprey*. I offered to fetch half of the remaining pie in exchange for a hunk of halibut. One of the men cut off a thick piece from the middle of the fish and wrapped it in aluminum foil.

On the way back to *Osprey* to fetch the pie, I held the halibut on my lap. It didn't sing to us, but later than evening it made a delicious dinner.

Ucluelet

A Beautiful Day

Steve and I like the no-nonsense attitude of this fishing and logging town. It has a paved highway from Port Alberni that makes it better supplied than Bamfield. And in addition to the Co-op, Ucluelet's general store, the town has a green grocer, a deli, a bakery and a laundromat—everything we need. The best place to moor is at the boat basin—a round shallow cove with a dredged area for docks. It's usually crowded with fishboats but it's the kind of place that always has room for one more boat.

The major attraction of the boat basin, besides the moorage, is the *Canadian Princess*, a former hydrographic vessel, moored on the west shore, which has been converted into a hotel and restaurant. The food is good and we always know we're eating on a ship. The deck where the restaurant is located is cambered; diners on the downhill side of a table risk getting everyone else's grilled salmon in their laps.

In 2001 we tied up at the boat basin as usual on our way north. It was a cloudy, cool day with little wind—a good day for town, for grocery shopping and laundry. We collected our grocery bags and headed up the hill where the stores are strung out along

The 52-step dock in Ucluelet is named for its 52-step stairway to the road. Steve counted them and insists there are only 51.

The *Canadian Princess*, a former hydrographic ship turned into a resort, shares the boat basin with fishing boats and yachts.

Salmon trollers in the Ucluelet boat basin. The boat basin has docks for both commercial boats and recreational boats.

the road. At the top of the hill we passed an elderly Native woman, so small that when I first saw her I thought she was a child. "Beautiful morning, eh?" she said and gave us a smile so friendly and wide it made up for the cloudy day. I smiled back, but after we passed her I looked at the cloudy sky, trying to see what made the day beautiful to her.

In the Co-op, I cruised the fresh fruit and vegetable section, planning for the next two weeks without access to a store. Should I buy enough tomatoes to last a week or would they go bad before then? And what about that lettuce that looked slightly wilted? The Co-op always reminds me of the grocery stores my mother took me to when I was a child; it makes me realize how pampered we are in the big cities with their huge supermarkets. The Co-op has baloney but not salami, spaghetti but not tortellini, zucchini but not eggplant. The lack of eggplant dismayed me, as I had planned to make a Moroccan stew with lentils and eggplant. Two years earlier we had bought eggplant in remote Queen Charlotte City, so I had assumed we would find it in the more populous Ucluelet. I asked a clerk who was busy putting tomatoes on the shelf if they had any.

"No. Lots of people ask for them. But we never have them."

At the bakery we bought two loaves of unsliced rye bread on the recommendation of the baker, who said it would last longer than sliced bread. When we asked for change in "loonies" (the Canadian dollar-coin with a loon on one side) for the laundromat, she raised her eyebrows in sympathy. "You have to do laundry on such a beautiful day? What a shame." Only a few scattered raindrops were hitting the pavement as we walked back to the boat burdened with our groceries.

We returned to Ucluelet (pronounced "Yoo'cloo'let") a month later on another flat grey day. The weather radio was predicting gales. In the boat basin fishboats were tying up to other fishboats, sailboats to sailboats, power yachts to power yachts. Engines roared as the boats backed down and the hum of generators and refrigeration systems reverberated down the dock. When the gale moved in during the night, I woke to feel the boat tugging at the mooring lines and hear the clack-clack of wires on trolling poles and the whine of wind through rigging. But I felt secure in the basin where no waves could find us. The word *ucluelet* means "safe harbour" in the Nuu-chah-nulth language. I thought the town was well named.

The wharfinger had been too busy the afternoon we arrived to collect our moorage fee, but the next morning we found him in his small office at the head of the dock, a dry spot in the rain and wind. A youngish-looking man with a blond crewcut, he sat at his desk surrounded by paper—receipt books, rate lists and miscellaneous faxes from the government.

"What'll it be? Do you want to pay by the week or the month?" he asked us.

Ucluelet waterfront. A fishing and logging town until recently, Ucluelet is becoming a tourist destination.

I was taken aback by this question, which no wharfinger had ever asked us before. Did he know something about this weather that we didn't? We assured him we would leave the next day.

"Well," he replied. "This storm is as bad as what we see in the winter. But anything you pay at the daily rate can always be applied later to either of the two long-term rates. Just keep in mind, four days of daily moorage is the same as a week."

When we had paid, he asked us what else could he do for us. Did we need a recommendation on a restaurant? Advice on shopping? We told him we had rented a car and planned to drive to Port Alberni for the day.

"You have a car? Going to the Port? You'll be all right, then. The only problem you'll have is fighting off the other sailboaters clinging to the bumpers and crying 'take me out of here!'"

As we walked out of his office we heard him say to himself, "I love gales."

Clayoquot Sound

Southeastern Portion

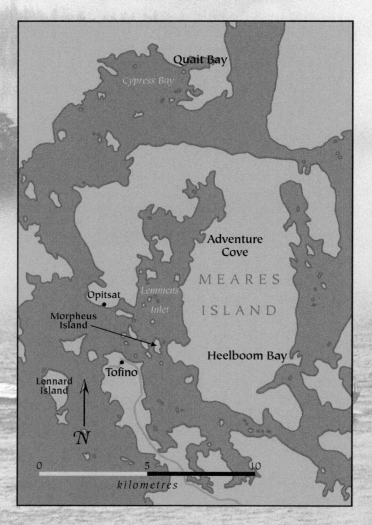

Quait Bay

Cypress Bay

Adventure Cove

MEARES ISLAND

Opitsat

Lemmens Inlet

Morpheus Island

Heelboom Bay

Tofino

Lennard Island

N

0   5   10

kilometres

We passed the distinctive needle-shaped light tower on Lennard Island as the fog lifted and entered Templar Channel, riding the incoming tide into Duffin Passage, a maze of sandbanks and islands. Eastern Clayoquot Sound fills through these constricted channels in a swirl of muddy water. The fur traders who came before us had only crude maps passed from one trader to another and only sails and ships' boats for manoeuvring. But we had the latest chart plus beacons and buoys for guides, and a diesel engine to push us through the calms.

Tofino

The Better View

"You're going to the west coast of Vancouver Island? You mean near Tofino? We went there last year-beautiful town," said my co-worker.

That land tourists sing praises of Tofino always surprises me. Tofino is a tourist town: its restaurants crowded; its shopkeepers preoccupied; its architecture a mish-mash of styles. For us Tofino is a provision stop, a place to get in and out of fast so we can move on to the really beautiful places-the inlets and islands of the sound. And to a sailboat, Tofino is a challenge. There is never enough room at the dock and tidal currents swirl through the harbour, which makes docking nerve-racking and anchoring difficult.

In 2001 we stopped at Tofino on our way home. After six weeks of quiet anchorages, we thought we were ready for art galleries and restaurants. To avoid the currents, we timed our arrival for slack water-before-the-flood and tied up alongside another Seattle boat at the end of a dock. There were very few other spaces available. Docks labelled "recreational boats" were full-of geoduck (clam) boats, tugboats, dive boats and others I would have classified as "commercial" while docks labelled "commercial only"

A fishing boat emerges from the fog off Tofino.

The Tofino waterfront is a departure point for whale-watching, bear-watching and eagle-watching.

were mostly empty. The geoduck boats and tugboats weren't really commercial, the wharfinger told us. The government defined "commercial" as possessing a commercial fishing licence. All other boats were by default "recreational."

We collected our shopping bags and headed up the hill into town. Coming toward us was a gaggle of tourists on their way to a whale-watching boat-all wearing identical red exposure suits. Tofino is the centre for whale-watching, bear-watching and eagle-watching, all done in high-speed boats that cover a distance in an hour that would take us two days. Tofino is also the end of the Trans-Canada highway, a significance that's marked by a sign on the waterfront.

We walked into town passing a fish-processing plant, miscellaneous houses, a church and an assortment of galleries and T-shirt shops. Just for fun we stopped at one of the galleries. Inside were oil paintings of the coast in brassy colours I couldn't remember seeing anywhere on Vancouver Island. In the bookstore, I browsed through the regional history books, finding one on seal hunters I had not seen before. To buy it I waited in line behind a woman who was negotiating a whale-watching trip for a family of six. In the bakery we took a number and waited in line to buy bread. When we finally reached the counter the clerk barely looked in our direction. Accustomed to the shopkeepers in Tahsis and Kyuquot, who have more time than customers, we felt out of rhythm with this fast-paced tourist town. But on the street we passed smiling tourists speaking French and German; they didn't mind the bustle.

On our way back to the marina, grocery bags full of bread and books, we stopped at a small grassy park at the edge of town to look at the harbour below. A tongue of fog was pushing up the inlet, weaving tendrils of white cotton among green islands and blue water. I was suddenly impatient to get back to the boat. I wanted to get my camera and come back to capture this scene.

I had just understood what my land-bound friends saw in Tofino. Coming from the land, they saw the sea-the fog, the islands, the water. Coming from the sea, I saw the land-the roads, the houses, the stores. Theirs was the better view.

Adventure Cove

The Boston Men

In October 1977 Steve and I were in Boston in *Velella,* visiting family and preparing to sail to Seattle via the Panama Canal and Hawaii. One evening we took time off from visits and preparations to see the movie *Star Wars.* I remember coming out of the theatre to see the first autumn leaves swirling around brick buildings. Images of spaceships sailing into the stars combined with thoughts of the voyage we would soon be taking and filled me with a mixture of fear and anticipation. I felt as if I too were starting on an epic adventure.

I didn't know it at the time but 190 Octobers earlier, on October 1, 1787, two American ships, the *Columbia Rediviva* and the *Lady Washington,* left Boston for the Northwest on a real epic adventure.

To the moribund shipping industry of post-revolutionary Boston the sea otter trade between the Northwest and China offered new life: the "*rediviva*" of *Columbia.* Although no one on the *Columbia* or the *Washington* became rich, other Boston ships soon followed. Free of the bureaucratic rules that encumbered the British traders the "Boston Men," or "Bostonahts," as the northwest Natives called them, became the most successful fur traders on the northwest coast.

The *Washington* never returned to Boston but the *Columbia,* under Captain Robert Gray, returned in 1790—the first American ship to sail around the world. In September

This steep-sided bluff on the northwest shore of Adventure Cove may have been the docking area where *Columbia's* men caulked the ship.

1790 the *Columbia* left Boston on a second trip to the Northwest, arriving in Clayoquot Sound on June 5, 1791. The *Columbia* spent the summer trading for furs and then began looking for winter quarters. For while other fur traders wintered in Hawaii, the *Columbia*'s owners, being from Boston where long winters were just part of life, had more industrious plans. In the *Columbia*'s hold were 2,000 Boston bricks and the stem, sternpost and floor timbers of a sloop—to be built and launched on the northwest coast and named the *Adventure*. Shipbuilding would keep the men busy through the long winter and two ships trading for furs could bring back twice as many as one.

For a winter shipyard Captain Gray chose the small cove, now called Adventure Cove, on the east shore of Lemmens Inlet on Meares Island in Clayoquot Sound.

During the winter of 2000–2001 I read Frederic Howay's *Voyages of the* Columbia *to the Northwest Coast, 1787–1790 and 1790–1793*, a compilation of journals of three officers on the *Columbia*: Robert Haswell, John Hoskins and John Boit. Their stories, reproduced with all the original misspellings, tell of the wilderness shipyard, of sailing through the narrow channels of Clayoquot Sound and of visiting remote villages. The stories seemed so real to me that I immediately wanted to see their winter quarters for myself. And I was intrigued by the Boston connection that Steve and I both shared with the men of the *Columbia* and *Washington*. Steve was born in Boston; I was born in Rhode Island to a Boston-bred mother. Although I had grown up in Seattle, Boston, or rather my mother's stories of it, coloured my childhood. Mention of "Boston" made me think of prim-and-proper aunts in stately brick houses, cold snowy winters, baked beans and brown bread every Saturday night and gaff rig sailboats tied to stone wharves.

"You won't see anything of the *Adventure* or the *Columbia*," Steve reminded me. "Not after 200 years."

I had to admit that in a climate where entire fish-processing plants had disappeared in the space of 20 years, the chances of finding any trace of the wilderness shipyard were slim. Still, I secretly hoped to find a broken piece of brick or perhaps the clearing where the *Adventure* had been built. And even if I found neither of those things, I still wanted to spend time at the cove, to relive its history in my mind.

I got my wish the next summer, in 2001. We travelled to Adventure Cove from Ucluelet on a calm, foggy day, motoring all the way. We passed the distinctive needle-shaped light tower on Lennard Island as the fog lifted and entered Templar Channel, riding the incoming tide into Duffin Passage and Clayoquot Sound. Duffin Passage is a maze of sandbanks and islands. Eastern Clayoquot Sound fills through these constricted channels in a swirl of muddy water. But we had the latest chart plus beacons and buoys for guides, and a diesel engine to push us through the calms. The fur traders had only crude maps passed from one trader to another and only sails and ships' boats for manoeuvring.

We continued past the town of Tofino with its whale-watching boats and tourist facilities, past the Native village of Opitsat with its row of modern houses strung along the beach, and into Lemmens Inlet. At mid-tide Lemmens Inlet was a large mud flat punctuated by islands and cut by narrow channels. At high tide it would be a broad open bay, its dangerous shallows hidden by the rising water. The currents made me uneasy; I felt that any minute *Osprey* could be swept onto the tidal flat.

Once we passed Opitsat, the only signs of civilization were several small floathouses tucked into coves and the blue barrels of an oyster farm. Distant mountains, still with snow patches from the previous winter, loomed above the green hills of Meares Island. It must have looked much like this when the *Columbia* sailed here.

We rounded Columbia Islet and entered Adventure Cove: two powerboats were rafted together in the south corner; two float houses occupied the northeast corner; rocks crowded the anchorage from the east and a sunken fish pen was just visible off

Opitsat village on Meares Island, 2001. Captain Robert Gray of the *Columbia* destroyed the original village and its magnificent artwork.

Columbia Islet to the west. As we were circling the cove, trying to decide where to anchor, a woman on the bow of one of the powerboats pointed to a large rock just beneath the water surface. Not all the rocks were on the chart, she warned us. We finally anchored in the middle, feeling uneasy about a rock off our stern.

When the *Columbia* made this same trip up Lemmens Inlet on a pleasant September morning in 1791, a crowd of Natives in canoes escorted it. A light breeze and a rising tide pushed the ship past the mud flats and into the upper reaches of the inlet. Assisted by her boats and those of the *Washington*, which was anchored in Clayoquot, the *Columbia* cast anchor and moored with cables attached to trees on two sides, "entirely lockt in an excellent cove." They called the cove Adventure Cove. The next day the *Columbia*'s men went ashore and began to clear land to build a settlement they called Fort Defiance—a complex of forge, boatbuilding shops, saw pits and a house with a brick fireplace. In this primitive shipyard Gray's men built and launched the ship *Adventure*—in time a modern shipyard would be proud of. When it rained especially hard, which it often did, they worked inside, sawing planks and building a yawl boat for the *Adventure*. Compared to a Boston winter, the weather was mild: the snow that fell was "little more than sufficient to bare [*sic*] the name."

Less than a month after the *Columbia* arrived in Adventure Cove on September 20, the men completed the sloop's frames. By January 17, they began to caulk the bottom. On February 22, they launched the sloop *Adventure*. On April 2, the *Adventure* headed north under the command of Robert Haswell. As the two ships left Clayoquot Sound, the *Adventure* outran the *Columbia*, testimony to the success of the wilderness shipyard. Once in the open ocean, the two ships separated. The *Columbia* headed south and discovered the Columbia River. The *Adventure* sailed north to trade in the Queen Charlotte Islands and Alaska.

Now *Osprey* was anchored in the cove where the *Adventure* had been built more than 200 years before. From our deck we could see a flat area beyond the beach that looked like a likely place for building a ship. We took the dinghy ashore there, nosing up a small stream onto a beach.

Robert Haswell described the cove as having "as compact a thicket as ever grew" with few trees "less than two fathoms round and many of them four." We pushed through a thicket of salmonberries and salal at the edge of the beach into a grove of cedar and spruce—tall and straight but not "two fathoms round." Scattered among the trees were immense stumps, green with moss. Notches in the stumps marked where loggers once stood to work their saws. The only other evidence of past habitation were fireplace circles left by campers and an abandoned white enamel gas cookstove, looking forlorn and out of place next to a fallen tree.

I was photographing the afternoon sun filtering through the trees onto the forest floor when Steve called me over to look at a spruce tree that had very tall stilted roots, the result of growing from a nurse log (a fallen tree on which new trees take root).

A snug anchorage, Adventure Cove has room for only a few boats.

The nurse log had rotted away long ago, passing its nutrients to the spruce and leaving a gap underneath. Steve pointed to some clamshells clinging to roots, their whiteness standing out against dark wood.

"Must have been a midden here," said Steve. I was puzzled. Trees didn't usually grow on middens. The usual sign of a midden was a small hill covered with grass and flowers. And the tree roots were unusually tall so that I couldn't imagine what kind of tree the nurse log had been. It was a mystery, but one that didn't seem important at the time.

As we were walking back to our dinghy, we saw several thick, newly cut planks just above the tide line. "Leftover planks from the *Adventure*," joked Steve.

Before getting into the dinghy we stood on the beach surveying the scene. I could see the resemblance to the sketch of the winter quarters in *Voyages of the* Columbia and could imagine the *Adventure* under construction on this beach and the *Columbia* at anchor where the *Osprey* now rode. I didn't need to see a physical structure to get a sense of history from this place: the landscape, unchanged from the days of the *Columbia,* was all I needed.

In our dinghy we motored toward a floathouse with two fishboats tied to its sides. A young man wearing sawdust-covered cords came out to greet us. He told us he was renovating one of the fishboats with the planks we had seen on the beach. The floathouse was a way to avoid a mortgage and raise a family without a day job. He was a carver of granite and wood. We asked him if the beach was where the *Adventure* had been built. He said it was, but "didn't much approve of Captain Cook."

"Gray," I said. "It was Captain Gray. Not Cook." I couldn't understand how someone could live at a historic site and not even get the names right. But I didn't tell him that he probably would have disapproved of Gray even more than Cook.

Clayoquot natives called Adventure Cove Clicksclecutsee. They visited Fort Defiance almost daily bringing fish, furs and freshly killed fowl to trade with the Boston men and to harvest the fish that swarmed in shoals in the cove. The officers thought their relationship with the Natives was good, but one incident marred the friendship. A sailor named Ottoo from the Hawaiian Islands deserted the ship and escaped to a village. To get Ottoo back Gray seized a chief as hostage. Gray didn't understand that seizing a chief could humiliate a village. When Ottoo returned, Gray considered the incident closed. But the Natives plotted revenge. They persuaded Ottoo to tell them the watch schedules

and the comings and goings at the fort. Fortunately for the men of the *Columbia*, Ottoo confessed the plot to Captain Gray.

The *Columbia*'s crew readied for an attack, loading the cannon and preparing arms. The *Columbia* had been tied alongside a rocky platform, out of sight of the fort and vulnerable to boarding. The crew quickly moved it to the ways near the fort. That night, while the tide receded the men stood to their waists in icy water, caulking the ship and waiting for the attack. They heard whoops and saw canoes off the cove's entrance, but no attack came.

What happened later is enough to make me ashamed of my Boston heritage. On March 27, as the *Columbia* departed Clayoquot Sound, one of Gray's mates, John Boit, wrote in his journal, "I am sorry to be under the necessity of remarking that this day I was sent with three boats, all well man'd and arm'd to destroy the Village of Opitsatah it was a Command I was no way tenacious off, and am grieved to think Capt. Gray shou'd let his passions go so far. This village was about half a mile in Diameter, and Contained upwards off 200 Houses, generally well built for Indians ev'ry door that you enter'd was in resemblance to an human and Beasts head, the passage being through the mouth…. This fine village, the Work of Ages, was in a short time totally destroy'd."

As if destroying Opitsat wasn't punishment enough, Gray then turned his cannon on a canoe of 20 men, killing them all.

The men of the *Columbia* and the *Adventure* never returned to Adventure Cove. The forest grew back around Fort Defiance. The house collapsed into the undergrowth and the brick fireplace sank into the forest floor. Even the Natives forgot the location of Clicksclecutsee. When a female relative of Captain Gray mistakenly burned his log, the only accurate record of Adventure Cove's location was lost. Only the journals of Gray's

Almost every cove in Lemmens Inlet contains a floathouse. An inexpensive way to live, floathouses are also controversial because of their sewage discharges.

officers and two paintings by George Davidson, a sailor on the *Columbia*, remained to describe Fort Defiance. Residents of Clayoquot knew the *Adventure* had been built in Lemmens Inlet, but not where.

In 1937, the historian Samuel Eliot Morison of Harvard University journeyed to Clayoquot in search of Fort Defiance and Adventure Cove. Finding a site near Morpheus Island that vaguely resembled the Davidson paintings, he published his discovery in the *Oregon Historical Quarterly*, concluding "we are quite certain as to the location of Fort Defiance and Adventure Cove." He noted, however, that "the artists have taken considerable liberty with the scene." One of the paintings even showed a triple-crowned mountain that couldn't be seen from Morpheus Island.

In 1966, Kenneth Gibson, a Tofino resident and amateur historian took up the search. Like Morison he used a photograph of one of the Davidson paintings as a guide. Gibson had spent his childhood exploring the coves and islands of Clayoquot Sound and thought he knew them as well as anyone. He was skeptical of the Morpheus Island site as Fort Defiance. It was too hazardous a location for an experienced captain like Gray: the channel was too narrow, the current too swift and it lacked drinking water.

"Winter Quarters," attributed to George Davidson. Reverse Painting on Glass, ca. 1790. Image size 26.5 cm H x 35.4 cm W. *Courtesy Massachusetts Historical Society*

The exact location of the *Columbia*'s winter quarters was forgotten until Kenneth Gibson, a Tofino resident and amateur historian, used a photograph of this painting to identify it.

Gibson searched the lower shoreline of Lemmens Inlet where Fort Defiance had been rumoured to be, looking for a break in the virgin timber and a spot where a ship could be easily launched. None of the beaches matched the photograph and he began to get discouraged. Most of the residents of Tofino thought his search a silly venture, but an 84-year-old handlogger told him he had seen bricks on the beach in a cove farther up the inlet where he had logged in the '30s.

On July 9, 1966, Gibson cruised into the glassy calm water of Adventure Cove and knew he had found Fort Defiance. Like the beach in the painting, the beach in the cove had a saw-tooth shoreline and the triple-crowned mountain in the background. Two creeks provided ample fresh water. There was deep water to moor a ship and a forest "as compact a thicket as ever grew." A depression in the shoreline marked the ways where the *Adventure* had been launched. Fifty feet above high tide charcoal and old

bricks marked the site of the cookhouse. News of the discovery travelled quickly and soon the cove was swarming with amateur and professional historians. Specimens of the brick were sent to Boston where experts declared them a match with similar bricks from the same period. Fort Defiance's location was confirmed. A local amateur historian had triumphed over a Harvard professor.

Although not one brick remained on the beach, we were satisfied that we had seen the site where the *Adventure* was built. We left Adventure Cove the next morning. But several days later I reread John Hoskins's description of Fort Defiance and saw a connection between the clamshells underneath the spruce tree and the fort. The men of the *Columbia* had used a mortar of burnt shells and clay between the logs of the house. Perhaps the house logs had become nurse logs and the shells we had seen were the remains of the mortar. The location, just above the creek, matched the location on the photograph. Could we have found something of the *Adventure*'s winter shipyard?

The saw-tooth beach in the painting by George Davidson is still visible today.

Quait Bay

Space for Art

In the northeast corner of Cypress Bay in the upper reaches of Clayoquot Sound is an almost landlocked little cove called Quait Bay. A small island in the entrance to this bay blocks waves from the south, keeping it calm, but it also makes getting in and out of the bay difficult. That's just the type of bay we like: perfectly protected once we're in, but a navigational challenge to get there.

On our first trip to the bay, in 1981, we looked at the collection of rocks smack in the north entrance and went around the back of the island to go in the south entrance. That entrance was so narrow that the trees on either side almost brushed the mast as we went through. After we anchored we looked back at the north entrance and thought about how much easier it would be to enter that way—a straight shot coming in from Cypress Bay. So we got out the dinghy and dragged a lead line through the north entrance. We discovered that if we hugged the northwest shore, we could avoid the rocks. Steve was pleased because it meant we would be able to sail in.

North entrance to Quait Bay. An island in the entrance makes navigation tricky—and ensures the anchorage is protected in all winds.

After that year we made Quait Bay a regular stop on our way north. We always had it to ourselves. I liked to row the dinghy along the shore in the quiet waters and in the afternoons we would hike up the creek bed to a lake where we went skinny-dipping among the water lilies.

Clayoquot residents know Quait Bay by the name of Calm Creek. But the creek that enters Quait Bay near its entrance is anything but calm. It tumbles down a steep rocky hillside and into a pool of rocks. From just about anywhere in Quait Bay, you can hear it roaring. The creek once powered a shingle mill operated by the Darville family. Anthony Guppy, an apprentice at the mill in the 1930s, described the mill and the Darvilles in his book, *Tofino Kid*. John Darville, the mill's owner, was a former foundry worker from Seattle. He was also a trained mechanic, a bit of a blacksmith, a good boat carpenter and a self-taught expert in gasoline, diesel and steam engines. Most importantly to Guppy, Darville was an excellent teacher who let his apprentice make his own mistakes, and then told him how to correct them in a way that made him want to do it right the next time. Guppy found Calm Creek to be a friendly, quiet place, even when the mill was operating. He speculated that the swishing of the water through the waterwheel harmonized perfectly with the whine of the saws.

We hadn't read Guppy's book before our first trip to Quait Bay and would never have guessed a sawmill had been there. The only evidence of human activity were some clear-cuts up in the hills and an old wooden water pipe snaking up alongside the creek. If we didn't know about the sawmill, we also didn't know what was ahead for the small bay, although we might have gotten some hint, in 1993, when we noticed a For Sale sign next to the creek.

In 1997 we stopped at Quait Bay on our trip north after an absence of several years. As we approached the entrance, I stood on the bow of the *Osprey* watching for rocks. Because the island blocks the entrance so perfectly, I couldn't see anything of the bay until we were almost in the entrance. As we entered, I expected to see the usual quiet scene and hear the dull roar of the creek. But the first things I saw were two other boats ahead of us in the anchorage. Then, a small powerboat roared out, sending *Osprey* rocking in its wake. We rounded the corner and I was astounded to see a large building complete with balconies, awnings, hanging planter boxes and an ornate green roof. Tourism had arrived in Quait Bay in the form of a floating hotel.

The hotel took up only a small corner of the bay next to the stream, but to our eyes, it dominated the entire bay. The rock where we had landed our dinghy was now the landing for the hotel. The lake where we had gone skinny-dipping was no longer private. The bay that we had once had to ourselves we now shared with the tourist industry. My first inclination was to turn right around and leave. But it was already late afternoon and both of us were tired from our sail from Ucluelet. So we stayed where we were, studiously trying to ignore the hotel.

When we are cruising inside the sounds of the west coast of Vancouver Island, it's our habit to spend the mornings, when it's too calm to sail, exploring the shorelines in our dinghy. We like to motor in and out of small coves and among the rocks where we can't go in our big boat. So the next morning when we awoke and saw that the sun was out and the water was absolutely flat and calm, we headed out the entrance in the dinghy.

The coastline of this area of Cypress Bay is rugged and rocky and the morning sun reflecting off the water gave rocks and trees an almost magical glow. We rounded a corner and there in front of us, enclosed in a tiny little cove surrounded by trees, was a fantastic floating complex of magenta and green buildings. Steve stopped the dinghy and we just stared. Had we drifted into some *Alice in Wonderland* world? At the centre

The Clayoquot Wilderness Resort includes a gourmet restaurant—for those with money to spare.

of the complex floated a small cottage of bright magenta with a multi-levelled roof that brought to mind the House-that-Jack-Built. Everything in sight was magenta or green: magenta and green docks, magenta storage sheds, green fuel tanks. Someone had even painted the roof shingles magenta. A sign over the door said "*Fireweed*."

A man and a woman were working in a garden on one of the floats, like two suburbanites in a backyard. As we gazed in astonishment, the man motioned us over to the dock. "Welcome to *Fireweed*," he said as he took our dinghy painter. He then introduced himself as Wayne Adams, the woman as Catherine King. I had the odd feeling that they had been expecting us.

Wayne is slender, of medium height, and sports a moustache. He told us he is a carver of buried ivory—ancient tusks and bones that require special government permits to obtain. While Wayne talked, Catherine glided around the floats, doing odds and ends, her long brown hair trailing out behind her. "Catherine is a painter, an apprentice carver and a former dancer," Wayne told us.

Wayne and Catherine built their home themselves, using materials rescued from the sea whenever possible. They painted it magenta and green to match the colours of the fireweed flower found in cleared areas of Vancouver Island. "Fireweed" was also Catherine's stage name as a dancer. Wayne told us that he is as proud of his home as he is of his art. The house *is* art. A walkway connects their house to the garden. Raspberries,

Opposite: Wayne
Adams and Catherine
King's house is named
Fireweed after the bright
pink flowers seen
growing on clearings
on Vancouver Island.

Left: Catherine demon-
strates a drawbridge
constructed so kayaks
from the Clayoquot
Wilderness Resort can
paddle through
Fireweed's garden.

lettuce and tomatoes grow over water. "We've got the only slug-free garden in British Columbia," bragged Wayne as he showed us around. No slugs can get from the land to his floats.

When we were getting into our dinghy to leave, I commented on the full-length mirror in a corner of their floating dock: "With that mirror, you could do yoga on this float." "Yes, Catherine does yoga here sometimes," Wayne said, "but usually she just dances."

If it hadn't been for Catherine and Wayne we might not have returned to Quait Bay—there were other attractive coves in Clayoquot Sound uncluttered by hotels. But we wanted to see Catherine and Wayne again and Quait Bay is the only good anchorage near their little cove. Over the winter we had time to get used to the idea of sharing the bay, so the next year we anchored there as usual, choosing a spot a little farther in to keep away from the hotel. But it was impossible to ignore the hotel and as we were putting away the sails we kept looking at it and talking about it.

"I wonder if they would let us hike up that road," I said to Steve as I peered at the hotel through binoculars. "It would be a lot easier than hiking up the creek bed. Maybe we can still go swimming. We'll just have to wear our swimsuits."

A hotel employee met us at the dock. "Go right ahead and take a walk," she told us. "Stop by on your way back, and we'll give you a tour." We walked by a horse paddock where several horses grazed, and up the steep dirt road to the lake. There we had our swim among the water lilies in the same clean water we had swum in years before.

Our tour guide, Erin, met us at the hotel entrance. She explained that the building had started life as a fishing lodge in Barkley Sound. New owners had towed it north in January 1996 and renovated it as a luxury hotel named the Clayoquot Wilderness Resort. Erin and her husband had followed the hotel north in their sailboat. They worked as staff at the hotel in the summer, as caretakers in the winter and lived in their sailboat anchored in Quait Bay.

We were amazed at the idea of such a big building under tow, especially in January when storms can come up without warning and the ocean swells can be huge. In

Seattle moving a two-storey building half a mile down the Lake Washington Ship Canal occasioned a front-page article in the *Seattle Times*, but on the west coast of Vancouver Island moving a building 30 miles was no big deal. The hotel was following a long tradition. In the 1930s and '40s logging camps routinely disappeared from one cove and popped up in another a few miles away. Bunkhouses, cookhouses and married men's houses were built on floats and towed with fishboats, tugboats, or whatever could be recruited for the job.

Like the logging camps, the hotel was self-sufficient: a state-of-the-art sewage plant hummed away in the bowels of the building; hydro power from the stream provided electricity, the lake provided drinking water from a pipeline at depth. Erin proudly pointed to the mouldings of the bedrooms and told us they had used nothing but previously cut logs abandoned by the mill to renovate the hotel.

The hotel was no rugged fish camp. Polished slate tiles covered the entryway floor and rough but artful wood panels lined the walls. By the time we reached the dining room on the second floor with its panoramic view of the bay, I was ready to register as a guest. White-uniformed chefs prepared dinner in an open kitchen. "Could we have dinner without being hotel guests?" I asked. Yes, if we made reservations ahead of time. A full five-course dinner was $45 Canadian. We gulped and headed back to our boat for a meal of black bean chili. "Forty-five dollars Canadian isn't really that bad," said Steve. "It's only $30 American." I didn't take much convincing. Dinner wasn't until 7 p.m. so we decided to visit Catherine and Wayne while we were waiting.

As soon as we stepped out of the dinghy, Wayne handed us a sheet of paper, titled "The Bower" that announced the marriage of Wayne and Catherine that April on his fiftieth birthday. In honour of the marriage, *Fireweed* had been renamed *The Bower* after the Australian bower bird—a plain brown bird that attracts his mate by making his nest from materials he finds in the wilds around him. The older the bower bird gets, the more elaborate his nest.

Wayne and Catherine had also become legal in another way: they had become legal squatters, paying the provincial government $100 a year to anchor their home in this small cove—a common lifestyle in Clayoquot Sound. Wayne proudly showed us the 1999 *Canadian Geographic* magazine with an article about Clayoquot squatters, complete with a full-page picture of Catherine dancing on *Fireweed*'s dock.

I had been so taken by all the magenta and green on our previous visit that I had brought colour print film just to take pictures of *Fireweed*. I asked permission to take pictures of them and their house. "I'm always happy to help a fellow artist," said Wayne, posing in front of his door. They invited us inside and we saw that the green and magenta motif continued inside with bright green walls accented by dark green curtains. In the center of the green floor is a Plexiglas panel. From their sofa, Wayne and Catherine could watch fish swim by below. Next to a window in their living room was one of Wayne's carvings: a life-sized foxglove with two small human feet sticking out of each flower.

On our way into *Fireweed*'s cove, we had passed a newly painted salmon troller anchored outside. Wayne told us he had purchased and rebuilt the troller through the Canadian government's buyout plan. "I'm glad the government gave us artists the opportunity to buy boats like that," he said. "Otherwise, I couldn't afford it." The troller gave them transportation to and from Tofino.

"We're always glad to see visitors," Wayne told us as we climbed into the dinghy to leave. "It's part of our jobs to welcome strangers to Clayoquot Sound. Most artists in Clayoquot Sound won't talk to you," he said. "They just want to be left alone. But we didn't come here for isolation—we came for space to do our art."

We returned to Quait Bay lulled by visions of Catherine and Wayne and their simple lifestyle. At 7 p.m. we were in a comfortable corner lounge next to the hotel's dining room, sipping glasses of chilled Chardonnay. A coffee table in front of us held several copies of *Country Living* magazine along with another magazine I'd never heard of devoted exclusively to growing and cooking with herbs. I felt as if I had stepped from *Alice in Wonderland* into the *Great Gatsby*.

Sitting next to us was another boating couple from Vancouver, BC. They were on their final leg of a circumnavigation of Vancouver Island in their powerboat. Like us, this was their first experience with the Clayoquot Wilderness Resort. They were congenial company and we shared a table for dinner. Except for three sport fishermen at the bar, the four of us had the dining room to ourselves.

Dinner was fresh leek and roasted onion soup, a salad of baby spinach and a choice of oven-roasted rack of lamb or grilled halibut with fresh asparagus. We could have been eating at a five-star restaurant in a city: white tablecloths, fine china and waiters hovering discreetly. Afterwards we relaxed in front of a fire, chatting with the hotel

owner. He wanted the hotel to welcome boaters and hoped we would come again: we were welcome to tie up to the mooring buoys in front of the hotel.

During dinner a thick fog crept into the bay. We hadn't expected to be so late and hadn't thought to put up an anchor light, but we found our way back to *Osprey* by heading for the anchor light of another boat nearby. It occurred to me on the way back that maybe having a hotel in Quait Bay wasn't so bad after all.

I couldn't help thinking about the hotel and Wayne and Catherine's house in terms of the planning and environmental issues I dealt with in Seattle. I had spent five years as a shoreline planner for the City of Seattle. There were

The Clayoquot Wilderness Resort has been adding facilities every year.

times when I felt like my job was holding back an army of floating hotels, houses and restaurants ready to invade Seattle's shorelines. The Washington State Shoreline Management Act, which it was my duty to uphold, maintained that over-water space should be preserved for water-dependent uses—shipyards, boatyards, cargo terminals— that couldn't logically be placed anywhere else. Floating structures shaded the water and damaged fish habitat, so they should only be allowed when absolutely necessary. Of course there were always exceptions to this rule, such as for Seattle's historic floating homes on Lake Union.

I wasn't at all sure this rule made sense on the west coast of Vancouver Island. There is no shortage of waterfront for water-dependent uses here and the floating structures seemed less damaging. No land had to be cleared and no trees had to be cut down to make room for them. The hotel and *Fireweed* could both disappear tomorrow, leaving their two coves quiet again.

Quait Bay remained a regular stop for us, but we only ate at the hotel restaurant one more time, in 2000. By then the dinners were $65, and the dining room was filled with a clientele that looked as if they had stepped off the streets of Vancouver or Seattle. In 2001 when Steve called from Ahousat to make a reservation for dinner, hotel staff asked, "Do you know we charge $100 now?" One hundred dollars, we decided, was too much, no matter how good the meal.

Anthony Guppy, the apprentice at the Darville mill, would not have recognized Calm Creek. Seaplanes droned overhead and then taxied by our boat on their way to deliver guests to the hotel. A constant stream of small powerboats raced through the narrow entrance to drop off tourists from afternoons of sightseeing and whale-watching. Offshore from the hotel an old tug served as the dormitory for hotel staff, its generator humming throughout the day. We actually had to stop and listen to hear the roar of the creek.

Every year afterwards when we returned we found a new addition to the hotel. In 2001, it was a longhouse. We went ashore to investigate and found workers putting finishing touches on a massive copper hood for an open firepit. Next to the longhouse several Nuu-chah-nulth were carving totem poles. We stopped and talked to them and learned they were from Ahousat. They seemed happy for the opportunity to carve. But the sense of luxury had grown even more noticeable and the resort was definitely out of our league.

At *Fireweed*, Catherine and Wayne had additions, too. Their pride and joy that year was an over-water chicken coop. "These chickens lay the best eggs," said Wayne, reaching into the hen house and pulling out an egg the size of a football. "That always gets people," he said when he saw my expression. "I get these ostrich eggs from a friend."

While Catherine, Steve and I sipped tea on their couch, Wayne lay on the floor and talked. He told us about the efforts to stop bear hunting and about the government's attempts to evict the squatters from Lemmens Inlet. Their sewage discharges were threatening the oyster businesses there. We told Wayne and Catherine about the $100 meals at the Clayoquot Wilderness Resort and said we thought it a shame that it was turning into an exclusive resort for the rich. Wayne had a different perspective.

"The kind of people the resort is attracting are good for Clayoquot Sound. They are people who take life easy. And they buy our art. Rich people are good for artists in Clayoquot Sound. At first, the resort tried to get tourists to come from Tofino. That didn't work. Now they arrange transportation from Vancouver or Seattle as part of the package."

We left with a statue of a funny little man made from a casting of two ostrich eggs. The statue had a teardrop in its eye and Wayne told us its name was either "Crying in the Wayne" or "Wayne Drop."

On our way back to our boat we stopped at the resort's gift shop to see a display of Wayne and Catherine's carvings. Wayne had contributed a small whale under attack by a squid, and Catherine a foxglove. Above the carvings was an 8 x 10 print of one of the pictures I had taken of them. Suddenly, it didn't matter as much that we couldn't afford to eat at the resort. Seeing my picture there made me feel as if I belonged in Clayoquot Sound.

That evening as we sat in our cockpit drinking wine and enjoying the evening sun, I thought about how Quait Bay had changed. I felt ambivalent about tourism in Clayoquot. I liked the fact that clear-cutting had stopped and I recognized that the people of Clayoquot needed jobs. Tourism filled a gap but provided mostly service jobs. Very few year-round residents of Clayoquot could afford to eat at the Clayoquot Wilderness Resort. And I wondered how many of the guests at the hotel ever met Wayne and Catherine, or anyone else in Clayoquot Sound who didn't directly serve them. But then getting to know people like Wayne and Catherine was one of the advantages of coming by sailboat.

Heelboom (C'is-a-quis) Bay

A Tribal Park

On a grey November day in 1984, an angry crowd of Tofino residents and Nuu-chah-nulth stood on the shore of Heelboom Bay facing a crew of loggers offshore aboard the boat *Kennedy Queen*. The loggers asked people to please get out of their way. The protestors stood their ground. Then Chief Moses Martin of the Tla-o-qui-aht First Nation (after whom Clayoquot Sound is named) stepped forward, welcoming the loggers to his garden—and asking them to please leave their chainsaws on the boat. This confrontation was the first of many protests that changed the logging industry in Clayoquot Sound and made Clayoquot a beacon for environmentalists around the world.

We visited Heelboom Bay, called C'is-a-quis by the Natives, in 2001. It was only the second time we had been to eastern Clayoquot Sound, which we considered to be powerboat country as it is full of shallow channels with swift currents. But while researching this book I had been astonished to learn that events here had made Clayoquot

A grey day at Heelboom Bay.

Sound famous around the world. In fact, a virtual library of academic literature had been written about them. We had known the protests were happening and had read of them in local newspapers on our summer trips, but hadn't realized the full extent or significance of those events. I knew that the subject of the protests was a controversial one and that there were many opinions about what had happened. I felt that to even begin to understand what happened I needed to see the site of that first confrontation.

We arrived at C'is-a-quis on a grey, cloudy day with a cold wind blowing up Fortune Channel and a drizzle that crept into my foul-weather gear and made me shiver. We anchored off a group of rocks at the entrance to the cove and took the dinghy inside, motoring past a plain wooden sign that said "Meares Island Tribal Park," and landing on a flat stretch of beach. Behind the beach we could see a small shingled cabin. We knew we had come to the right place when we saw a sign on the cabin's front wall reading,

In a bid to prevent its being logged, Chief Moses Martin of the Tla-o-qui-aht band declared Meares Island a tribal park.

"STOP Clear-Cuts." It was a sentiment I had to agree with. On our first trips to the west coast of Vancouver Island, we thought we had come to a wilderness, only to realize the wilderness was disappearing around us as patchworks of clear-cuts spread along the coast like a malignant cancer.

In Checleset Bay we had gazed in horror at Mount Paxton, shaved from top to bottom, slashed with logging roads, blotched with landslides and gullies. In Kyuquot Sound we had sailed into promising little coves, then sailed right back out to escape their bleak shorn shores. In Nootka Sound we had looked across from Captain Cook's first anchorage and seen barren mountains where once there had been green forests.

But the wilderness had been only in our imaginations. The history of this coast from the time of first contact with Europeans has been one of exploitation for profit of one resource after another. First came the fur traders, carrying away so many otter furs they drove the sea otters to near extinction by 1820. Sealers came next, chasing seals far out at sea. When an international treaty ended fur sealing in 1911, sealers turned to whaling. By 1920 the whales too were gone. Then the pilchards, a sardine-like fish, disappeared, followed by halibut, herring and salmon. Forests, the very foundation of the ecosystem, would have followed, if the people of Clayoquot Sound hadn't started the "war of the woods."

The controversy at C'is-a-quis began in 1980 when the British Columbia lumber company MacMillan Bloedel announced plans to log Meares Island. Residents of Tofino, who relied on the watersheds of Meares for their water and could see its forested slopes from their houses, formed Friends of Clayoquot Sound to save Meares.

For almost four years the Friends of Clayoquot Sound and Nuu-chah-nulth tribal members negotiated with MacMillan Bloedel and the BC government. But when the provincial government announced its decision, the only concession made was to delay a mere 10 percent of the logging—a decision the government deemed a compromise. Residents of Clayoquot Sound rallied in outrage and at a gathering in April 1984 the Tla-o-qui-aht band declared Meares a tribal park, open to all who followed the laws of the band's ancestors. The residents gathered in C'is-a-quis Bay where the logging was to start. There they carved cedar canoes and built a cabin while helicopters buzzed overhead. And there the MV *Kennedy Queen* found them.

From C'is-a-quis the battle moved to the courts. MacMillan Bloedel obtained an injunction against the protestors. The protesters filed an appeal—and stayed put at C'is-a-quis. Then the Tla-o-qui-aht band showed they had learned white men's tricks: they filed their own injunction, claiming ownership of the land.

British Columbia First Nations do not have treaties with the Canadian federal government as Natives do elsewhere in Canada or as tribes in the United States have with the US Government. Nor do British Columbia bands have reservations equal to those of US tribes. Instead, they have numerous small reserves scattered up and down the coast at river mouths or the entrances to inlets. The total area in reserves on all of the west coast of Vancouver Island is barely equal to the area of the Makah Reservation at Neah Bay in Washington State. These small reserves give access to traditional fishing grounds, but leave the fish runs and other resources vulnerable to damage caused by logging upstream. As a result Natives across the province had filed land claims. In 1980 the Canadian government agreed to negotiate. They are still negotiating today.

When the BC court approved the Tla-o-qui-ahts' (Clayoquots') injunction pending the results of treaty negotiations, it bought time for the people of Clayoquot Sound to come up with a new way of managing their resources.

In 1987 a report by the United Nations-sponsored World Commission on Environment and Development called on all nations to promote "development that meets the needs of the present without compromising the ability of future generations to meet their needs." "Sustainable development" became the guiding principle of environmental groups, including those at Clayoquot.

Clayoquot residents soon found that defining sustainable development isn't easy. Environmentalists, the Nuu-chah-nulth, townspeople and forest companies met, discussed, and discussed some more. Even those who agreed that clear-cut logging needed to stop couldn't agree on what to replace it with. Tourism was growing in Clayoquot Sound, but not everyone welcomed it. Some saw problems in skyrocketing property values and the clash of cultures as latte-drinking urbanites replaced fishermen in plaid shirts. Some even wondered if a land of housing developments and tourist hotels was worth saving. As word of the controversy spread, experts in politics, economics, sociology and ecology came to the Sound, but few could agree on what to do.

A freshly logged clear-cut in Millar Channel. 1980.

Abandoned logging
gear rusting on the
rocks.

Then in 1993 the BC government released its solution to the problem: the Clayoquot Sound Land Use Decision. It was a compromise solution that protected many pristine watersheds but left others unprotected. Once again environmentalists were outraged. The Nuu-chah-nulth were angry that their land use claims were left unresolved.

That summer a daily ritual of protest and arrest took place on a bridge over the Kennedy River, just a few miles east of Heelboom Bay. Every morning protestors blockaded the road and the RCMP arrested them. Students with backpacks, grandmothers in tennis shoes, people from all walks of life and from all over the world were arrested that summer. It was the largest mass arrest in Canadian history. Celebrities including Robert Kennedy Jr. made visits in support of the protests. And two major paper companies cancelled newsprint contracts with MacMillan Bloedel as a result.

Events accelerated after that summer. Legal decisions in British Columbia and elsewhere in Canada had strengthened the legal status of Native land claims. As a result of those decisions and in response to the protests, the BC government concluded an Interim Measures Agreement with the Nuu-chah-nulth. The agreement established a regional board that gave both First Nations and other residents a say in resource decisions with the ultimate objective to promote economic and environmental sustainability for Clayoquot.

Also, as a result of the mass arrests, the BC government established a blue-ribbon scientific panel of biologists, foresters, fishery scientists, and Nuu-chah-nulth elders expert in traditional resource use. Their task: review forest practices and recommend changes. The panel's recommendation: stop clear-cutting and destructive road building and instead log so as to keep the natural age and species distribution of trees in the forest. In effect, the scientific panel sided with the protestors.

Discussions continued. Environmentalists and the tourism industry saw Clayoquot as an untouched pristine wilderness. Forest industry representatives saw the forest as a source of profit and jobs. In the middle were Nuu-chah-nulth tribal members whose ancestors thrived in the forests, but to whom the idea of a wilderness free of humans would have been alien. The Nuu-chah-nulth didn't like clear-cuts, but they needed jobs. They saw Clayoquot forests as a resource to be managed for the good of the people.

In my work in Seattle I have observed that environmental groups with radical agendas can balance business groups with equally radical agendas on the other side. But I have noticed that the best way to get real progress on an issue is for a moderate group with a vested interest in the issue to step forward. The moderate group gives the others a focus, and paves the way for a compromise. From reading the literature on the Clayoquot controversy, I believe that the Nuu-chah-nulth may have played that role here.

In 1999 MacMillan Bloedel, the Nuu-chah-nulth and several environmental groups signed a Memorandum of Understanding. MacMillan Bloedel and the Nuu-chah-nulth forest companies agreed to operate within the spirit of the principles of the scientific panel and to identify areas for ecologically sustainable commercial forestry. The environmental groups took a rare step away from their absolute positions and agreed to help develop markets for forest products harvested with sustainable forestry. The Memorandum of Understanding cleared the way for an event on May 5, 2000, that many refer to as the end of the "war in the woods." The United Nations officially declared Clayoquot Sound a Biosphere Reserve. The only sour note was a boycott by the Tla-o-qui-aht due to stalled treaty negotiations.

The biosphere designation won't save Clayoquot Sound—the people of Clayoquot Sound must do that. And it remains to be seen what effect it will have on the rest of the coast. The biosphere doesn't establish new laws or enforce old ones. What it does is formalize the vision of Clayoquot Sound that its people had developed: a vision of pristine areas protected from industrial forestry, but used to support the economic health of the region in other ways—in healthy fish runs and locally controlled ecoforestry.

The small cabin in front of us on the beach at C'is-a-quis has become a symbol of triumph. "Nobody messes with that cabin. It's a special place," our friend Wayne Adams of Quait Bay told us. We pushed gently on the cabin's wooden door. It swung open and we walked gingerly inside. To our right we saw a crude wood-burning stove made from oil drums. Running around the walls were rough shelves with crude benches. Neat stacks of pots and pans occupied one shelf. On another I found some photographs varnished onto a board. They looked like photographs anyone might take on a group camping trip: people chopping wood, carving a canoe—ordinary people who had taken a stand and accomplished something.

We put the pictures back and walked out, carefully closing the door behind us. In back of the house we found a trail that went uphill and across a stream past giant cedars and spruce. On the slope above the cabin we found several cedars with long vertical bare strips where bark had been stripped off. The Nuu-chah-nulth once carved these strips from the trees to use for clothing, mats and baskets. By only cutting a narrow vertical strip, they left the tree to grow and serve future generations. The Nuu-chah-nulth claim these trees, called "culturally modified trees" or CMTs by anthropologists, as evidence of their historical ownership of the land. I can't think of a better example of sustainable development.

We walked up the hill, breathing in the smell of cedar and feeling layers of evergreen needles springing beneath our feet. Under the trees the drizzle was only a mist, the ground almost dry. Old-growth forests are more open than second-growth because the massive canopies of the large trees shade the forest floor and prevent new growth, so we found it easy to walk among the trees. It was beautiful, even in the rain. I tried to imagine what C'is-a-quis would be like today if the protests had failed—bare ground scraped of trees and exposed to the rain. The thought of it made me grateful to the people of Clayoquot Sound for helping to preserve all of this and awed at what they had accomplished. It was like walking through a park—a tribal park.

Clayoquot Sound

Northwestern Portion

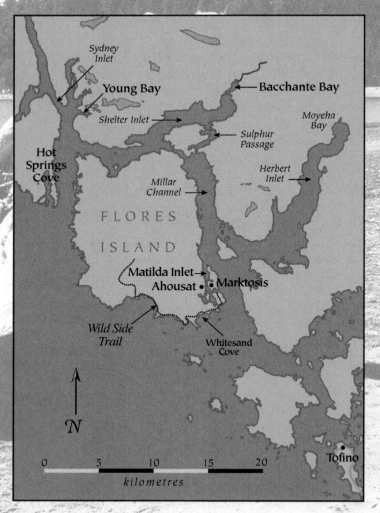

When we turned the corner into Sydney Inlet, we saw a wall of white fog creeping in from the ocean. I liked the drama of the fog streaming toward us as we sailed toward it. Each time we tacked I looked south to check the fog's progress. I felt as if we were in a race, the fog against Osprey. We were battling the wind; the fog was battling the sun. As the fog moved north, the sun burned away its leading edge, so that the fog, always moving, never advanced. The race was ours.

Matilda Inlet

Wild Side Heritage Trail

We like to anchor in the small basin on the west side of Matilda Inlet near its head. It's a pretty place and just a short dinghy ride to the warm springs at Gibson Marine Park. On the west shore of the basin an old cedar snag supports an eagle's nest. Through binoculars we can watch the eaglets begging their parents for food. A large salt marsh fringed with trees extends across the bottom of the inlet, cut by a line of abandoned telegraph poles. I have puzzled over the poles, wondering who used them. The only settlements on Flores Island are the Native village at Marktosis and Ahousat across the inlet, and they're close enough to each other that even a canoe can get back and forth in a few minutes.

Each time we passed the entrance to the village of Marktosis on our way into the anchorage at the south end of Matilda Inlet we were intrigued by the narrow rocky channel and the glimpse of the village beyond. But we had heard yachts and their

The remains of an old telegraph line can still be seen crossing the marsh at the head of Matilda Inlet.

owners weren't welcome at this village, the home of the Ahousaht band of the Nuu-chah-nulth. Like so many communities on the west coast of Vancouver Island, Matilda Inlet is divided into a Native village and a non-Native village, which had the store, fish plant, post office and fuel dock. We had no reason to go to the Native village, so we stayed in the basin or shopped at the Ahousat General Store.

Then in 1998 we heard that the Ahousaht band had built a trail, the Wild Side Heritage Trail, that was touted as an example of a new entrepreneurial spirit among the Nuu-chah-nulth. The 11 km hike crossed sandy beaches and climbed forested headlands on the ocean side of Flores Island. Because so much of the west coast of Vancouver Island is impenetrable forest, the chance to hike appealed to us.

To walk the trail, we would have to take our dinghy through the narrow rock-strewn entrance into Marktosis. On our way to the anchorage, we stopped at the general store to ask about the route into Marktosis. We found Hugh Clarke, the store owner, cleaning fish in front of the fish plant, a box of salmon at his feet. He advised against going to Marktosis. The village children would wreck our dinghy, he told us.

The Wild Side Heritage Trail winds through the forest on a path of cedar boards.

They had broken the oars and damaged engines of other visitors' boats. "They're good kids," he said, "but they've never been told not to play with other people's boats." Most tourists visited Marktosis in the tour boat from Tofino—with a tour guide near them at all times. If we really wanted to go there we could take the trail across the isthmus to Whitesand Cove and walk backward to the heritage trail.

We had tried to walk to Whitesand Cove once before and had given up when we found ourselves knee-deep in mud. So we left Matilda Inlet to explore Herbert Inlet instead.

But I didn't give up on the Wild Side Trail. From time to time I would talk about it with Steve, wondering if we couldn't pay a Native child to watch our dinghy or hire a water taxi to cross the inlet. But to Steve the idea of paying someone to watch the dinghy or to ferry us a distance we could easily travel ourselves was too much like extortion. Then, two years later we met a powerboater at Hot Springs Cove who had ignored Hugh Clarke's advice and taken his dinghy to Marktosis without incident. We decided to just go. Besides, this time we were on our way home. If our dinghy were trashed, at least we wouldn't be without it for a whole vacation.

The next morning was perfect for a hike—blue skies and warm sunshine. We motored the dinghy through the narrow entrance leaving a light to starboard and a treacherous-looking rock to port. The fishboat *Solander Isle* was inching its way out as we went in. Beyond the narrow entrance, the channel opened to a round basin with a multi-fingered public dock surrounded by a mud flat. Abandoned fishboats rested haphazardly on the mud. We tied our dinghy next to the ramp where a little boy of about 10 with the dark hair and round face of a Nuu-chah-nulth was standing. "Good morning," we said. He walked up the ramp without acknowledging our presence. I thought uneasily of Hugh Clarke's advice.

The history of the Ahousaht could make anyone nervous. They once lived on Vargas Island where there were no salmon streams while a band called the Otsosaht lived on Flores Island, where the Ahousaht live now. The Otsosaht owned many salmon streams all around the area. In the early 1800s the Ahousaht went to war with the Otsosaht to win rights to the salmon, chasing down the Otsosaht as far away as Neah Bay to make sure they wouldn't come back.

As we walked through town, I expected to be accosted at any moment by someone demanding to know what we were doing there. But passersby merely ignored us, except for one young woman with a baby who gave us a welcoming smile. We followed a winding dirt road past unpainted wooden houses set haphazardly close together among unmown grass and blackberries. Plastic coolers, gas tanks and other miscellaneous gear littered the small porches. Every house had its satellite dish. There was nothing picturesque about this village, except possibly the strings of Christmas lights still decorating many of the houses.

We found the band Council building and went in to ask directions. A young man in a T-shirt and jeans introduced himself as James and volunteered to take us to the Wild Side office. Outside the band office James's dog, a black Labrador-like puppy named Tica, was waiting on a leash—the only dog in Marktosis on a leash, James told us. Indeed there seemed to be dogs running free everywhere. As we walked, James gave us a running commentary on the village. About 300 people lived there. He pointed out the new school, a modern building with northwest Native designs on its upper storey. They had built two new classrooms themselves and the government didn't even know they had done it. They had also built their own store and were no longer dependent on the Ahousat General Store for all of their needs.

When we reached the top of a hill, James pointed us to the office of the Wild Side Heritage Trail in a two-storey red building. The office was a small shop with carvings of paddles and masks on the wall. A round-faced Native woman, who introduced herself as Ramona, was working at a desk. She told us the fee to walk the trail was $20 Canadian apiece, $30 if we wanted a guide. She also had guidebooks for $17. We hadn't imagined the trail would be that expensive. We had only $50 between us so we paid $40 and asked for directions.

I listened with dismay to Ramona's vague directions. She said something like, "Go behind the school, then go this way, then that way, then over a bridge." The first problem came when we got to the school: which side was "behind"? We chose the side fronting the road and followed that road past the school and across a field of stumps to an abandoned sawmill. We were lost. We retraced our steps until we found the bridge, crossed it and then followed a road constructed of small round logs laid crosswise in the road. We were walking a corduroy road, something I had heard about but never seen before. The road ended at the head of Matilda Inlet with no trail in sight. We had left *Osprey* more than an hour ago and now we were just a few hundred feet from the anchorage. The morning was disappearing fast. I wondered if we would ever find the trail. Why had no one thought to put up a sign?

"We paid $40 just to get lost?" Steve turned quickly and strode off in the direction we had come, presumably to give the Ahousaht a piece of his mind. I followed, worried that he might get us into a battle. But just before we came to the bridge, we saw the entrance to the trail all but hidden by bushes.

With a solid boardwalk under our feet our moods improved. The trail led through a swamp, into a forest and from there onto a broad sandy beach with a view of islands and blue water. Piles of pungent red seaweed squished under our feet, each step sending hordes of sand fleas leaping into the air. We learned later that the Ahousaht call this beach "stinking seaweed beach." At the far end of the beach we spotted a West Coast trail sign— an orange crab buoy hanging from a tree. Ducking underneath overhanging branches of spruce, we entered the forest. A six-foot-tall, green-painted sign confronted us:

Ahousaht Wild Side Heritage Trail
Treat with Care and Respect
You are in Ahousaht Territory

Nine different organizations had put their names on this sign, including the Ministry of Environment, MacMillan Bloedel and the Western Canada Wilderness Committee. Nine organizations had helped construct the trail; none had thought to post a single directional sign.

We followed the split-cedar trail as it wound through old-growth forest of cedar, spruce, hemlock and fir. Where the trail led up steep slopes, it became stairways complete with handrails made from tree branches. Each board was hand split, sawed to length and nailed in place. Forty dollars to hike the trail was a bargain. We stopped in front of an old cedar. Like the cedars that we had seen in Heelboom Bay, a narrow strip of bark had been peeled from it long ago exposing bare wood. An interpretive sign on the trail explained that the tree was a culturally modified tree and provided evidence of early aboriginal occupation.

Whitesand Cove is part of the Gibson Marine Park.

Eventually the trail left the forest and emerged onto the beach at Whitesand Cove. Low surf curled onto the broad sandy beach, which stretched for half a mile. From the beach we could see west toward the open ocean, south across the blue waters of Russell Channel studded with rocks and islands and east to the high rocky cliffs of the Catface Range—a beautiful view. I was glad we had made the effort to find the trail.

Walking through the town on our way back, I looked again at the houses that had seemed so alien. Although miscellaneous junk littered the porches, the streets and yards were clean, the houses weathered but not dilapidated. They reminded me vaguely of suburban houses—set close together at various angles, rather than in neat rows like city houses.

We stopped to admire a canoe outside a house under construction. A man working on the house told us there were more canoes in the boathouse. We followed his directions to the large rambling structure and stepped through a dark doorway. Inside were five or six canoes in various stages of construction. There wasn't anyone around so we ran our hands over the bare wood and sniffed the fresh cedar.

On our way back to the dock we saw a sign saying "Deaf Children's Play Area." I realized the boy on the dock hadn't been unfriendly; he just hadn't heard us.

Our dinghy was still tied safely to the dock, our outboard and oars undisturbed. Children played around the dock, diving in the water and spraying each other with a hose. "We wondered whose boat that was," said a little boy. We watched as an adult standing on the dock reached down into the water to retrieve a painted paddle from one of the swimming children. "Give me that," he said. "It's not a plaything." Someone was telling the children not to play with other people's boats.

EPILOGUE. The Heritage Trail now has a website, a guidebook, T-shirts and an annual trail run. The locations of office and trailhead are subject to change; ask for help in finding the office. Beware! Hikers have sighted bears, cougars and wolves on the trail.

Matilda Inlet

Shopping without a List

The native village of Marktosis is accessible only by boat through a narrow rockbound channel.

We visited the Ahousat General Store for the first time in 1981, arriving in the middle of a sunny afternoon. A steady stream of boats was coming and going from the Native village of Marktosis and a parade of shoppers walked up and down the ramp to the store. Children seemed to be everywhere, playing on the dock and eating ice cream bars in front of the store. We squeezed *Velella* into a space at the dock between a fishboat and an aluminum skiff, grabbed our shopping list and shopping bags and joined the shoppers.

The store was a real general store, a holdover from another era. As if to emphasize this, a mounted cougar head glared down at shoppers from the wall. Post office boxes lined the wall behind the cash register. Engine belts hung over the counter. Canned goods vied with boots and fishing gear for room on the shelves. To get to the flour I had

to step over boxes of potato chips and cereal. The whole place needed a good cleaning. I looked at the two men behind the counter and thought—a woman would never have allowed this chaos. Shopping list in hand, I searched for flour, eggs, green pepper and fruit. Flour and eggs were no problem, but the green peppers were sold out. For fruit there were only a few withered apples. The delivery boat had obviously not been here recently. Discouraged, I put my list in my pocket and just explored the store, finally buying zucchini, lettuce and onions because they looked good.

That was the last time I bothered with a list at Ahousat General Store. In subsequent years I just looked to see what they had that I could use and bought whatever it was. Unwittingly I had stumbled on a truth long known by housewives on this coast. Margaret Sharcott, who travelled through this area in the 1950s with her fisherman husband and wrote *Troller's Holiday*, summed up a typical salt-water village store in one sentence: "One can buy nearly anything but the exact item one wants."

The Ahousat General Store sells everything from boots to zucchinis.

Ahousat is a one-man enterprise. Hugh Clarke, called Hughie by the locals, owns and operates the store, the fuel dock, the marine ways, the small fish-processing plant and the small motel over the store. He also owns the café next to the store run by his sister Pat Mosely, called Patty. A stocky man with straight greying hair, Hughie is usually dressed in jeans, a plaid shirt and suspenders. Someone once told me that you could write a whole book just about Hughie. If so, I won't be the one to write it. His taciturn nature has always intimidated me and his brief answers to my questions have discouraged me from asking more.

In 1998 we stopped at the store after an absence of several years. The first thing we noticed was a large For Sale sign across the storefront. Small print on the sign told us that not only the store, but the café and other businesses were all for sale. For a minute I thought the store was closed, the dock was so quiet. Where fishboats had once queued up for fuel, there was now only one lone motor yacht. Across the inlet aluminum skiffs still buzzed in and out of the reserve, but few stopped at the store.

Inside the store Hughie still reigned and the shelves were as crowded and chaotic as ever. A box of tomatoes on the shelf looked abandoned, the tomatoes soft and squishy and smelling of mould. Seeing me sorting gingerly through them, Hughie pointed to a second box on the floor. Those tomatoes were still firm. Then I noticed the flats of raspberries. Red and ripe and dripping with juice, some were already mildewed. But there were enough good ones left for raspberry shortcake that night. Among our purchases was a box of Grape-Nuts. When we opened them the next morning they tasted stale. We didn't know how to read the Canadian date codes, but the "83" in the midst of the numbers alarmed us. Could the Grape-Nuts have been on the shelf for 15 years?

When we left Ahousat that year, we wondered how long the store could last. We didn't see how Hughie could keep it open nor could we imagine who would want to buy it with so few customers. The Ahousaht band now had its own store and with commercial salmon fishermen gone, there wasn't much of a white community left in this part of Clayoquot Sound. And Tofino with its roads and supermarkets was only an hour away by speedboat. The few yachts that stopped at Matilda Inlet would never be enough to keep the store running. I felt sad that a store that had been an institution in Clayoquot Sound had to close and I didn't look forward to shopping at Tofino with its hordes of tourists and crowded docks.

So it was with a feeling of trepidation that I looked toward the store whenever we entered the inlet. But each year the store was still open. The For Sale sign, we decided, had become a permanent fixture.

One year when we arrived, we found the store sporting a new coat of blue paint and the For Sale sign gone. The store was closed for lunch, so we went directly to the café. As we opened the door, we noticed it still had the familiar sign on it from past years: "No Shoes, No Shirt, No Service Women Topless Okay." We assumed the store had been sold, so we were surprised to see Hughie and Patty eating at a table in the middle of the empty café. Sunlight streamed through clean windows with fresh clean curtains. Chairs and tables sat in orderly rows. Neatly framed posters and photographs decorated the walls. I was amazed that anything this neat and clean could be run by the same family as the general store.

We didn't want to interrupt Patty and Hughie's lunch, so we wandered around the room looking at the prints on the wall. I stopped to admire a print of an old-fashioned steamship. Patty saw me looking at it and came over to talk to me. "That's the *Maquinna*. My parents were married on that boat. Right here in Ahousat."

I had read the story of Patty and Hughie's parents in George Nicholson's *Vancouver Island's West Coast, 1762–1962*. Their father had started the general store at Hot Springs Cove where Patty, Hugh and their six siblings had grown up. But I didn't know the parents had been married on the *Princess Maquinna*. I thought maybe this was an opportunity to learn more about the history of Hot Springs Cove. I asked Patty if she would be willing to talk to me about her childhood.

"I won't talk about it," she told us. "Ask Hugh. He'll tell you. My childhood wasn't happy. I can't say anything good, so I won't say anything at all." I thought that probably Patty's story would be more interesting than Hughie's, and I was sorry she wouldn't say more.

We sat down and Patty brought us menus. A stocky woman with short greying hair, she wore a pink T-shirt, jeans and an apron. I asked her how the fish and chips were.

"Good choice," she told us. "The batter is my own personal recipe, the best on

Fishing boats like this one lay abandoned on the mudflat on the way into Marktosis.

the West Coast." When she brought the fish to our table they were crisp and golden with moist flaky flesh.

"How do you like the batter?" she asked us a few minutes later.

"Delicious."

"I plan to go into the business of selling that batter. I just haven't got around to it," she said. "I'm going to call it Battle Axe Batter. People call me a battle axe and that's what I'll call the batter."

While we ate, Patty talked. We had been wondering how the café stayed in business with so few customers, but we learned that they often had groups of tourists and that in addition to café customers Patty regularly cooked for a crew of workers.

Native children of Marktosis playing in the water near the public dock.

She asked us about our trip. We were on our way south after almost two months north.

"How did you like the store at Kyuquot?"

"Best general store on the west coast of Vancouver Island," I said. I stopped talking as I realized my mistake.

Patty looked knowingly at me and said. "They have a nice cold box for fresh food. Hugh bought a new cold box this year. Went all the way to Victoria to get it. Be sure to tell him you like it."

With new paint and a new cold box, I wondered if Hughie had given up selling and was trying to improve his business. But Patty told us he had a deal to sell the store to the Ahousaht band. It just hadn't been signed yet. They were reviewing the books. As we walked back to our boat, I thought what a good solution the sale to the Ahousaht would be. It would stop the competition between the two stores and give the Ahousaht more businesses for their entrepreneurial projects.

Later that afternoon we took the dinghy to the small public dock near the entrance to Marktosis and followed a dirt road up a hill to the trail office. Ramona wasn't there, her place at the desk taken by a young man. We bought the guidebook that we had wanted to buy on our last visit and an art print. On our way back we passed the band store in the downstairs of the same building. "Let's go in," I told Steve, although we had gotten just about everything we needed at the general store in Ahousat. We opened a glass door and walked into a small supermarket. Neat stacks of cans and boxes lined the shelves in orderly rows. The floor gleamed with polish. In the back a clean cold box held fresh milk and eggs. I could shop here with a list. Now I knew why the dock at Ahousat was so empty.

EPILOGUE. The small supermarket at Marktosis lasted only a few years before going out of business. As of 2014, the Ahousat General Store is still operating—and still for sale.

Bacchante Bay

Cat Overboard!

A sailboat motoring cautiously through the entrance to Bacchante Bay. For years the chart showed a nonexistent rock in the entrance.

Whenever anyone asks for our favourite anchorage in Clayoquot Sound, we always answer, "Bacchante Bay." It's not so much a bay as a short extension of Shelter Inlet protected from the afternoon winds and by two rocky promontories. Inside the bay steep rockbound cliffs climb straight up out of the water, so high they put the west side of the bay in shadows by early evening. At the head of the bay, Watta Creek comes down from the mountains and spills across a wide green marsh. From the anchorage near the marsh, you can look up the valley to Splendor Mountain with its distinctive hooked top. The bay is so beautiful and peaceful we almost always spend two nights there on every trip. We like to fish for rockfish at the bay's entrance, take our dinghy up the creek to pick blueberries or just relax in the sunshine.

In 2003, we arrived in Bacchante Bay late one sunny afternoon and anchored in our favourite spot in the southeast corner near the marsh. We were both tired from our sail so we settled down in the cockpit with our books while our cat, Jigger, sprawled on the floor. I didn't get much read because I kept stopping to listen to the clonk of a raven in the forest, the rush of a waterfall high up on the hillside or the honk of geese on the marsh. And just as I was settling down to read once again, a fly landed on my bare foot. I had forgotten about the flies, Bacchante Bay's only flaw. Big, beefy-looking flies with grey striped abdomens, they are larger, meaner and more persistent here than anywhere else. And they like to bite. I swatted the fly with my book but it was too fast for me, so I went below to get the fly swatter that we had last used in this same bay two years ago. I had returned to the cockpit and was flailing away with the swatter when I heard the "snap" of a cat jaw at my feet. I looked down to see Jigger licking his chops.

Jigger, our sailing companion, always gives his opinion of our choice of anchorage.

"Did you see that?" I asked Steve. "The cat just caught a fly." I couldn't believe a cat could catch something with his bare paws that I needed a fly swatter to get. But as I watched, Jigger reached out with one black paw and snagged another one.

We had gotten Jigger from the Seattle animal shelter the summer before as a replacement for Koala who had sailed with us for 17 years. There couldn't have been two more different cats. Koala had been a small teddy bear of a cat with long fluffy fur, blue eyes, Siamese markings and a laid-back disposition. I had made a special bunk for him on the shelf above the quarter berth, complete with a lee cloth to hold him in when we heeled. The only thing that could lure him out of it during the day was an open can of tuna fish. Jigger, on the other hand, is large and lanky with thick black fur and lots of energy. He likes to run around the boat with a toy mouse in his mouth and take flying leaps onto our shoulders. In port, he perches on top of the dodger and surveys the world, loudly meowing his opinion of whatever bay we are in.

That evening when we went to bed, Jigger was perched on the edge of the fantail outside the stern pulpit, still batting at flies.

"I hope he doesn't fall overboard," said Steve.

"Well if he does," I answered, "we'll be sure to hear him." I had never known a cat that meowed so loudly.

The night was peaceful and I slept well, waking up only once or twice to see the stars through the open hatch above us. But I was annoyed in the early morning when a wet paw touched my face. "Go away," I muttered and pulled the sleeping bag over my head. A minute later I was instantly awake. I had rolled into a puddle of icy cold water. I sat up and looked at Jigger and couldn't believe what I saw. He sat staring reproachfully at me, looking very bedraggled. His coat was slick with water and his normally bushy tail looked as skinny as a rat's. I couldn't figure out where the water had come from. I could still see the last of the morning stars shining through the hatch so it couldn't be rain. The only explanation I could think of was he had fallen overboard. But how had he gotten back on board?

"Steve, Steve, wake up. Did you know the cat fell overboard? Did you pull him out?" I felt foolish as soon as I said it. Surely Steve wouldn't have pulled Jigger out then just gone back to bed without drying him off. Steve was as surprised as I was and got up to look around. He found a trail of wet paw prints leading across the cabin floor from the cockpit.

Osprey, like all fibreglass sailboats, has a slick shiny hull with nothing for a cat to grab. There were only two ways to get on board: up the stainless steel boarding ladder on the port side or onto the dinghy that we had left tied to the starboard side. The ladder was steep and slippery, with rungs spaced far apart, impossible for a cat to negotiate. He must have used the dinghy. I imagined Jigger in the water, paddling furiously, grasping at the dinghy, which would have skidded away as he lunged for it. Somehow he had managed to reach up and set in his claws enough to hoist himself up. Once in the dinghy, it would have been an easy jump up to *Osprey*'s deck.

"We'd better check the dinghy," I told Steve. "Make sure it's floating."

The dinghy was floating but the next afternoon we noticed the starboard pontoon was decidedly soft. Steve mixed up a solution of soapy water and painted it on to look for leaks but not a bubble broke the surface; the leak was either too slow to see or located in some inaccessible spot. We didn't find it until three weeks later when we got home.

Since we couldn't find a leak to fix we had to pump up the dinghy twice a day for the rest of the trip. But although I knew Jigger had surely used at least one of his nine lives and taken at least a year of life off the dinghy, every time I put my foot on the pump, I couldn't help laughing. What a cat, to have climbed back on board on his own. And he hadn't even meowed!

Bacchante Bay

Watta Creek

No visit to Bacchante Bay is complete without a trip up Watta Creek in the dinghy. We planned our trip for the late morning when the water reached half-tide-rising. From our anchorage we watched the tide rise until it covered the last of the mud at the edge of the marsh. We knew that would give us enough water in the creek to float the dinghy but leave enough time in the tide cycle to get up and back before the tide went out again. We climbed into the dinghy with enough equipment for an expedition: rubber boots for wading, bells to scare off bears, plastic bags for picking berries, jugs for collecting fresh creek water and a camera with enough film to produce a book on Watta Creek alone.

We headed for the west side of the marsh where a deep-water branch of the creek skirts the edge of the cliffs before entering the forest. At the creek entrance several large trees lay beached on the marsh where they supported small gardens of salal and fireweed. As we rounded one of them a flock of Canada geese flew up in front of us, startled by the sound of our engine.

A dinghy trip up Watta Creek is always a highlight of a visit to Bacchante Bay.

Once past the marsh, the creek crossed to the east side of the valley to follow a rock wall upstream. The creek ran narrow and deep here with eddies swirling in its depths where fresh water from the creek met the denser salt water coming in from the sea. We continued up the creek until we came to a pool at the foot of some shallow rapids. It looked like the end of the creek but we knew it was only the dividing line between sea and forest. We nosed the dinghy onto a cobble beach next to the rapids and then carried it to the creek above. I was thankful that we have only a small dinghy with a five horsepower engine that is not too heavy for the two of us to carry. At the top of the rapids the creek stretched ahead wide and deep and running fast. We climbed back in the dinghy and motored over to the east bank. Blueberries and huckleberries grow on the rock wall above the rapids under the shade of old cedar trees. We motored beneath them, surveying the crop to see if they were ripe. It looked like a good year, but we would wait to pick them on the return trip.

Stately trees crowded either side of the creek in an impenetrable jungle. I marveled at the different colours: the bright green of hemlock with yellow tips at the end of their branches, the yellow-green of yellow cedar, the darker green of red cedar, the bluish green of spruce, the dark green of pine. I took my eyes from the trees to look down at the water. Water bugs skittered away from us and dragonflies hovered above the surface. An occasional small fish darted out from under rocks as we motored through the clear water. Watta Creek is a perfect salmon stream: cool, clear, running water, cobble bottom and shade.

We were approaching shallow water when suddenly the boat jerked and a horrible clatter came from its stern. Steve swore and stopped the motor to set it on its shallow setting. Now we progressed more slowly with the propeller churning the water at the surface. Within a few minutes the propeller clanged on rocks even at the shallow setting. We abandoned the engine for oars, then finally got out to wade, towing the dinghy behind us. It reminded me of Humphrey Bogart towing the *African Queen*, except that unlike Katharine Hepburn, I was pulling too. The shallow creek bed along the shore was slick with algae and mud and we slipped and slid among the rocks as we walked.

Bacchante Bay is a great place to watch eagles.

After what seemed like miles but was actually only a few hundred feet, the creek bed widened to provide a small beach for walking and we tied the dinghy to a tree and walked on without it. We crossed a small tributary where the water flowed so swiftly I had to wedge my boots among the rocks to keep my feet from being swept out from under me. A few minutes later we crossed a large gravel bar with the creek gurgling quietly beside us. Just above our heads, an eagle flew from a tree, so close we could hear its wings beat. Its high-pitched trills filled the air.

As we were crossing the gravel I looked down and saw an ugly pile of pinkish-brown gunk: bear scat, and soft enough to have been deposited recently. I looked around nervously and jingled my bear bell. This was definitely bear country, with lots of berries for them to feed on. In addition to the blueberries and huckleberries near the rapids, salmonberries crowded the underbrush and thimbleberries bordered the creek. Vancouver Island's bears are all black bears, not the more dangerous grizzlies, but we were in their territory near their food source so we needed to be careful.

Each time we come up here we see bear scat, but only once have we actually seen a bear. We rounded the corner in the dinghy and there he was, standing on a log at the creek edge just a few yards away. And once we came uncomfortably close to a bear den, on the marsh, not the creek. We had gone ashore at low tide and were wandering around the marsh. Near the edge of the forest we stopped to admire hedges of pink Nootka rose when we noticed a small cedar tree with a missing strip of bark. It was like a culturally modified tree, except this was a bear-modified tree: claw marks raked the bare spot, starting at a point higher than either of us could reach. I was taking a picture, when Steve said in a low voice, "Hurry up and take your picture and let's get out of here." Just a few feet from where we were standing was the bear's bed: a depression in the grass lined with tufts of fur.

I thought about that bear bed and gave my bell an extra jangle. Above the gravel bar a massive pile of tree trunks straddled the creek—fir and spruce more than four feet in diameter with root balls still intact. Swept downstream in winter storm fury, they had been piled like a child's pick-up-sticks. We climbed over and around these to continue upstream. There was no trail here and we had no destination except to see what was there: to catch a glimpse of mountains up ahead, or admire a quiet pool in the stream. The view up the creek here is awe-inspiring: tall trees frame steep rock walls and the hooked-top Splendor Mountain looks down from the end of the valley.

The blueberries were calling us. It was time to head back. When we got to the dinghy, we found the tide had pushed far enough upstream to float the dinghy easily over the rocks and we let the current carry us down until we came to the blueberries. Next to the rock wall the water was quiet and we could cling to the bushes above to hold the dinghy in place while we picked. We went for the big blueberries first, picking all we could reach, then added the dark blue huckleberries and finally, for variety and colour, the bright red huckleberries. Even with all the varieties to choose from it was hard to get enough, so many were out of our reach over our heads.

Onboard the *Osprey* we picked twigs and spiders out of the berries as we discussed what to do with them. We needed two cups for a pie but didn't quite have that. We did have enough for breakfast the next morning: blueberry pancakes or Steve's specialty—blueberry biscuits called "biscuitos."

Whenever Steve talks of his biscuitos I think of our friends John and Maureen Alvarez who came north with us in *Velella* one year, flying up from California to join us. John's Hispanic surname was the inspiration for the name "biscuitos." That trip was only their

This BMT (bear-modified tree) on the marsh near Watta Creek looks like a culturally modified tree (CMT) with claw marks.

At its outlet Watta Creek crosses a salt marsh, home to Canada Geese.

second sail in *Velella*; their first had been an afternoon sail in Boston Harbor six years before. But before that, when we had all lived in New Jersey, they had spent hours on the boat on dry land, helping us do a major overhaul. The trip was our thanks to them for that help.

We hadn't seen them since that afternoon in Boston six years before so we had a lot to catch up on. John and Maureen had finished degrees in Boston, taken jobs in San Francisco and had two children. John is Puerto Rican; Maureen is Chinese. Steve asked them, "What kind of food do you feed your kids?" The answer in chorus: "Chincorican!"

The next morning Steve baked blueberry muffins, delivering them with a flourish to the table. "Here you go," he said. "Biscuitos del mar chung-wa avec fruit de saison." We laughed. Chincorican! But what was that French doing in the name? Steve insisted his biscuitos were not Chincorican, that he had gotten the recipe while working in the Swedish merchant marine from a Spanish sea cook who had served in the French legation in Shanghai during the Boxer Rebellion. This was the first I had heard of that story. And in our bookcase is a Fannie Farmer cookbook with an identical recipe called "baking powder biscuits."

Young Bay

Where Have All the Pilchards Gone?

On a breezy afternoon in 2001, we sailed north up Sydney Inlet into Stewardson Inlet. We were looking for evidence of the Indian Chief Mine, a copper mine that had operated in Stewardson Inlet during the 1920s and '30s. We had with us a book, *Clayoquot Soundings, A History of Clayoquot Sound, 1880s–1980s* by Walter Guppy, which showed a picture of the mine from the water. We thought surely there would be something remaining of the large wharf, warehouse and factory-like building in the picture. But although we found a place on the shore with hills in the background that matched the shape of the hills in the photograph, we saw no signs of buildings or wharves.

There was no place in Stewardson Inlet to anchor for the night so we turned and sailed back into Sydney Inlet toward Young Bay, a small funnel-shaped bay on the east side of the inlet just south of Adventure Point. When we turned the corner into Sydney

Young Bay offers a perfectly protected anchorage behind a group of small islands.

Inlet, we looked toward the south and saw a wall of white fog creeping in from the ocean. The fog didn't worry me. Sydney Inlet is deep with few dangers and I knew we would be able to find our way. I liked the drama of the fog streaming toward us as we sailed toward it. Each time we tacked I looked south to check the fog's progress. I felt as if we were in a race, the fog against *Osprey*. We were battling the wind; the fog was battling the sun. As the fog moved north, the sun burned away its leading edge, so that the fog, always moving, never advanced. The race was ours. We passed Adventure Point and headed east across Sydney Inlet into Young Bay. Inside the bay the wind died to a whisper while outside in the inlet wisps of fog streamed by. We motored to an anchorage off Cecilia Creek and behind a cluster of small islands.

We made our first trip to Young Bay in 1983 in our 32-foot boat, *Velella,* with Maureen and John Alvarez. On that trip the islands gave us quite a fright: they weren't supposed to be there. We were following small area chart 3648, which showed a wide-open bay with no obstructions. When we saw the islands, we slowed down and crept carefully into the bay. I kept my eye on the depth sounder while the others watched out for rocks. Where there were uncharted islands there could be uncharted rocks or sandbars, but once we anchored, the islands charmed us. Some had little thatches of trees while others were no more than large rocks. We named two of them "Velella" and "Velellalita" Islands—"Velellalita," according to John, would be Spanish for "little *Velella.*" The next morning when we got out the large area chart, 3640, we found the islands where they belonged. A cartographer's error must have left them off the other chart. To this day we still call the islands Velella and Velellalita.

While Steve settled in *Osprey*'s cockpit with a book, I launched the inflatable kayak and paddled off to photograph the islands. On the previous trip I had seen an old cement

This deserted little bay was once the site of a bustling pilchard reduction plant, and later hosted a copper mine.

Abandoned mining machinery visible at low tide.

platform on one of them and I wondered if it could be part of the pilchard reduction plant reported to have been in this bay. I found the cement platform on an island close to shore. A brick column supported one corner. A second island sported a row of cement footings. It looked as if the islands had served as foundations for a series of piers criss-crossing the bay.

I was drifting with the current, admiring the play of light on the old bricks when a large piece of rusty machinery only six inches beneath the kayak caught my attention. I peered into the water. Whatever it was, it was large, cylindrical, eaten away by corrosion and covered with barnacles. Could it be a boiler from the pilchard plant?

George Nicholson, in *Vancouver Island's West Coast, 1762–1962*, described the rapid rise and fall of the pilchard fishery on the west coast of Vancouver Island. Pilchards are the same species as the sardines once caught off the coast of California, but larger and oilier. Vancouver Island fishermen first sighted pilchard schools acres in size inside the sounds in 1925, recognizing them by fish tails flipping above the water or by the dark shadows the schools made beneath the surface.

By 1927 there were 26 pilchard reduction plants between Barkley and Kyuquot Sounds, many located in small bays like Young Bay where there was shelter from the waves and plenty of fresh water for processing. Fishermen in small boats brought the pilchards to the plants where they were rendered into chicken feed, fishmeal and oil. Shipyards cranked out seiners and scows; shipping companies sent fleets of small freighters to take the fish products to market. Temporary villages sprang up every summer as Nuu-chah-nulth men came to fish and Nuu-chah-nulth women came to work in the reduction plants.

Just a few years after they were first sighted, the pilchards moved offshore. By 1944 the offshore schools started to decline too, and by 1946 pilchards had almost disappeared from the entire west coast of Vancouver Island. In California the sardines disappeared at the same time. George Nicholson wrote that biologists had debated for years the reason for the disappearance of both species. He could have added, however, that biologists often blamed overfishing.

In 1968, when I was a college student, I spent the summer studying marine zoology in Monterey, California, the former centre of the California sardine industry. It was a time of political awareness on campuses across the United States. The Vietnam anti-war movement was building and although the first Earth Day, in April 1970, was still a few years away, hints of the environmental movement were stirring. My classmates and I were fascinated by the story of the sardines' disappearance. In the evenings, when we tired of our books and microscopes, we went for walks to Cannery Row. Restaurants and hotels occupied many of the old canneries, but there were just enough vacant and dilapidated ones left to fire our imaginations. We were particularly curious to see the site of the laboratory belonging to Ed Ricketts, the model for the eccentric "Doc" of John Steinbeck's *Cannery Row*. As marine biology students we spent our days messing around in tide pools and the idea of doing that for the rest of our lives, as Ricketts had done, appealed to us.

One evening a bunch of us were sitting on a rocky promontory on the shoreline next to one of the deserted canneries, listening to a rock band practising in a renovated cannery nearby. Tuni, one of my roommates, stood up as if in a trance, walked down the rocks toward the water and disappeared under the pilings of the old cannery. When she didn't return after five minutes, one of the young men in our group went after her. The rest of us were anxiously waiting for them to reappear from under the cannery, when to our surprise they came up behind us. They had crawled into the old cannery through a hole in the floor and walked out the cannery's front door.

After that night we became curious trespassers. In between studying for tests and treks to Big Sur to hear Joan Baez sing anti-war songs we headed down to Cannery Row. In the canneries we prowled among old machinery, inspected cases of empty sardine cans and unused labels, walked up conveyor belts to the roofs and leafed through papers in abandoned offices.

As potential marine biologists we debated the sardines' disappearance. Our professors told us that no one really knew why they had disappeared. But we had all read a reprint of a 1948 newspaper article by Ed Ricketts in which he advanced the unpopular idea that poor fishing practices—overfishing, taking undersized fish, fishing in spawning grounds—had caused the sardines' demise. He admitted that climate changes might have had an effect but pointed out that while we had no control over that, we could control the fishery.

"Ricketts is right," someone would argue. "Look around you." And we would look around at the vast empty factories and imagine the estimated one billion sardines that had moved up the conveyor belts each season. It was hard to believe any fishery could withstand such an onslaught of machinery.

"But that's too simple," someone else would say. "If it were overfishing, surely the sardine catches would have declined more gradually. And what about the changes in sea temperature?"

Thirty years after my classmates and I debated the disappearance of the sardines, scientists still don't know exactly what happened to either the sardines or the pilchards, but they know more about the effects of overfishing and about how changes in ocean temperatures can affect fish populations. El Niño and La Niña are household names in the Northwest, but there's a lesser known phenomenon called Pacific Decadal Oscillation that refers to longer lasting changes in ocean temperature. Before the pilchards arrived in 1925, the ocean was relatively cool; from 1925 to 1946, the years of pilchard abundance, it was relatively warm. Scientists have linked temperature changes like this to sudden waxing and waning of populations of salmon, smelt and dolphin. Add overfishing and the result is a death knell for a fishery.

Implements from the copper mining operation.

The next morning at low tide I took Steve out in the dinghy to see the machinery and was disappointed when he declared it too thin to be the boiler of the old pilchard plant. He pointed to large gears on one end whose presence implied that the whole round structure turned. We were probably looking at mining machinery.

Among the rocks near the platform, we saw globs of copper slag and on top of the platform we found several black electrodes and some small rake-like implements left there by previous explorers. According to Walter Guppy's book there was once a copper mine in Sydney Inlet, in addition to the one in Stewardson Inlet. He didn't say where in the inlet it was located, but it must have been here. I had hoped to find evidence of the pilchard plant on land near the islands, but the trees were so tall and the underbrush so thick, we didn't even see any rusty machinery. Dreams disappear fast on the west coast of Vancouver Island; lumber and machinery is often cannibalized for the next dream. The pilchard plant and the copper mine had shared the same site—and the same fate.

I once thought the disappearance of the pilchards and the sardines was unique to our time. But the Nuu-chah-nulth predicted the loss of the pilchards in 1946 when thousands of small blue jellyfish appeared in swarms off the coast. Oral history, passed down through generations of Nuu-chah-nulth elders, holds that the arrival of swarms of these small jellyfish predicted the departure of the pilchards. Today's Nuu-chah-nulth call the jellyfish Portuguese men-of-war, but since Portuguese men-of war aren't found in these waters these are more likely a closely related jellyfish: "sailors by the wind" or *velella*, the jellyfish for which our boat was named. Perhaps Velella and Velellalita are good names for the islands in Young Bay after all.

Pilchards began returning to the west coast of Vancouver Island in the 1980s, when hake fishermen started finding them in their nets. By 1997 biologists from the Department of Fisheries and Oceans reported that roughly 250 million pilchards lived off the coast. Sardines began returning to California at the same time. Experimental fisheries are underway in both British Columbia and California.

How long will the pilchards stay this time? I'll look for swarms of *velellas* to tell me.

Hot Springs Cove

Fishing for Ice

Sometimes when I open *Osprey*'s icebox, I think of my grandmother. A frugal woman, she understood that with every opening of the refrigerator door, cold air spilled into the kitchen and the electricity bill went up. After a meal she would marshal the butter, the milk or the leftover broccoli on the counter. Not until everything was assembled would she open the refrigerator door. She saved money in other ways too— by keeping used paper napkins to wipe up spills and using a pressure cooker to save gas. She once told me she had done things like that all her married life. And then with a rueful look at the carpet in the living room said, "And while I was saving pennies, your grandfather was out buying oriental carpets for hundreds of dollars."

On our trips north up the west coast of Vancouver Island, I copy my grandmother's frugality and open our icebox as infrequently as possible. But it isn't pennies I'm concerned with: it's ice. My grandfather would have approved of our priorities, for until the year 2000, *Osprey* had an oriental carpet, but no refrigeration. Ice, its availability and

its melting rate, set our itineraries. Two blocks of ice lasted six or seven days. Three or more blocks lasted eight or nine days but didn't leave much room for food.

We always topped off with ice in the town of Ucluelet before leaving Barkley Sound for the north. Around day five I would check the ice level and estimate the days to go. If we were in Friendly Cove, would the ice last until Tahsis? If we didn't stop in Tahsis, would it last until we reached Zeballos? And what if we got there and the ice truck hadn't come?

Then one year we waited out a gale in Hot Springs Cove and ran out of ice. We looked around at the salmon trollers waiting out the gale with us and saw a fleet of floating ice trucks. The trollers didn't have refrigeration either but they had plenty of flake ice made from sea water and purchased at fish-packing plants up and down the coast. Hoping to make a trade, Steve took several bottles of beer and a bucket and walked down the dock. Half an hour later he returned with a bucketful of ice. The flake ice filled the bottom of the icebox and smelled faintly of fish. Because it was made from salt water, it was the coldest ice we'd ever had.

We stopped planning our itinerary around the towns and started watching for the salmon trollers. They would come into the harbours in the evening, their trolling poles spread out like the wings of great water bugs. At night their anchor lights were a comforting presence bobbing at the outskirts of the harbours. We would take our bucket and our bottles of beer and row over to a fishboat and ask, "How was fishing? Could you give us some ice?"

Salmon fishing, they told us, was bad and getting worse. The government was to blame—or the fish-processing companies, or the logging industry, or the First Nations. Sometimes it was even other fishermen. What to do about it was never clear.

In 1997 salmon treaty negotiations between Canada and the United States broke down and BC fishermen blockaded an Alaskan ferry in Prince Rupert. Meanwhile, boat basins at Ucluelet and other small towns filled with idle fishboats as fishermen stayed in port waiting for an opening that never came. The next year wasn't much better. By 1999 the trollers had all but gone, the docks were empty and the packing plants closed. I realized we had witnessed the end of an era.

The next winter we installed refrigeration in the *Osprey*. Ice no longer sets our itineraries. But we miss the fishermen.

Fisheries statistics tell the story. In 1982, the first year for which detailed catch data is available, salmon fishermen on the west coast of Vancouver Island—from Barkley Sound to the Brooks Peninsula—caught 45.37 million pounds of salmon. By 2001, their catch shrank to 1.1 million pounds—only 2 1/2 percent of the 1982 catch.

The decline of salmon is a regional problem affecting British Columbia, Oregon, Washington and California. On Vancouver Island's west coast where small towns rely on fishing to make their living and First Nations rely on salmon for food, the loss of the fisheries is devastating. With no other industry to replace fishing, populations of both non–Native and First Nations people are declining. To lose a fishery in an urban area is sad; to lose a fishery in the wilderness is enraging.

Opposite: Bathers sunning themselves on the rocks around Hot Springs Cove. Once visited primarily by fishermen and sailboaters, the Hot Springs are now crowded with tourists coming by seaplane, water taxi, and helicopters.

A salmon troller at anchor in Hot Springs Cove. Its trolling poles hold fishing lines away from the boat when fishing.

Idle salmon trollers tied up at the boat basin in Ucluelet. With salmon populations at an all time low, boats spend more time at the dock.

In Oregon and Washington, we blame dams and urban development for the salmon's decline. But on the west coast of Vancouver Island, we can only blame logging and poor management. The clear-cut has become as much a symbol of this area as its rocky shores. Logging along rivers and creeks increases erosion and sedimentation, destroying spawning grounds and feeding areas for young fish. Without trees to shade them, the streams heat up, and salmon won't migrate up rivers when the water is too warm.

We tend to think that before the white man arrived, North America was pristine wilderness left to its own devices. But on Vancouver Island's west coast 25,000 Nuu-chah-nulth nurtured and cared for the salmon. At every change of season, they checked the rivers, cleaning up fallen trees and inspecting spawning beds. When they found young fish stranded in shallow pools, they caught them in baskets and carried them to the river. And they fished with traps near the mouths of rivers for one species at a time, not out at sea with nets that catch many species indiscriminately as today's fishermen do. When they caught all they needed, they let the rest swim upstream to spawn.

The Nuu-chah-nulth had a word for this caring for resources: *Hishukish Ts'awalk*, everything is one. This concept is the Nuu-chah-nulth's basis for respect for nature. It promotes the need to be thrifty, to be conscious of actual needs. My grandmother would have understood.

Hope lies with the salmon itself—and with our willingness to listen to the "grandmothers" among us. Salmon have survived volcanoes, floods and tsunamis. If we give them a chance, they may yet survive us.

Hesquiat Harbour

Hesquiaht beliefs have evolved over thousands of years along with the salmon. Beliefs that seem silly to us helped to preserve the salmon runs. To the Nuu-chah-nulth, fish, seals, trees and other natural resources were gifts that must be respected, not wasted. We looked across the harbour where clear-cut hills rose above the blue water, slashed with zigzags of forest roads. I thought how ironic it was that we were in one of the most remote areas of the coast and so much of our view was taken up by clear-cuts.

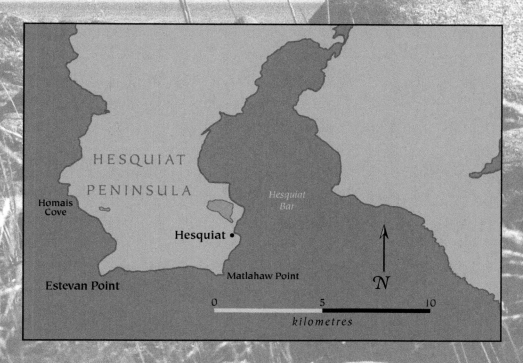

Hesquiat Village

"Taking Charge of the Indians"

The anchor bounced across the rocky bottom of Hesquiat Bar, sending a horrible grating noise up through the water to the deck of the *Osprey* where I crouched next to the anchor windlass, my hand on the brake. If I couldn't get the anchor to grab soon, we would have to pull it up and re-anchor, or perhaps leave without going ashore. Quickly I released the brake, letting more chain rumble across the anchor roller. The chain pulled taut and the boat stopped. We had anchored over a shallow rocky bar in front of the ancient village of Hesquiat on the east side of the Hesquiat Peninsula, a flat featureless land mass that juts out into the Pacific between Clayoquot Sound to the south and Nootka Sound to the north. Only a small rocky point of land and a fringe of kelp protected us from the full force of the open ocean.

We knew no other boaters who had visited Hesquiat—that, in fact, was one of its main attractions to us. It also made me uneasy. We would be going ashore on a Native reserve. Would the villagers welcome us or send us away? A low ocean swell, the dull roar of surf on the rocks and the mournful hoot of a whistle buoy reminded me how precarious our anchorage was.

The morning breeze barely ruffled the water; a cloudless blue sky and a high steady barometer promised calm seas. Conditions were as perfect as they could be for anchoring on an open roadstead and taking a walk. We had on board chart 3640, which showed a road leading from the village around Matlahaw Point to the Estevan Point lighthouse. We hoped to find that road and hike to the lighthouse, a distance of less than five miles.

Hesquiat Village, 2004. Most members of the Hesquiaht band now live at Hot Springs Cove where the anchorage is more protected.

The village didn't look like much—four or five houses and a scattering of blue and orange tents bordering a shallow cove. A low concrete breakwater jutted out from the beach in front of the village providing safe landing for canoes (and dinghies) but not much more.

Friendly children helped us pull the dinghy up the beach and accepted our arrival without questions. My anxiety evaporated in their sunny smiles. But when we asked the way to the road, they gave us blank stares, then pointed toward a footpath and shrugged. We followed the footpath past an unpainted wooden smokehouse where we met a woman and a teenaged boy who introduced themselves as Dianne and Mark. Dianne had light skin, light brown hair and blue eyes. In her skirt and blouse she looked like a suburban housewife out for a stroll. Mark had the olive skin, dark hair and round face of a Nuu-chah-nulth. Dianne pointed us toward the small rocky point to the west of the village where the trail started. They used to clear the brush away every year but hadn't gotten around to it for several years, she told us. It might be too overgrown to use, but we could always walk on the beach. "Stop by for tea when you get back," she said, gesturing toward a red shingled house.

It took us awhile to find the road. We were looking for an obvious sign, a clearing in the woods or even a road sign. We finally gave up and just headed inland, crashing through the underbrush until we came upon the road a short distance from the beach. It was a road like no other we had ever seen, like none I would ever want to drive. It consisted of two wooden tracks exactly one axle-width apart, suspended one to three feet above the marshy ground on trestles.

We climbed up on one of the tracks and started walking. Salal, that ubiquitous green underbrush, grew between and beside the tracks so tall and thick it formed a canopy above our heads. We had to push it aside to walk and it scratched our bare arms and faces. Salmonberry brambles grabbed at our clothes. Still, we pushed forward. The farther we went, the thicker the brush grew. The old wooden track creaked and bounced beneath us. I knew how quickly wood rots in the forest and worried that the track would give way, sending us to the marshy forest floor.

A pickup truck once drove this road regularly, balancing carefully on the slippery planks, bringing mail, food and personnel to the Estevan Point lighthouse. It was a precarious route: first a landing at a shallow rocky beach too rough for a dock then a ride on a rotting wooden road through the wilderness. In the '70s the Coast Guard abandoned it in favour of helicopter deliveries.

At the rate we were moving I figured it would take us a week to get to the lighthouse. "Let's give up. What's the point?" I said to Steve. But Steve was not as easily defeated; he had come for a hike on the road to the lighthouse.

"Let's just go a bit farther," he said. "I want to see what's around the corner."

I gritted my teeth and pushed on. I knew it was fruitless to argue. Steve would always want to see around the next corner, walk to the top of the highest hill or sail to the farthest bay while I would be content with a lesser view, a lower hill, the closer bay. With Steve as *Osprey*'s skipper we would be sailing to windward long after others had turned downwind. In his perseverance he was well-suited for the west coast of Vancouver Island.

One man whose strength and perseverance permanently marked, some would say scarred, Hesquiat and the entire West Coast was Father Augustin Joseph Brabant of Belgium, founder of the first mission in this area of Vancouver Island. An imposing man over six feet tall, Father Brabant was capable of enduring hours of discomfort in open canoes, surviving on dried fish and biscuits, all to bring the word of God to the "savages" of the West Coast.

Father Brabant arrived at Hesquiat in the sloop *Thornton* on a stormy day in May 1875. He had selected Hesquiat for his mission because in previous visits the people had welcomed him and seemed eager for his message. Prepared to settle in permanently, he brought with him three small calves, one bull, two heifers and a young Newfoundland dog.

Father Brabant believed he had been sent to Hesquiat to "take charge of the Indians." So when he discovered Chief Matlahaw was absent and none of the Hesquiat present dared to give him a site for the mission, he forged ahead anyway, selecting the site himself. To construct the mission he employed Native labour and commandeered lumber that had come ashore from the wreck of the lumber schooner *Edwin* the December before. The Hesquiaht had used some of this lumber to construct new houses, but "after much trouble and some reasoning" Father Brabant persuaded them to give it all to him.

On July 5, 1875, Father Brabant read the first mass in the new church, noting exultantly in his journal that all the Hesquiaht and their neighbours the Muchalaht, attended. Then he set about converting and "civilizing" the Natives. For the beliefs and rituals of the Hesquiaht people Father Brabant had nothing but scorn. "Their superstitions are so numerous and absurd as to be almost incredible," he wrote.

Custom forbade the Hesquiaht to carry salmon in a basket, feed it to dogs or cut it with a knife. Under no circumstances could salmon be given to a white man, including a priest, lest the white man cook it in lard in an iron pot. Any Hesquiaht who broke these rules risked driving the salmon away and bringing starvation on the entire village. Father Brabant considered these rules a challenge. He recruited two young boys and a canoe and, in a short time, caught a large salmon. He returned to the beach, where he put the salmon in a basket and gave the basket to his dog to carry, predicting, rightly, that no Hesquiaht would mess with his dog. In the mission kitchen a crowd of Hesquiaht watched, aghast, as Father Brabant cut the salmon with a knife and cooked it with lard in an iron frying pan.

Dianne Ignace canning sockeye salmon in her front yard. Dianne and Dave Ignace and their children live year-round at Hesquiat.

The village chiefs predicted famine. At first it looked as if their predictions would come true: the winter started stormy and canoes stayed stormbound on the beach, unable to fish. But storms gave way to calms and soon the canoes were out bringing hundreds of fish to the village. The village chiefs met, argued and decided to make peace with the priest.

Father Brabant didn't understand that the Hesquiaht beliefs had evolved over thousands of years along with the salmon. Beliefs that seem silly to us now inadvertently helped to preserve the salmon runs. To the Nuu-chah-nulth, fish, seals, trees and other natural resources were gifts that must be respected, not wasted.

Father Brabant's perseverance paid off. By the close of 1888 he was able to write in his journal that there were only three or four families of real pagans at Hesquiat; the rest had become Christians.

Perhaps if Father Brabant had been with us on our walk to the lighthouse, we would have continued on the old road to our destination. But, looking for an easier route, Steve climbed down from the track and pushed his way through the underbrush to the beach. I followed close behind.

We came out of the woods onto the beach. From there I looked across the harbour to see *Osprey* rocking gently in the swell, looking as if it were far out to sea. Across the harbour clear-cut hills rose above the blue water, slashed with zigzags of forest roads. I thought how ironic it was that we were in one of the most remote areas of the coast and so much of our view was taken up by clear-cuts.

The beach was only a slight improvement over the road. Rust-coloured boulders, rounded by eons of surf and ranging in size from basketballs to VW beetles, littered the foreshore. Only giants could comfortably walk this beach; we had to jump from stone to stone, risking turned ankles and sore knees with every leap. The sight of Matlahaw Point ahead kept us going. From there, we hoped to see the lighthouse. But when we

Rust-coloured boulders, rounded by eons of surf, litter the foreshore on Matlahaw Point on the Hesquiat Peninsula.

reached the point, we saw only more boulders stretching before us to the next point. We remembered the tea promised by Dianne and decided to turn back.

A journey back is never as long or as far as a journey out on an unknown road. We took a shortcut across a point of land and came upon a stretch of road we had missed on the way out—not a wooden track but a cleared area of firm ground for easy walking. We followed this trail until it ended near the village. A sign marking the road said:

ROAD ABAND
USE AT OWN RI

Dianne met us at her front door and led us upstairs to the kitchen. While we relaxed at her kitchen table, she made tea on a large wood-burning stove and served us fresh apple pie. We talked, or rather Dianne talked and we listened. It was as if she had so few visitors that she had stored a treasure trove of talk.

From their front window the Ignaces can watch bears scavenging on the beach.

Dianne told us that she and her husband, a Hesquiaht, chose to live in the village year-round because they didn't want to raise their four children in town. She home-schools her children; her oldest daughter had graduated from high school that year. We asked Dianne where she got groceries. She explained that Tofino is only a couple of hours away by speedboat, weather permitting. In the winter the Coast Guard delivers food by helicopter, a benefit to her husband, a Coast Guard retiree. I pictured a list of benefits encoded in a government document: pension, insurance, helicopter deliveries, then dismissed that picture as preposterous. The "benefit" was probably informal.

Afternoon was turning into evening when we left Dianne's house and walked back through the village to our dinghy. We saw no sign of the church. In 1911 Father Brabant replaced the original simple church with an elaborate gothic structure complete with buttresses, gables and a bell tower. A succession of priests occupied the mission after Father Brabant, but none was as successful as he had been and the church gradually deteriorated until it was replaced by a smaller structure in the 1930s. During this time the Hesquiaht were replacing their canoes with gasoline-powered fishboats and leaving the village for Hot Springs Cove with its safe anchorage. Lacking a congregation, the mission closed and the church went the way of all structures abandoned in the rain forest. The mission cattle, originally brought to Hesquiat to teach the Natives agriculture, broke from their pastures to roam through the forest. Rumours of cattle running wild on the peninsula still persist today.

The anchorage that wasn't good enough for the Hesquiaht fishermen wasn't good enough for us, either. We raised *Osprey*'s anchor and motored through a sea of crab pot buoys, around Antons Spit and into the protected Hesquiat Harbour where we anchored off a pebble beach. The anchor grabbed easily in the muddy bottom.

Nootka Sound

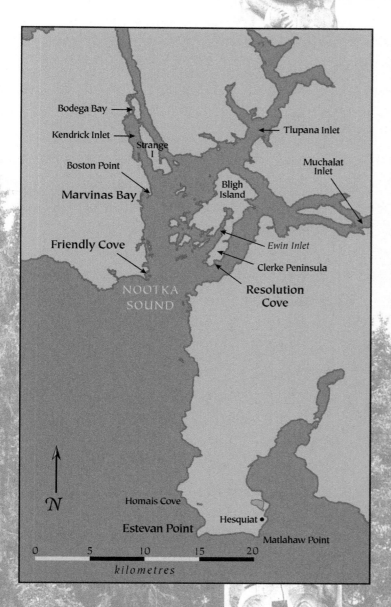

Bodega Bay

Kendrick Inlet

Strange I

Boston Point

Marvinas Bay

Friendly Cove

NOOTKA
SOUND

Tlupana Inlet

Muchalat
Inlet

Bligh
Island

Ewin Inlet

Clerke Peninsula

**Resolution
Cove**

N

Homais Cove

Estevan Point

Hesquiat •

Matlahaw Point

0   5   10   15   20

kilometres

Ahead we could see the faint white dot of Nootka light and the mountains of Nootka Sound beyond. By the time we passed San Rafael Island and entered the Sound, the seas had subsided to a gentle roll. We anchored in Friendly Cove almost in the shadow of Nootka light. As I waited for the boat to swing to its anchor, I looked with pleasure at the lighthouse buildings with their red roofs, at the white church against the green forest and at the totem pole rising above the beach. I was glad we had come.

Rounding Estevan

"It's Lumpy out There"

T he roar of an engine on the fishboat tied next to us at the Hot Springs Cove dock woke me. That fishboats were leaving was a good sign. It was 1984, and we had been waiting out a northwest gale here for three days, hoping for a break in the weather before heading north to Nootka Sound. Perhaps this would be the day. I slipped out of our bunk and into *Velella*'s main cabin to turn on the radio. I heard, "west coast Vancouver Island, south part: wind, northwest 25–35 knots." It would be windier than I had hoped for our first trip north of Clayoquot Sound, but not as bad as gales. We could go. Time was running out on our three-week vacation. If we didn't leave today, we probably wouldn't go at all.

After breakfast, while Steve got the sails ready, I cleaned the galley and stowed everything loose, putting pots and pans safely away in their bin behind the stove, wedging books into corners and carefully latching port lights and hatches. I wanted to be ready

Approaching Nootka Sound on a breezy day. The Sound's easy entrance made it a popular stop for the early fur traders.

for whatever the seas gave us. Satisfied that everything was secure, I went out on deck to help Steve deflate and store the dinghy.

A breeze was already darkening the water, breaking up the morning calm. Several of the fishboats that had left earlier had already returned as the seas had been too rough for fishing. One of the fishermen who had returned, a hefty man in a plaid shirt and worn jeans, stood on the dock, watching us work. He looked out toward the harbour entrance, then back at *Velella* and said, "It's lumpy out there."

"Sailboats are made for rough weather," said Steve. "*Velella*'s a good boat. We've been in worse than this."

"I guess that big keel makes her stable, eh?" said the fisherman.

The flag halyard was now going rat-tat-tat, slapping against the mast in the breeze. It made me nervous. Despite Steve's assurances I doubted the wisdom of venturing out where fishermen feared to go. The wind would only increase during the day, and our course would take us around Estevan Point where winds blow stronger and waves run higher than just about any other place on the west coast of Vancouver Island. The *BC Sailing Directions* warns, "This part of the coast should be given a wide berth." We would be sailing far offshore, but it could still be rough. We untied the lines and motored out the harbour. As we passed the hot springs at the cove's entrance, I could see bathers already relaxing in the hot water. I shivered in the wind and went below to don boots and foul-weather gear.

At first *Velella* rose and fell comfortably on the seas, her main and 120 jib pushing her easily through the water as she heeled slightly in the freshening breeze. Then we passed Barney Rocks and entered open water. The first spray hit the dodger as *Velella*'s bow crashed into the waves and we heeled so far over that water buried the lee rail and washed across the port lights. We reefed the mainsail, but water still rushed across the rail. We would have to change the jib, and it was my turn.

Velella's self-tending working jib sat on its boom on the foredeck, permanently hanked to the forestay. When furled its top hank attached just below the bottom hank of whatever sail was flying. To change sails we had only to take down and stow the 120 and raise the self-tender. It was an arrangement that works well for a fast sail change at sea, one that we have since duplicated on the *Osprey*. I inched my way to the mast on the sloping, pitching deck to release the jib halyard while Steve uncleated the jib sheet. The sail came down with a rush, flailing in the wind. Almost instantly *Velella* stopped pounding into the seas and began instead to plunge up and down in place. I ran to the bow to gather the sail. It had fallen partially in the water and had to be hauled in wet and heavy, then lashed down with sail ties. I crouched at the forestay and hung on as the bow heaved up and down with each succeeding swell, sometimes diving so far into the waves that cold sea water swept over me. With each plunge of the bow I wondered what I was doing out there. However had I let Steve talk me into coming out here? "Sailboats are made for rough weather, indeed!" I muttered to myself, struggling to knot a wet sail tie.

Finally I had the 120 tied down and could go back to the mast and raise the self-tender. Once the jib was up I retreated to the cockpit where spray still flew over the dodger and into our faces. I moved to a seat on the uphill side close under the dodger and braced my feet against the opposite seat while Steve adjusted the self-steering vane. We seemed to be expending more energy bouncing up and down than going forward. It was indeed "lumpy" out here.

Just as I was wondering if I should suggest turning back, I looked at the knotmeter and saw it was running a steady four to five knots. I looked astern and saw an unbroken white wake snaking out behind us and boiling with bubbles as the land receded. *Velella* had settled down to a long slow slog to weather. And I settled down with

Built in 1908, the Estevan Point Lighthouse towers 150 feet above the land.

her. The fears that had haunted me at the dock had disappeared in the immediacy of working the boat. And, although we were going to weather, tacking was easy. When we pushed the tiller over, mainsail and self-tending jib followed. We had only to reset the self-steering vane.

By noon Estevan lighthouse was off our beam, a thin white line against the green forest. Built in 1908 of reinforced concrete with flying buttresses to withstand wind and earth tremors, the lighthouse is among the tallest towers on the coast and makes an impressive sight, soaring 150 feet above the beach. Estevan lighthouse also marks one of Canada's historic sites: the only place in Canada to be attacked by the Japanese in World War II. According to official records, on June 20, 1942, Japanese submarine I-26 surfaced off Estevan and fired 25 five-and-a-half-inch shells at the lighthouse, every one of which missed.

To this day some British Columbians doubt that story. Donald Graham, author of *Keepers of the Light: A History of British Columbia's Lighthouses and their Keepers* (and a lighthouse keeper himself) wrote that west coasters have always been skeptical about the shelling. They didn't understand why a Japanese submarine would shoot a lighthouse that was useful to the Japanese as well as to the Canadians. And if they did shoot at it, how could they have missed it 25 times? Graham pointed out that Americans, who wanted Canadians to join the war against Japan, had more of a motive to stage an attack than did the Japanese. But there may be a simple reason why the Japanese gunners missed the lighthouse: they weren't aiming for it in the first place. Sub and crew survived the war and the captain explained he had orders to strike a radar/radio-direction-finding installation he believed to be just beyond the lighthouse.

We continued tacking back and forth offshore, keeping our distance from the perilous shallows of Estevan Point. As the white line of the lighthouse grew smaller, the seas no longer seemed so threatening. Soon we could see our second historic site of the passage: Perez Rocks, a cluster of drying rocks almost a mile and a half off the Hesquiat shore. Historians believe that Juan Perez, on the Spanish ship *Santiago*, the first European ship to visit the west coast of Vancouver Island, anchored near these rocks on a quiet day in August 1774.

Two versions of this event survived. In a story passed down through generations, Nuu-chah-nulth tell of Hesquiaht from the village of Homais near Estevan Point who looked out to sea and saw what looked like strange housepoles floating out in the ocean. The Hesquiaht paddled out in their canoes to investigate and saw the Spanish ship *Santiago,* which to them looked like a floating house. Inspired by this sight the Hesquiaht composed a song whose words included, "I got my walls of a house floating on the water." The Hesquiaht told this story to their neighbours up and down the coast, which explains how Europeans became known as *maamałni* which means "living on the water, floating around, having no land."

Sea Lions crowd Perez Rocks on a rare quiet day. Juan Perez, the first European to approach Vancouver Island, anchored near here.

In the Spaniards' story, written in the *Santiago*'s log and in the diaries of priests on board, nine canoes full of stout Indians came out and bartered salmon, meat, and furs for iron. Planning to send a party ashore with a wooden cross to claim the land for their king, the Spaniards launched the ship's boat. But before they could get ashore, a wind came up and the anchor dragged. The boat returned and the ship cut its anchor cable and left in a hurry. Historians have argued for years whether Perez's failure to return was reasonable, or the sign of cowardice.

The honour of being the first European to step ashore on Vancouver Island was left to Captain James Cook four years later and several miles east. If the wind had not come up, if the Spaniards had persisted, if they had returned the next day and gone ashore, we might be carrying a Spanish phrase book on our boat today.

Perez Rocks marked our turning point. Steve took bearings off the rocks and lighthouse with the hand-bearing compass, calling them out to me to plot on the chart. When our plot showed us clear of the rocks, we headed off the wind and let out the sails. The boat straightened up and started moving with the waves instead of against them. Ahead we could see the faint white dot of Nootka light and the mountains of Nootka Sound beyond. By the time we passed San Rafael Island and entered the Sound, the seas had subsided to a gentle roll.

We anchored in Friendly Cove almost in the shadow of Nootka light. As I waited for the boat to swing to its anchor, I looked with pleasure at the lighthouse buildings with their red roofs, at the white church against the green forest and at the totem pole rising above the beach. I was glad we had come. And glad the trip was over.

Resolution Cove

An Inconvenient Anchorage

Resolution Cove is just a small notch carved into rockbound Clerke Peninsula on the south side of Bligh Island, but Steve and I like to visit historical sites when we go cruising. We knew Captain Cook's two ships had sheltered there in March 1778 and we figured if Cook's two ships could stay there a whole month during unsettled weather, we could spend one night in July 1994, when the weather was good.

We anchored in the centre of the cove in 45 feet of water, not too far from a moss-covered knoll with a bare flagpole on top. We wanted to do some exploring so we set off in the dinghy intending to land there. As we approached the shore, a surge sent the dinghy hurtling toward a rock wall. Then it yanked us back like a ball on a string. On the next pass I grabbed a tree branch to keep us in place and jumped out onto a ledge with dinghy painter in hand. The *BC Sailing Directions* says, "Resolution Cove … is an inconvenient anchorage." Now we knew why.

We scrambled up the rocky shore to the top of the knoll where we saw two plaques mounted in gold braid. One commemorated Captain James Cook; the other, his landing

The view out Resolution Cove has changed little since Captain Cook's visit.

108

RESOLUTION COVE

TO COMMEMORATE THE VISIT OF CAPTAIN COOK R.N., F.R.S.,
WHO SHELTERED WITH H.M. SHIPS RESOLUTION AND DISCOVERY
31 MARCH–26 APRIL 1778 AND REPLACED TWO LOWER MASTS
WITH TREES FROM THIS ISLAND.

THIS WAS THE FIRST BRITISH LANDING IN WHAT IS NOW
BRITISH COLUMBIA.

PLACED ON THE OCCASION OF THE CAPTAIN COOK
BICENTENNIAL 26 APRIL 1978 BY THE COMMANDER, OFFICERS,
AND MEN OF THE MARITIME FORCES PACIFIC.

Captain Cook's two ships, the *Resolution* and *Discovery*, spent a month in Resolution Cove in March of 1778.

in this cove. When Cook's two ships, *Resolution* and *Discovery,* entered Nootka Sound, crowds of Natives greeted them. Cook wrote in his journal, "a person in one of the two last [canoes] stood up and made a long harangue, inviting us to land as we guessed by his gestures …. At the same time he kept strewing handfuls of feathers towards us, and some of his companions threw handfuls of red dust or powder in the same manner." The next morning Cook found Resolution Cove, later named for his ship. He described the cove as, "a convenient, snug cove, well suited for the purpose." It was close to the ocean, easy for sailing ships to enter and offered good timber for ships' spars. "Convenient" clearly meant something different to Cook, who had sailed across the Pacific to get here.

After almost two years at sea, Cook's men badly needed clothes and blankets. So when the Natives offered them otter skins for only sixpence-worth of goods each, they snatched them up. Two years later they sold them in China for $100 each. Word of these riches spread quickly and within a few years ships from many nations converged on Nootka Sound. Resolution Cove, however, faded into history, eclipsed by the better anchorage in nearby Friendly Cove. We stood on the mossy knoll and looked out on a scene little changed since Cook's landing. Tree-covered shores and rugged rocks framed our sailboat. It was a beautiful setting.

I awoke in the night to the sound of anchor chain grating across rocks. I got up and looked out the cabin door. The water was glassy smooth, but the boat was swinging in a wide arc around the anchor, as if towed by an invisible force.

That was to be our last night in Nootka Sound, but in the morning we found that the anchor wouldn't budge. We finally got free by powering in a circle, unwinding ourselves from the rocks below. "It's a message," Steve said. "Something's trying to keep us here." I thought it was probably just an inconvenient anchorage.

Friendly Cove (Yuquot)

Machiavelli at Nootka

The Mowachaht band, who once lived at Friendly Cove, call it *Yuquot*, "place of many winds." It's an unsettling name for an anchorage that has provided refuge to so many boats.

The time I most appreciated the protection of Friendly Cove was in 1993. We were on our way home, heading for Hot Springs from Nuchatlitz, when light southerlies blew up to gales. Off Bajo Reef, just north of Nootka Sound, the mast started to wobble. Each time we hit a wave, the mast jerked back and forth until we were afraid it would jerk right apart. Earlier that trip we had run hard aground in Sulphur Passage in Clayquot Sound and, although we didn't realize it at the time, had knocked loose the gum rubber wedges that protected the mast where it went through the roof of the cabin. We needed a place to shelter from the gale and to make repairs. Friendly Cove was close and easy to enter with good protection from the waves.

Inside the Sound, gusts of wind skittered across the water and a low swell curved around the point. The little cove looked crowded to us. A log-and-plank float snaked

A centre of commerce during the fur trade, Friendly Cove, or Yuquot, now has only one resident family.

its way out from the beach and divided the anchorage in two. The public pier and two salmon trollers occupied most of the eastern half. A third salmon troller swung at anchor near the western shore. We chose a spot in the northwest corner as far from the other boats as we could get.

We spent most of the afternoon on deck, repairing sails and hammering the gum rubber wedges in between the mast and the deck. As we worked, more trollers came in, seeking shelter from the gale. By 3:00 p.m. when the coastal steamer *Uchuck III* arrived, it had to thread its way through an obstacle course of trolling poles to get to the pier. At dusk we counted 12 boats in an anchorage that feels crowded with three.

As we got ready for bed Steve looked out at the fishboat off our starboard side and said, "I hope he doesn't drag. Those trolling poles would make a mess of our rigging." Trolling poles are designed to hold fishing lines away from the boat. When fishing, they extend out from the hull at an angle, but at a dock they can be stowed vertically. Unfortunately, the vertical position raises the centre of gravity and makes the boats roll, so most fishermen prefer to leave the poles down when at anchor. All of the trollers had left their poles out that night.

Steve went to sleep while I lay awake with visions of trolling poles tangled in our shrouds. Finally, I got up and looked out. I could see the loom of the Nootka light sweeping over the cove while fishboats swung in the gusts, their trolling poles outstretched like the arms of dancers. Reassured by the way the boats moved together in the wind, I went back to bed and slept well, rocked to sleep by the low swell.

We have never before or again seen Friendly Cove so crowded with boats. But its waters are crowded with history.

Residents of Nootka Sound, especially those in the tourist industry, are proud of that history. Tourist maps call the Sound "Historic Nootka Sound." "Birth Place of British Columbia" proclaims one tourist brochure—never mind that Vancouver Island wasn't even part of British Columbia when the colony was first established in 1858. "Site of the first contact between Europeans and First Nations of British Columbia" proclaims a pamphlet about Yuquot—never mind that the first European ship to visit the northwest coast, the *Santiago* of Spain, traded with the Haida of the Queen Charlotte Islands before proceeding south to Nootka. Never mind that the first contact on Vancouver Island, between the *Santiago* and members of the Hesquiaht band, actually took place off Estevan Point, almost 10 miles to the south. And never mind that the first landing by a European took place not in Friendly Cove but in Resolution Cove, three miles to the east.

Captain Cook's report of sea otter furs—"softer and finer than that of any others"—set off an international rush for furs. Friendly Cove's easy entrance, its protection from the worst of the ocean swells and its friendly inhabitants eager for European goods made it a natural gathering place for ships from all over the world.

But Friendly Cove wasn't just a place of commerce. Events here affected Europe half a world away. It was the actions of a British fur trader named John Meares, sometimes called the "Machiavelli of the fur trade," that propelled Nootka Sound into history. Meares first landed at Friendly Cove in 1788 in the ship *Felice Adventure* with a crew of Chinese carpenters. In the northeast corner of the harbour, Meares built what he called "a structure of uncommon magnificence"—and what others called a hut. On the beach the Chinese crew built and launched the ship *North West America*, the first sailing ship built on the northwest coast.

I've always been fascinated by the history of the places I've visited. Oddly, history appeals to the scientist in me: it so often explains, or pretends to explain, why a place is like it is today. So when I learned that Friendly Cove was famous for its history, I set

Fireweed on the foreshore of the beach north of Friendly Cove. Fees charged by the Mowachaht-Muchalaht band for landing on their reserve help maintain walking trails and other amenities.

out to learn more about it. Historians have written whole libraries of books about what happened at Nootka the next summer (1789), translating and analyzing the journals of all the players. My first stop was at the University of Washington Library Northwest Collections, where a librarian brought me a leather-bound copy of Captain Cook's journal, so fragile I had to prop it open with foam rubber wedges. Reading it I was transported right back to Nootka Sound. Even with all of the "s"s written as "f"s, I felt as if the events depicted had happened only yesterday. From there I went on to read other journals of other adventurers, many of whom were at Friendly Cove in the summer of 1789.

Some of the journals included sketches by members of the expeditions. I was surprised to see that sometimes the trees in the sketches looked deciduous, with broad spreading branches like no trees I had ever seen at Nootka. I concluded that the artists, seeing trees, drew them as they had known them in their native countries, not as they were at Nootka.

Making sense of all of these journals is a challenge. Derek Pethick, author of *The Nootka Connection,* on the subject of Meares stated, "a historian who claimed to have unraveled all the facts of the matter might really have done no more than enroll himself in the lengthy list of this shrewd manipulator's dupes." And then there's the view of the Mowachaht. "The history books are neither accurate nor kind to us," the Mowachaht wrote in an agenda paper presented to the Historic Sites and Monuments Board of

Canada in 1997. From the standpoint of First Nations, historians are outsiders who stole their history from them and mistakenly believe they know all about them. The First Nations believe these "experts" lack the context to understand what really happened, and point out that these histories discount the Natives' oral history in favour of written history. With so much controversy, I am compelled to issue a disclaimer: my story of the events that took place in Friendly Cove is just my interpretation, and may include deciduous trees.

That summer of 1789 the Spaniards, who believed their sighting of Nootka in 1774 gave them ownership of the land, sent Estéban Martínez to Nootka in the ship *Princesa* with instructions to "prevent [other] nations from enjoying … commerce with natives." Martínez had been aboard the *Santiago* when it made its first contact with Natives and may have had a proprietary interest in the Spaniard's ownership as a result. John Meares, who believed that ownership was earned by occupation, not discovery, sent four ships to Nootka. To avoid the restrictions of Great Britain's East India and South Seas Companies Meares gave his ships Portuguese flags.

The American ships *Columbia* and *Lady Washington* were also at Nootka that summer. The *Lady Washington* came and went on fur trading expeditions while the *Columbia* swung at anchor, doing nobody knows exactly what. Her captain, John Kendrick, thought there was enough land for Americans and Spaniards, but had no interest in friendship with the British, from whom the Americans had recently won independence.

Also in Friendly Cove that summer were over a thousand Mowachaht, occupying a village of magnificent longhouses. The early years of the fur trade had been good to them. They had a monopoly on trade with the European ships and had become one of the most powerful nations on the coast, and their leader, Chief Maquinna, one of the most powerful chiefs. The Mowachaht would have been astonished to learn that anyone other than their chief claimed ownership to Nootka Sound—after all, they had lived there over 4,000 years.

At first relations between the various ships' officers were friendly; they dined regularly with each other and with Chief Maquinna. But the Spaniard, Martínez, was only biding his time. When more Spaniards arrived, he made his move. He first seized Meares's ship *Iphigenia*, then released it with a warning to leave the coast and never return (she didn't leave). Next, he seized the *North West America*, then the *Princess Royal*, and finally the *Argonaut*, until he had taken all of Meares' remaining Portuguese flagged ships. He imprisoned the officers and men, and on shore he built two forts with gun emplacements. Chief Maquinna, who saw no advantage to his people from this squabble, shuttled among British and Spanish ships in a vain attempt at canoe diplomacy. For his efforts, he lost his brother, Chief Callicum, shot by a trigger-happy Spaniard. Only the *Columbia* and the *Washington* escaped capture. No one knows why. In his diary, Martínez admitted that he "treated this enemy as my friend."

In Europe the seizure of Meares's ships and imprisonment of their officers and crew nearly caused a war between Great Britain and Spain. His claims for $600,000 in damages, however, angered officials of the East India Company who considered him no more than a scoundrel. Spain and England signed the first Nootka Convention in Europe in October 1790. In this document, Spain agreed to restore buildings and land at Nootka to Meares and his associates, but left the exact reparations for Captains Vancouver of Great Britain and Quadra of Spain to resolve at a historic meeting in Friendly Cove in August 1792.

That meeting is depicted in one of two stained glass windows donated to the village of Yuquot by the Spanish Government in 1957 and located in the church in Friendly Cove.

The Spanish government donated these two stained glass windows to the church at Yuquot.

We first visited that church in 1984, walking up from the beach on a path lined with blackberries. We didn't see anyone around, so we walked up the stairs and tried the door; it was open. We entered a small foyer panelled in knotty pine. The stained glass windows marked either side of the foyer with display cases of newspaper clippings in the middle. The window to the left of the door showed a picture of serious-looking men in gold braided uniforms and tricorn hats pondering important papers, while in the background two ships rode at anchor. At the bottom of the window were the words, "Reunion de los Capitanes Bodega-Quadra y Vancouver." The window to the right showed a picture of a brown-robed priest preaching to Natives in cone-shaped hats.

We looked at the windows and read the newspaper clippings, then walked into the chapel. Rows of pews sat empty under a watermarked ceiling and it didn't look like anybody had done much preaching there for quite a while. There wasn't anybody to preach to. Tuberculosis, venereal diseases, smallpox and warfare with other tribes had reduced the Mowachaht to just another small band. Eventually the few survivors moved to a reserve near Gold River and joined forces with the Muchalaht band. Only one family lives at Yuquot today. The whole church seemed out of place in this wilderness.

From the newspaper clippings, I had assumed the events the windows portrayed were important. Then I read Vancouver's journal and learned that Vancouver and Quadra made no decisions and signed no papers at their meeting. Vancouver would not believe that Meares's shacks and puny piece of land was all his government wanted him to claim while Quadra refused to give up more. The second Nootka Convention, signed in Europe in 1794, finally resolved Meares's claims. In 1793, France declared war on Great Britain, and Britain and Spain became allies. Both nations had more important things to worry about than compensation to someone of doubtful character. The Spaniards paid Meares $210,000, which some said was more than he deserved.

In 1794 Britain and Spain signed yet a third Nootka Convention in which the Spaniards agreed to withdraw their garrison and disband their settlement at Nootka. Spain had always blown hot and cold over the Northwest anyway—had, in fact, already abandoned and reclaimed Nootka once before. Spain's withdrawal cleared the way for Great Britain to claim what is now British Columbia and set the stage for the United States to later claim Oregon and Washington.

Friendly Cove

Fallen Totem

One of the highlights of our first trips to Yuquot was to visit the totem pole that until 1993 stood just above the beach to the north of the houses, not too far from where John Meares built his "structure." It was thrilling to stand below a real totem pole and look up at the intricately carved figures and imagine what the village must have been like when totem poles lined the beach.

When we heard in 1996 that the pole had fallen during a storm in 1993, we imagined it lying in the forest, rotting away in isolation. Determined to find it and photograph it, we pushed through the thick undergrowth of salal and blackberries toward the spot where we thought it was, but found nothing but more blackberries. Finally, we returned to the house of the one family that still lives at Yuquot, the Williams, and asked Terry Williams where the pole was. "I haven't been to visit it since it fell," she said. She directed us to a clearing around a clump of trees just a few yards from her house. The totem pole lay next to a pile of lumber for a new house, blackberries growing indiscriminately around both totem pole and lumber.

Tourists enjoy visiting the fallen totem and studying its intricate carvings.

The totem pole had stood watch over Friendly Cove since 1929 when, according to George Nicholson in *Vancouver Island's West Coast, 1762–1962*, Chief Napoleon Maquinna presented it to Lord Willingdon, the Governor General of Canada. Chief Maquinna made it clear that the pole was a potlatch gift and that custom demanded the Governor General give a gift in return. The Governor General dutifully sent a power saw on the next steamboat. The totem pole, however, remained in Friendly Cove as the Department of Indian Affairs discouraged the removal of totems from their native environments.

When we saw the pole lying unattended, we didn't understand how the Mowachaht could just abandon a work of art. But to them the pole's fall and decay is part of a natural cycle, best left undisturbed.

Thinking we had seen everything there was to see at Friendly Cove we stayed away for several years. In 1999, we returned because we had seen pictures of new carvings decorating the church. We walked through the foyer into the chapel and stood in awe. Sunlight streamed through coloured glass windows onto brightly painted carvings of bears, whales, ravens and thunderbirds. The wooden pews no longer faced the front, but instead had been rotated 90 degrees to face the centre of the church and each other. The altar had been shoved into a corner, its surface a jumble of hymnals and altar cloths. The church had become a museum and meeting place for the Mowachaht–Muchalaht band. The band had reclaimed Yuquot.

Drawn by the carvings we returned to the church two years later. On the trail we met Ray Williams. When he collected the $10 landing fee from us, we asked him to come back to the church with us and explain the carvings. Ray sat in one of the pews and pointed to the large thunderbird above the doorway and a whale just below it. They were replicas of a memorial for a Chief Maquinna, he told us. In the original memorial the whale had been large enough to hold the chief's body.

The Mowachaht-Muchalaht band has turned the former Catholic Church into a meeting room and cultural centre.

I asked Ray if the animal figures on the totems had stories connected with them. "Yes, but I don't know them. They're not my stories, they're Chief Maquinna's stories. No one else knows them."

He told us that all of the Mowachahts' great chiefs had been named Maquinna. This was a very sad time for the Mowachaht, because just a few days earlier Chief Ambrose Maquinna had died. The chief's son would be the new Chief Maquinna.

As Ray got up to leave I asked him if I could take a picture of him in front of one the totems. "You can take a picture," he said. "But not here. I'm not a Maquinna. It wouldn't be right."

In 2003 we stopped again at Friendly Cove. We brought Ray a copy of the picture I had taken of him two years before. "Who's that?" he asked. "Some crazy Indian?" Then he told us about his son, Sanford, who had set up a carving shop in the house next door. We looked in and found Sanford and a friend sitting at a workbench. Shavings littered the floor and the pleasant smell of cedar filled the room. On the wall were several masks already complete. Friendly Cove seemed to be getting better every year, I thought, as we walked down a freshly paved walkway to our dinghy.

On our way home in the summer of 2004, we stopped at Yuquot on a Sunday afternoon. We had heard that the Mowachaht–Muchalaht bands were holding a Spirit Festival that afternoon and, for $25, we could attend. We were looking forward to a lunch of salmon and an afternoon of watching Native dances.

New friends, Dave and Sherry of the sailboat *Alrisha,* had agreed to meet us there and the four of us dinghied ashore before noon. We found a scene of festive activity. Rows of tents lined the field below the church and children played on the grass. In the centre of the field sat an open-sided tent surrounded by church pews that had been moved out of the church for the occasion. Women were setting out boxes of watermelon and cakes and a young man in a golf cart was carting luggage to the dock.

At noon the *Uchuck* arrived, disgorging a full load of 100 passengers onto the dock. They swarmed over the field, visited Sandford Williams in his carving shop, wandered in and out of the church and milled around the tent. We joined them, looking over the tables of T-shirts and other memorabilia. We finally settled into the pews when a group of young men gathered in the centre of the tent to sing a welcome song. Children in red and black capes served us paper plates of smoked salmon and potato salad.

"We're here to celebrate the history of Yuquot, our history, your history, everybody's history," announced Margarita James, the festival organizer, after everyone had been served. She then told us that the Mowachaht–Muchalaht had held the first Spirit Festival in 1992, the bicentennial of the Vancouver–Quadra meeting. Dignitaries from Spain and England attended. That first festival was such a success they had repeated it every year since. The festival was the Mowachaht–Muchalaht's way of thanking people who helped them during the year.

Chief Mike Maquinna spoke next. I leaned forward to get a closer look at this descendant of the great Chief Maquinna—a solid-looking man dressed casually in shorts and a fleece vest.

"Yuquot is the centre of our world," he told us. "From the beginning we knew Yuquot would be the centre of our efforts to attract tourists. We built tourist cabins, renovated the church, fixed the dock. And now we will reclaim the Whaler's Shrine." He was referring to an open shed house—holding 88 human carvings, four carved whales and 16 human skulls—that now resides at the Museum of Natural History in New York. According to the band's Agenda Paper, the Mowachaht–Muchalaht saw bringing home the shrine as a way to reclaim their history.

Chief Mike Maquinna (left) is a descendant of the great Chief Maquinna of fur trading days.

Maquinna then turned the microphone over to another member of the band who proceeded to award plaques and other gifts to a long list of people. Each person receiving a gift gave a speech. I shifted in my seat impatiently and looked guiltily at Dave and Sherry. What had I gotten them into?

The announcer was talking about someone named Tsu-xiit. At about the third referral to Tsu-xiit, I figured out he was talking about the young male orca, called Luna by the non-native press, who had strayed from his family's pod three years earlier and had been swimming the waters of Nootka Sound ever since. The Department of Fisheries and Oceans (DFO) had been trying to reunite the orca with his pod. From all around the world people had taken up his cause, raising money and posting news about him on websites.

Although we hadn't seen Tsu-xiit ourselves, every day we had heard the Tofino Coast Guard radio warn boaters to avoid the inlets of Tlupana and Muchalat, which the whale frequented, announcing that the "whale appears to pay particular interest to sailing vessels' keels and rudders and has been reported to have caused substantial damage."

The Mowachaht believed that Tsu-xiit was the reincarnation of Chief Ambrose Maquinna, who had died only three days before Tsu-xiit arrived in Nootka Sound. They wanted Tsu-xiit to stay in Nootka Sound, or at least to make his own choice. When the DFO tried to lure Tsu-xiit into his pen, the Mowachaht took to their canoes paddling furiously, singing and drumming their paddles against the canoes to lure Tsu-xiit away from the pen. For eight days they paddled. The press began to pay attention and the tide of public opinion shifted. Finally, the DFO agreed to negotiate for the whale's future. In a battle of traditional canoes against motorized zodiacs, the canoes had won. And today the Mowachaht–Muchalaht was celebrating that victory. In a small way, Nootka Sound had again become important beyond its boundaries. (In September 2004 the DFO agreed to let Tsu-xiit stay in Nootka Sound on the condition that the Natives would run patrols to keep whale and boats apart.)

When the last gift was given and the last elder thanked, the dances started. A line of women in black and white fringed capes entered the tent to the sound of drums, dancing in a circle with slow deliberate motions. Next, children in white capes painted with butterflies whirled and stamped, their capes flying out from their bodies to show jeans and T-shirts beneath. After a few minutes of dancing, the children sat in a circle as the drummers chanted and beat a rapid rhythm. A black-robed woman called out names. As each child's name was called, he stood up to dance, hopping up, down and sideways to the rhythm. I didn't understand the words of the chants, but I understood the fun the children were having and the laughter of the audience. When all the children

had danced, the woman called another name and one of the drummers joined the circle, doing the same dance, to the laughter of the other musicians. Then she called on one of the elders, a bent old man in a baseball cap who got up and gave a little hop. Finally, she proceeded to the audience, first pointing to Dave, sitting next to me in the front row. He shook his head and shrunk back. She then pointed to Steve, who shrugged and got up and gave a passable hop to good-natured laughter.

When the dancing was over and the *Uchuck* with its load of tourists had steamed out of the cove, we joined Sherry and Dave for a walk out to the ocean beach. The trail followed a row of stately spruce trees, past the group of small tourist cabins and down to the beach. We climbed over driftwood logs and through a field of pink fireweed to the beach. It was a balmy sunny day and the sun sparkled on the water. Offshore, a crowd of small white sport fishing boats bobbed among the rocks—customers for the cabins.

As we stepped onto the beach, the ground gave way beneath us in a rattle of rolling stones. The smaller stones worked their way between our sandals and feet until it felt like we were walking on pins. I leaned down and picked up a handful of stones. Some were rust-coloured while others were grey or green, but all were smooth and shiny. How much history had had to pass, I wondered, for the waves to round off the sharp corners and turn the rocks into things of beauty?

EPILOGUE. The friendly young killer whale Luna, or Tsu-xiit, was killed by a tug boat's propeller in 2006.

Dancers at the annual Spirt Festival, a celebration of history.

Marvinas Bay and Bodega Cove

Adventures and Suffering

The sport fishermen were just returning from their morning bite in their small white kicker boats as we left Friendly Cove. Already some of the men were gathered on the float holding up their fish for others to admire. On land a Mowachaht band member rumbled along the trail in his golf cart, ensuring that no one went ashore without paying the landing fee. Glad to put the bustle behind us, we raised anchor quickly and motored out toward Cook Channel.

Steve had the mainsail up almost before we cleared the lighthouse and soon we were raising the jib and sailing past the rocky entrance to Santa Gertrudis Cove. The westerlies pushed us easily up Cook Channel. We passed the green chain of the Saavedra Islands to port while to our starboard we could see the humps of the large archipelago of the Spanish Pilot Group. In less than an hour we were off the entrance to Marvinas Bay, five miles from Friendly Cove.

We were following the path of the American fur traders who once frequented Marvinas Bay. Out of reach of ocean swells and away from the Spanish and British ships crowding Friendly Cove, Marvinas Bay offered the Boston men an easy entrance,

Marvinas Bay was once the favourite anchorage of the "Boston Men" (American fur traders). Modern sailors scorn it for the west winds that blow right into it.

drinking water, firewood and an anchorage all to themselves. Captain John Kendrick of the ships *Columbia* and *Washington* liked it so much he built a house on shore and called it Fort Washington.

We sailed past the small island near the bay's entrance and circled the bay, looking for a place to anchor. I wanted to experience the bay as the Boston men had experienced it. At its head we could see a small marsh and I wondered if that was where the Boston men had gotten their water. As for the wood they had sought, there was still plenty there, but the hills had that patchy, ragged look, like a bad haircut, that is evidence of past clear-cutting. Nor would we have the anchorage to ourselves. While we circled the bay a small white motorboat left a float in front of a building onshore and went roaring by us, sending *Osprey* rocking. This wasn't the Marvinas Bay of 200 years ago.

Of all the Boston ships that anchored here, the most famous was named after the city itself. On March 12, 1803, the fur trader *Boston* anchored here in 12 fathoms of water, so near to shore they secured to a tree. The crew spent several days gathering wood, filling water casks and trading with the Mowachaht who paddled up from Friendly Cove. One day Captain Salter gave Chief Maquinna a rifle. The next day Chief Maquinna brought nine pairs of ducks as a present for Salter, but the gun he returned, complaining that one of the locks was broken. He called it *peshak*—"bad." Salter was offended, called Maquinna a liar and accused him of breaking it. To the Boston men it was just a few angry words over a rifle, but to Maquinna this was the last straw in a long series of insults: Boston men had held him hostage as ransom for deserters, had ignored Mowachaht traditions and had trampled on their sacred sites.

Despite their chief's anger, the Mowachaht pretended to remain friendly. The next day they lured part of the crew off the ship by promising them good fishing for salmon in Friendly Cove. Once the crew was divided, warriors overpowered the crew on board and seized the ship while their tribesmen killed those who had gone fishing. Only the ship's armourer, John R. Jewitt, an Englishman, and the sailmaker, John Thompson, who were working below at the time of the raid, escaped death.

Mowachaht warriors found Jewitt shaking with fear and brought him to Maquinna. Maquinna realized the advantage of having his own armourer and over the objections of his men, determined to save him. He demanded that Jewitt be his slave for life—to fight his battles and repair his muskets—or be put to death. When Jewitt consented, Maquinna then had his men bring the grisly heads of the ship's crew to Jewitt for identification.

Jewitt determined from his first day of captivity to adopt a conciliating manner to his captors and conform to their way of life. He befriended the chief's young son and made himself useful, hauling firewood, making bracelets for the chief's nine wives and forging knives and axes. When the Mowachahts found Thompson hiding in the ship's hold, he convinced the chief to save Thompson by claiming that Thompson was his father.

Among the other bands the capture of the *Boston* was a public relations coup. With Jewitt's help the Mowachaht sailed the *Boston* to Friendly Cove and within a few days, canoes of 20 bands filled the cove to celebrate the ship's capture and to receive gifts of muskets, looking glasses and cloth. Maquinna paraded Jewitt and Thompson in front of his visitors as symbols of victory and status. But word of the massacre spread among the fur traders, too, and no ships came to Friendly Cove to trade for furs or to rescue the captives. And when the *Boston* burned and sank in Friendly Cove, the captives' last ties to civilization sank with it.

Jewitt learned the Mowachaht language and earned the affection of Chief Maquinna. Throughout his captivity Jewitt kept a journal, recording the details of his new life in a ledger he had rescued from the *Boston*, writing with blackberry ink and raven quill pens. Maquinna wanted Jewitt to forget his past life and insisted he and Thompson wear

Mowachaht clothing and eat Mowachaht food. Seeing that Jewitt was unhappy, Chief Maquinna ordered him to marry. But although his bride was comely, bore him a son and sought to please him, Jewitt could not accept either her or his new life.

Rescue finally came in July 1805, in the form of the brig *Lydia* of Boston. As Maquinna had spared Jewitt, so Jewitt spared Maquinna, arguing to the *Lydia*'s captain that to kill Maquinna would only extend the cycle of revenge and cause the loss of many more American lives. Jewitt and Maquinna parted amicably, with Maquinna promising to care for Jewitt's son.

Jewitt and Thompson returned to Boston on the *Lydia,* but Jewitt was unable to settle into the life he had longed for. Instead, he published his journal and travelled throughout the country selling it from a peddler's cart. His journal caught the attention of a writer, Richard Alsop, who interviewed Jewitt extensively and published, *A Narrative of the Adventures and Suffering of John R. Jewitt*. The book in turn caught the attention of the playwright James Nelson Barker, who wrote a melodrama titled, *The Armourer's Escape*, starring John Jewitt himself.

Jewitt's *Narrative* is still in print today. Scholars quote from it and schoolchildren read it. Because of Jewitt's story, the Nootka Indians (as the Nuu-chah-nulth were called then) became a household word in Boston and beyond. And because of his capture we know many details about the early-contact Nuu-chah-nulth. Reading it I was struck by Jewitt's horror at being marooned in a strange land and his fascination with the very people who had killed his shipmates.

One sail through Marvinas Bay was all we needed to experience it. The easy entrance, so important to the fur trading ships, left the bay open to westerlies that stirred up a short chop and caused me to pull my jacket tighter against the cold. We left in search of a more protected anchorage, one better suited to a modern yacht.

We motored out past Boston Point and set sail again, heading northwest up Kendrick Inlet with the wind behind. We were in logging country. Both sides of the inlet had

Giant machinery shove logs into the water at Kendrick's Camp in Kendrick Inlet.

Metal teeth on the bow of this log pusher aid in moving logs.

been clear-cut, some areas so recently we could still see the grey slash left behind. To our right Strange Island sported newly planted trees, making it look strangely out of scale. Between Funter and Matute Islands we caught glimpses of a logging camp: docks, workers' housing and log dumps. A log pusher was making up a log raft at the entrance to Plumper Harbour. At Kendrick Camp near the head of the inlet, we stopped to watch giant yellow machines dump bundles of freshly cut logs down skids into the water.

We headed for the northeast corner of Kendrick Inlet and entered a narrow channel formed by Bodega Island on the right and Nootka Island on the left. With the wind still behind we sailed into a perfectly protected cove. Unnamed on the chart, it was no more than a wide spot in a narrow channel with room enough for one or two boats. The shores had been logged some time ago but were growing back nicely. A thrush sang from the shore and a raven clonked in the distance. Later, Steve went out in the dinghy to Princesa Channel and caught three greenlings for dinner. I took my inflatable kayak farther up the channel and watched seals cavorting among the eelgrass. It was a perfect spot to wait out the evening before heading north to Tahsis the next day. It was our Marvinas Bay.

Esperanza Inlet

Oclucje
Zeballos
Espinosa Inlet
Zeballos Inlet
Tahsis
Steamer Point
Esperanza
Catala I
Tahsis Narrows
Nuchatlitz
Tahsis Inlet
NOOTKA ISLAND
N
0   5   10   15   20
kilometres

The westerlies pushed us up Esperanza Inlet and around the corner into Zeballos Inlet, following the twists and turns of the channel as if the wind too planned a visit to town. The farther up the inlet we went, the stronger the wind blew until the water almost boiled with foam. It was one of those rare days on the west coast of Vancouver Island when the air was warm enough for shorts and T-shirts and I was enjoying the downwind ride.

Tahsis

Waiting to Live

We heard rumours of a Canadian armada heading toward us as we headed north in the year 2000. Twenty-seven boats from the Royal Victoria Yacht Club were circumnavigating Vancouver Island in a group millennial cruise. The storekeeper in Hot Springs Cove warned us, "They're in Walters Cove [Kyuquot] tonight. They'll be here the day after tomorrow." The next day we sailed to Nootka Sound and anchored in Ewin Inlet, away from Friendly Cove where we expected the boats to be. In Ewin Inlet we met Elaine and David on the sailboat *Astrosight* of Vancouver.

"Have you heard about the Victoria Yacht Club?" they asked. "They'll be in Tahsis tomorrow."

We groaned. Tahsis was our destination, too. There are only two places in Nootka Sound and Esperanza Inlet to provision and Tahsis, just a short distance from Tahsis Narrows is the most convenient and the best stocked. And there's only one place for cruising boats to stay in Tahsis: Westview Marina. When we had stayed there two years

Motoring up Tahsis Inlet in the morning calm. By noon the wind can be blowing 25 knots.

before, small sport fishing boats had packed the marina. We didn't know where 27 cruising boats would fit—28 counting *Osprey*.

Victoria Yacht Club boats were jockeying for space outside the marina when we arrived. We waited until a teenager wearing a dark green T-shirt with "Westview Marina" on its front directed us alongside two Victoria sailboats. More green-shirted teenagers helped us tie up. A plump girl in braids and green T-shirt asked if she could take my garbage. Astonished, I automatically said no. Then I saw she wanted to do it, so I handed it over.

We soon saw how the marina could accommodate 28 cruising boats: the fleet of sport fishing boats was gone. A complicated red-, yellow- and blue-striped fisheries map posted outside the marina office announced salmon fishing closures almost everywhere in Nootka Sound and Esperanza Inlet.

Tahsis was in trouble. The Tahsis sawmill operated fewer days every year. Commercial salmon fishing, Tahsis's second industry, was nearly dead. The sport fishing business, centred in Westview Marina, had been the town's best hope. The marina had expanded to fill its new role. Cathy Daynes, the owner, had added slips, built a small tackle and gift shop, a café, a convenience store and laundry facilities. Westview Marina had impressed us as unusually friendly and attractive. But when I saw the hordes of sport fishing boats here two years before, I had wondered how long they would last. It didn't make sense to me to turn from one kind of salmon fishing to another and expect to prosper. So I wasn't surprised at the absence of sport fishermen—just sad.

With sport fishing boats gone, who would fill the marina? There wouldn't be 28 cruising boats every night. One or two a night was more likely. And Tahsis seemed an unlikely destination for other types of tourists. Although the view from the dining room window of the Maquinna Resort is spectacular—red rock cliffs interrupt green forested slopes on mountains that rise straight up from the shore—getting here is a challenge. Tourists from Vancouver or Seattle first take a ferry, then drive up the east coast of Vancouver Island to Campbell River, then drive 40 miles across the mountains to Gold River. The final 30 miles from Gold River are on bone-jarring, dusty, tortuous logging roads. And once tourists reach Tahsis, they have another 20 miles by boat to

Westview Marina in Tahsis is a popular destination for sport fishermen from Washington State.

reach fishing or whale-watching grounds in Nootka Sound or Esperanza Inlet. Tahsis would have a tough time competing with Tofino and Ucluelet farther south. These two towns are both closer to the cities, are reached by paved highways and have ready access to the ocean.

We had come to Tahsis to provision, as we needed fresh fruits and vegetables and other supplies. We knew from previous years that when the sawmill wasn't running, provisions were scant. With 27 other cruising boats in town, would we find anything left in the stores?

The town of Tahsis stretches along the west shore of Tahsis Inlet until it reaches the inlet's head, where it sprawls out onto the flood plain of the Tahsis River. The Maquinna Resort and a small shopping mall are at the narrow end of the town to the south, while the sawmill, workers' housing, grocery stores, bakery and hardware store are at the north end. A small public dock and the Westview Marina are near the middle. It's an inconvenient arrangement for visiting boaters who must navigate the town by foot in search of supplies.

We started our shopping at the mall where we hoped to buy some wine and a flat of beer requested by friends we would be visiting the next day in Nuchatlitz. We walked past empty storefronts with brown paper on the windows. The bank we had seen two years before was boarded up. Besides the liquor store only the post office, a gardening store and an appliance–hardware store were still in business. We looked in at the garden store and saw scraggly-looking plants looking forlorn on nearly empty shelves. In the window of the appliance store, faded boxes of coffee makers and hair dryers gathered dust. Only the liquor store looked prosperous, but it was closed for the day. It was Monday and a sign on the door said to come back on Tuesday.

Next on our list was the grocery store. It was too far to walk, but we knew how easy it was to hitch a ride in Tahsis. On our first trip here we had started walking with laundry

The Tahsis sawmill was the town's primary industry until it closed in 2002.

bags over our shoulders. Within a few minutes a car stopped and its driver, a housewife with two kids in the back, offered us a ride. Since then we had hitched on almost every visit. Always we had met someone interesting and learned something about Tahsis and this year was to be no different. The third car around the corner, a late-model maroon Subaru, stopped.

"You want to go to grocery store?" the driver asked, in heavily accented English. A stout woman with curly grey hair and glasses, she was wearing a T-shirt that said, "If women have to admit their age, men should have to act theirs."

Her name, she told us, was Dora. "I take you there. I take you back, too," Dora announced. "I have time, more time than money."

While she drove toward town, Dora told us about herself. She and her husband Ivan, both from Croatia, had lived in Tahsis for 27 years. Ivan was an oiler at the mill, but was now unemployed, waiting for the mill to start up again. Today Ivan was fishing and Dora had time on her hands. She pointed at the mill, surrounded by empty parking lots, as we went by.

Dora had put her house up for sale. "If it sells, fine; if not, we stay here."

She drove by the grocery store and out the road a ways to show us where she lived: a small white clapboard house in a row of similar houses. Many, like Dora's, had For Sale signs in their front yards.

At the grocery store Steve and I contemplated mouldy-looking grapes, soft-looking apples and brown-tinged iceberg lettuce. The once-a-week grocery truck delivered on Tuesday night so this produce was a week old. We finally bought the least mouldy looking bunch of grapes and some of the better looking apples. Dora bought a loaf of bread.

Dora dropped us off at the top of the bumpy dirt driveway to the Westview Marina. "If you ever need anything in Tahsis, just call Dora. Next time you come to Tahsis, I take you to grocery store."

"But how will we find you?" I asked. "We don't know your last name or your phone number."

"I'm Dora, just Dora. Everybody knows Dora and Ivan. Ask at the marina. They call me for you."

The mill where Dora's husband worked had been the dream of Gordon Gibson, a hard-drinking, hard-working, loud-voiced man from Ahousat with only six years of schooling. His grammar school teacher had told him he was a hopeless student and in so doing made him so angry he was determined to be first in everything for the rest of his life—a life he described in his book *The Bull of the Woods*.

Gibson dreamed of ocean-going ships loading lumber in Tahsis—ships that would do away with log rafts and the loss of logs at sea. He and his brothers built the sawmill without plans, using rough lumber and used equipment. When that mill burned down in 1948, the Gibsons rebuilt it in partnership with the East Asiatic Company, a Danish shipping firm with international markets. The new mill didn't have the same appeal to the Gibson brothers and in 1952 they sold out to the East Asiatic Company, which operated the mill as Tahsis Company, Limited.

Tahsis was a true company town. Tahsis Company, Limited owned and built the sawmill, the roads, the water system, houses, schools, even the churches. The Company set the rules. Among other stipulations they decreed that Volkswagen Beetles were too large for their roads. It was not until 1969 that the town incorporated and workers could buy their own houses.

On our first visit to Tahsis in 1984, we hiked up a steep street called Cardiac Climb and walked among residences of mill managers and supervisors. There we found a small park where we looked down on a scene of noisy activity: pipelines spewed wood chips into barges for towing to the pulp mill at Gold River; piles of fresh lumber waited to be loaded onto ships; the smell of fresh cedar filled the air; the parking lot at the plant was full of workers' cars.

Now that parking lot was empty and the mill was quiet, silenced by economic recession in Japan and other Asian markets. I knew the quiet mill meant forests saved from clear-cutting, but I missed the activity. The old Tahsis was much more interesting than this empty, forlorn town.

In the evening we walked from the marina to the Maquinna Resort for dinner, hoping to beat the Victoria crowd by arriving early. On the way we noticed a new building constructed just a few feet from the old Tahsis hospital and wondered if the hospital were expanding. We waited to ask a woman carrying a briefcase up the drive what was happening.

She told us that she managed the Tahsis clinic and the clinic in Gold River. The new building was a replacement for the old building—a flat-roofed structure with leaks that couldn't be stopped—which would be torn down when the new one was completed.

We asked her about the town, noting that it obviously wasn't doing very well. She agreed. Tahsis needed, she believed, high-technology companies like we have in Seattle. But the town didn't have the infrastructure to support them—their phone systems and roads weren't good enough.

The mill hadn't closed for good, just for the summer. Workers couldn't leave because they owned their houses; they were hoping that if the mill closed, the company would buy out the houses as they had at Gold River, where the same company had closed the pulp mill and where retirees had bought the workers' houses at bargain prices. Gold River was now recovering. But at Tahsis the workers were in limbo.

"The town is waiting to die," she told us.

"Waiting to die? No, waiting to live!" said Bob Devault of Nuchatlitz two days later when we told him of this conversation. According to Bob, retirees and other people were buying houses in Tahsis already and more would do so if the mill closed. New businesses were moving in, like the company that took people skin diving in the winter and whale-watching in the summer—businesses run by "people that know how to make a living without killing fish or chopping down trees."

I just hoped their customers would brave the logging roads.

In October of 2002, the Tahsis Mill closed permanently. The company bought the workers' houses and in November put 50 houses on the market at once. By January all of them had been sold to retirees and summer residents. Dora's house was among the houses the mill purchased. Ivan and Dora retired to Port Alberni.

In December 2002, the population of Tahsis had fallen below 400, and the Canada Health Act regulations meant a full-time physician could no longer be supported. The clinic was combined with the Gold River Clinic to comprise a population of 1,800 and a second physician was added to the consolidated clinic. When we visited Tahsis in the summer of 2003 we found The Savage Biscuit, a bakery that had once been on the outskirts of town, occupying one of the storefronts in the mall and selling dairy products and a few miscellaneous fresh vegetables, as well as some of the best whole grain bread on the coast. The grocery store in town was still operating, its shelves looking even more barren than before. Westview Marina was bustling, filled to almost overflowing with small sport fishing boats. They were having a good fishing year. Residents told us they were doing well but they anticipated a quiet winter.

By 2004 the mill had been demolished and the town was planning to use the mill dock for a cruise ship terminal.

Esperanza Mission

Lunch with Fuel

"God doesn't make bad things. He made the world good." At these amazing words from Kevin, the Esperanza missionary, I shifted uncomfortably in my chair and looked around the room. The words made me wonder what Steve and I, two non-churchgoers, were doing here. The room, with its upright piano, folding chairs and Bible verses on the wall reminded me of the basement of the Lutheran Church where my father had been organist and choirmaster during my childhood. Only the children's drawings next to the Bible verses, of northwest Native designs, showed it for what it was: the dining room of a mission on the west coast of Vancouver Island. The missionary's words, on the other hand, reminded me of Sunday school lessons at my mother's Christian Science Church. I thought I had left all that behind. I couldn't believe anymore that if I prayed hard enough, or believed the right thing, that God would make everything work out all right.

Teenaged Nuu-chah-nulth from Zeballos and Kyuquot were sitting at tables around the room. I couldn't tell what they were thinking; their faces showed no expression. A few of them were looking around the room, but most seemed to be listening attentively.

Just before noon that day we had stopped at Esperanza's fuel dock. After the young man operating the fuel dock had helped fill our diesel and water tanks, he invited us to lunch. It was a Tuesday toward the end of July and a camp for Nuu-chah-nulth youths was in full swing. We were now listening to a pre-lunch pep talk while delicious aromas of soup and grilled cheese drifted out from the kitchen.

A fuel dock helps support the Esperanza Mission.

At Esperanza an invitation to a meal comes with almost every tank of fuel. But even after many trips I'm still amazed at the idea of a combination fuel dock and mission. The fuel sales help support the mission—and serve a need by providing fuel to a population dependent on their boats for all their transportation.

We made our first visit here in 1984 on a beautiful sunny day with a strong northwesterly wind. From Tahsis Inlet we had sailed into Tahsis Narrows, tacking back and forth in the winding channel. The water in the narrows is deep right up to the edge so we sailed close on each tack, flirting with the rocks before turning. An RCMP boat followed us through the narrows, staying politely behind all the way, perhaps expecting to pick up the pieces if we missed a tack. Steve thought it was amusing. I found it unnerving; I kept looking back over my shoulder every time we turned, expecting them to pass us or arrest us for blocking their passage.

We rounded the corner and saw the white houses and green lawns of the mission. They looked inviting and peaceful. We were curious: a mission in 1984 seemed like an anachronism. So we decided to stop and find out more.

On the fuel dock a sign announced "out of fuel." At the head of the dock a young man was chopping wood. He put down his axe to talk to us. We were welcome to walk around, he said. And we could stay at the dock. He explained that Esperanza had once been a hospital mission, providing medical and dental services to the whole area. Now it provided religious camps for First Nations and local non–Native children and outreach to their parents.

We had arrived between camp sessions and the mission was almost deserted. We crossed a wooden bridge over a stream and walked through a small orchard, enjoying a peaceful

summer day and the view of the inlet. The mission reminded me of a small village with its rows of neat white houses, an old schoolhouse up on the hill and a boat shed with workshop. There was no church.

That evening we were invited to one of the houses for popcorn. At first, I was leery of the missionaries. Neither Steve nor I had been to church in years, and I didn't want to get into a discussion about why not. But when no one asked our religion or requested a donation, I relaxed. We sat on cushions on the floor in a bare room that reminded me of student housing and talked to several young mission workers. Our polite inquiries about the religious affiliation of the mission were met only with, "non-denominational." In fact, it was not until several years later, after we had visited the mission several times, that we learned it was run by an organization called the Shantymen's Christian Association whose purpose is to take the gospel to isolated communities in Canada.

The visit had satisfied our curiosity and we might not have come back if we hadn't seen the fuel dock open in 1987. We needed diesel and water, so decided to stop. As we were paying the bill, a woman ran down the ramp. "I saw your flag," she told us, gesturing at *Osprey's* American flag on the stern, "and just had to come down to talk to you. I'm an American too. I hope you can stay for awhile."

The woman's name was Virginia, and she and her husband Mike were from Nebraska. Virginia was an energetic woman in her forties with short dark hair and an infectious

The Esperanza Mission started its life as a hospital mission, providing health and later dental care to residents of Nootka Sound, Esperanza Inlet, and Kyuquot Sound.

smile. Mike was a solid-looking man with brown hair and a beard. To my surprise, we became instant friends.

In Nebraska Mike and Virginia had owned a farm machinery business before one of the Midwest's many farm crises caused its failure. From farm machinery they had turned to missionary work or, as Virginia put it, "the Lord had sent them to Esperanza." Over coffee they laughed as they told us tales of how as farmers, they had struggled to adapt to West Coast life. Mike, wearing cowboy boots, slipped on the wet dock, landing in the water. They had gone to town for propane at low tide only to find the tanks too heavy to push up the steep ramp. They had even tied their dinghy to a piling at high tide and found it dangling in the air six hours later. But they spoke in awe of their first winter in the rain forest—how it had rained and rained but the water had just rolled off the land instead of making mud. Despite their inexperience with salt water, their mechanical know-how and business sense got the fuel dock working again.

That night Mike stoked the wood-burning hot water tank in their small house so I could take a real bath. In the morning they served us breakfast of pancakes and fresh raspberries. As they walked us back to our boat, our arms laden with fresh lettuce from their garden, Mike pointed out several sailboats motoring toward Tahsis. From the direction they were going, we surmised they were circumnavigating Vancouver Island.

"I see them going by under motor all the time. Why don't they sail?" he asked. Shaking our heads at the foolishness of motoring in a following breeze, we asked Mike if many sailboats stopped at the mission. He told us that only a few stopped for fuel and even fewer took the time to visit.

"They don't know what they're missing," I said.

As we were raising sail in the channel, I looked back and saw Virginia and Mike on shore, waving goodbye. I reflected on how amazing it was that we had spent almost two days with two missionaries and never been asked our religion or even if we believed in God.

The founders of the Esperanza Mission, Dr. Herman McLean and his wife Marion, had dreamed of going to Africa as missionaries, but when their application was rejected, they turned to the West Coast instead. Depending on your perspective, the McLeans' story, told in *Not Without Hope* by Louise Johnson, is either the story of immense faith and determination or of religious fanaticism.

When the McLeans arrived at Esperanza in 1937, Nootka Sound and Esperanza Inlet were busier than they are now. Fish plants at Nootka, Ceepeecee and elsewhere did a booming business in pilchards and salmon. A sawmill cut logs in McBride Bay and miners dug gold in Zeballos. The area had no hospital and logging and fishing accidents were taking their toll. Children were dying of diseases medical science had found a cure for long before. Dr. McLean's first hospital was no more than a shack, the McLean's house no more than a lean-to. While Dr. McLean tended the sick, Mrs. McLean and the children (eventually there were eight) cooked, cleaned, carried water and chopped wood. Mrs. McLean also commuted by boat to Zeballos where she taught school. By 1939 they were able to build a larger hospital with 16 beds and to add regular nursing staff.

Dr. McLean never forgot that he was a missionary, not just a doctor. Margaret Sharcott, a fisherman's wife from Kyuquot, in her book *Troller's Holiday*, described the two weeks she spent at Esperanza waiting for the birth of her son. The patients shared meals with the staff. Before each meal the staff prayed, while the food cooled. After each meal they sang a hymn or read the Bible. In between treating patients the medical staff queried them on the state of their souls and urged them to give up "evil pleasures." Sharcott wrote that the experience made her understand why the other women at Kyuquot preferred to go to Victoria or Vancouver to give birth.

The McLean story that generates either awe or anger today is the story of a boat trip in October 1948. Dr. McLean and his 15-year-old son, Bruce, flew to Chamiss Bay in Kyuquot to retrieve their motorboat, *Messenger II*, which they had left there a month earlier. They had tried to return earlier on two separate occasions but each time had been beaten back by the weather. Finally they had left the boat in Chamiss Bay and flown home. Now they needed the boat at home and the weather looked promising.

But as they left Kyuquot Sound at 12:45 p.m., the wind howled and the waves broke across the pilothouse. Bruce became seasick and hung out the cabin door. Dr. McLean had dreaded the trip—he was not a sailor but a farmer at heart. Still, he kept on. For five hours they slogged south against the wind and waves. Fifteen minutes from the safety of Rolling Roadstead the engine sputtered and died. Water had gotten into the bilge and onto the batteries. Wind and waves pushed the boat toward the rocks. McLean frantically tried to start the engine, then work the pump, both without success. With a crash of a massive wave the doctor and his son were thrown from the boat into the stormy sea.

Only Dr. McLean survived. Thrown by the waves onto the top of White Rock he lashed himself there with line from the *Messenger II*, withstanding the battering of waves and cold for two days until being rescued by a passing salmon troller.

Dr. McLean saw his survival as proof of God's will, the loss of his son as the sacrifice he had to bear to carry out that will. On a coast where every trip in the ocean risks death, and a boat can be a family's only tie to civilization, I can understand why Dr. McLean left Chamiss Bay. What disturbs me is his belief that his survival and the loss of his son were God's will—that he had no responsibility in them.

The hospital closed in 1972. A dental clinic continued for several years longer and later the mission opened a school. Both have since closed.

We never saw Mike and Virginia again; they left the mission before our next visit three years later. But meeting them had sparked an interest in the mission and we stop there almost every trip we make. And the fuel dock has never been out of fuel again.

Churches in general, and missionaries in particular, are out of favour on the west coast of Vancouver Island. The Roman Catholic missionary Father Brabant and his crusade to civilize the Hesquiaht is considered at best the work of a misguided zealot, at worst the evil destruction of a culture. When I think of Christianity and the Vancouver Island's west coast, I think of the altar in the church at Yuquot, pushed into the corner to make room for traditional Native carvings.

In addition to missions, churches ran residential schools, paid for by the Canadian government. The purpose of the schools was to assimilate First Nations children into the dominant white culture. Children were forcibly taken from their homes. Some were beaten for speaking their own languages. Some of them were sexually abused. Even children who were not abused rejected the cultures of their parents and grandparents, refusing to learn the dances and stories passed down through generations.

But the Esperanza mission continues. On one of our visits I asked one of the mission workers how they dealt with the negative reputation missionaries had among Nuu-chah-nulth people. He replied that unlike the early missionaries, the Shantymen respected the Native culture.

Like Father Brabant, the Esperanza missionaries are trying to change a culture—albeit a culture broken by alcoholism, drug abuse and family breakups. Ironically, much of the damage perpetrated on Native culture can be blamed in part on the residential schools—institutions of the Christian religion the mission represents. Despite this, I find myself hoping the mission will succeed, at least in some small way. And "hope" is what the word *Esperanza* means in Spanish.

Nuchatlitz

Entering Nuchatlitz

Steve likes to sail through even the tightest passages. But the day he decided to tack through the rock-bound channel to the village of Nuchatlitz, I thought he had gone too far. The village of Nuchatlitz sits in a maze of reefs and islets just outside the entrance to Esperanza Inlet.

We first ventured through the rocks of Nuchatlitz during our fourth summer on this coast. The description of Nuchatlitz in the cruising guide, *West Coast of Vancouver Island* by Don Watmough, intrigued us: a seldom-visited Native fishing village whose inhabitants included an old woman who wove reed baskets in the traditional manner. Thinking about going there made me feel like an explorer, as if we were more than summer vacationers. Not even Watmough's warning, that "only cautious mariners, canoeists, or those with local knowledge can safely enter this isolated and placid anchorage," discouraged us. In our four summers of sailing this coast in *Velella,* we had grown increasingly comfortable in these waters. We were still wary of the coast's fog, rocks and strong winds, but we didn't let them stop us.

Numerous rocks make navigation challenging in the waters of Nuchatlitz.

The night before we were to go there, we got out the chart for Esperanza Inlet, the *BC Sailing Directions* and Don Watmough's book. The chart showed Nuchatlitz light on a small, unnamed island. The light faced up inlet, not out to sea as we would have expected. Between the light and Rosa Island to the northeast stretched a string of rocks. Watmough advised, "go around the north and east side of Rosa Island, avoiding the drying rocks." The *Sailing Directions* advised differently: "Nuchatlitz is approached ... through a narrow and tortuous channel entered between Rosa Island and Nuchatlitz light ..." We studied the chart. In the middle of the string of rocks, we saw a narrow band of deep water which we assumed was the entrance described by the *Sailing Directions*. Whichever route we chose we faced a maze of rocks, islands and sandbars. We chose the *Sailing Directions* route because it was shorter.

As we approached the entrance, the northwest winds blew 20–25 knots into Esperanza Inlet. The wind would be against us in the narrow channels. I waited for Steve to round up into the wind so we could take down the sails. But Steve adjusted the mainsheet and pointed to a rock on the chart.

"Keep your eye out for this rock. At this tide it should be just below the surface. We have to go between it and this other one to the south. It's going to be tight."

I felt a knot growing in the pit of my stomach as I realized he intended to sail all the way in.

"Are you crazy?" I asked, "Most people wouldn't even motor through this channel and you want to sail!"

"We've sailed through tighter channels than this. *Velella* is a good boat."

I remembered those tighter channels and wasn't reassured. One mistake, a tangled line, or the tiller pushed to leeward too late, and we'd be on the rocks. But there wasn't time to argue—we were already approaching the first of the rocks.

Fish packers used to enter Nuchatlitz through this narrow kelp-clogged entrance.

We entered the channel on a starboard tack. Steve headed *Velella* as close to the wind as he could; I cranked in the jib as hard as I could.

"Can you see that drying rock?" Steve asked as he pulled in the mainsheet.

I peered anxiously beneath the sail but saw only choppy water and the coastline ahead. "I don't see it. Shouldn't we turn?"

"Not yet. We're okay. We must have passed it already."

I barely had time to think about what would have happened if we had hit the rock with our keel. The rocky shore was getting closer fast. I waited for Steve to give the order to tack. He kept sailing. I bit my tongue, trying not to say anything. We were sailing so close to the rocks I could see individual barnacles growing at the water's edge. I couldn't stand it any longer. I yelled, "Come on, turn!" More seconds dragged on before Steve finally pushed the tiller to leeward. I kept the port jib sheet tight, letting the wind backfill the jib to push the bow through the wind. The jib filled, the boat heeled sharply onto the other tack and I scrambled for the starboard sheet as the jib flapped madly in the breeze.

Three times we tacked; three times I was convinced we would strike rock; three times we cleared with inches to spare. When we finally turned the corner, my heart was pounding as if I had run all the way.

We passed two red spar buoys marking a sandbar, glided by a low grassy island with its collection of small houses and drifted into the most beautiful anchorage I had ever seen. Only the barest ripple disturbed the water's surface, yet we could see all the way to the ocean across a field of blue water studded with rocks and green islands. To the east rose the forested mountains of Nootka Island. As I went forward to release the anchor, I heard a loon laugh in the distance.

As we were putting away our sails, a man came out of a small cabin on the shore, climbed into an aluminum skiff and rowed out to talk to us. He introduced himself as Dan Devault.

"You're the first boat I've ever seen sail through that entrance," Dan told us. "Not too many sailboats come in here, and the ones that do always use their engines."

We found the anchorage as fascinating and tranquil as the guidebook promised. Three years later we returned—this time in *Osprey*. Once again, the west wind blew strongly up the inlet. Once again, Steve decided to sail. "We aren't in *Velella*," I protested. "*Osprey* can't turn as fast." But Steve insisted; he had a reputation to keep up. *Osprey* did fine. I was a nervous wreck. As before, we cleared the rocks with inches to spare. And as before, Dan rowed out to greet us. He didn't recognize us at first in the new boat.

"About three years ago, another boat sailed in here," he said. "It was green just like this but smaller. That was the only other boat that has sailed in."

Steve was proud that we had sailed in and, now that the danger was over, even I felt a bit cocky. We had sailed through a difficult channel without that famous "local knowledge" that the guidebooks always say you should have but never tell you how to get.

It seemed to me, however, that without much effort, the Coast Guard could have made the entrance a lot easier. The buoys on the sandbank struck me as a joke: who cared about soft sand after sailing through a rock maze? And why hide the light among the rocks?

I asked Dan about the light.

"The light? That marks Entrance Island; that's where the fish packers used to come in."

Out came the chart again and this time we inspected it with a magnifying glass. We could see a thin channel next to the light, but it looked too treacherous even to Steve. So that afternoon at low tide we explored in our dinghy. Between the light and the rocks we found a narrow kelp-filled channel leading straight from the inlet to the anchorage. With a lead line I measured 15 feet—plenty of water for *Osprey*. The mistake we had made in planning our first entrance was assuming the Canadian Coast Guard used the US practice of marking the dangers. We had avoided the light when in fact it marked the safe entrance.

Our third entrance into Nuchatlitz three years later was easy. I had only a brief moment of panic approaching the light. Was that narrow channel really the entrance? Were we really going to sail through that kelp at seven knots? But a cluster of rocks broke the seas outside the entrance, the island blanketed the wind and *Osprey* coasted through, sails drooping.

On that third visit to Nuchatlitz we were greeted, not by Dan, but by C.L., a tall lanky man in his fifties, whom we had met on our two earlier trips.

"I saw a boat sailing through the entrance and knew it had to be you," he told us. And then, "I was going out to the burial canoes. Have you seen them? Have you seen the burial cave?" When we told him we hadn't seen them, hadn't even known they were there, he volunteered to give us a tour.

An hour later we were skimming across the quiet water of Nuchatlitz harbour in C.L.'s outboard-powered aluminum skiff. At the base of a small island C.L. cut the power and pointed up. Two weathered wooden prows stuck out from a rocky promontory above our heads. They were empty now, but had once held the bones of Nuu-chah-nulth tribal members.

From the burial canoes we headed toward Nuchatlitz's outer islands. C.L. beached the boat on the sandy beach of a small island and we waded ashore through low surf. We hiked along the beach to a rocky cliff with a yawning black hole at its base. We climbed

The Nuu-chah-nulth buried their dead in canoes such as these or in burial caves.

A burial box. Burial caves can be found up and down the coast and are considered sacred areas by the Nuu-chah-nulth.

over a pile of driftwood and crawled into the cave. Cold damp air smelling of seaweed and decay flowed out toward us, making me shiver.

Inside the cave, C.L. swept his flashlight around the chamber, lighting up a jumble of wooden boxes and bones. The flashlight beam moved across the dark walls of the cave, then to a far corner where it lit a rough-hewn wooden box. Steve reached out and lifted up the box lid. My blood froze when I saw four green mouldy skulls staring back at us.

We left the cave, walked across a beach of mussel shells piled into blue dunes by the waves. Shells cracked and clinked under our feet. Around the corner, we found an old timber barge shipwrecked on the sand. Small yellow flowers grew among massive timbers—bones of another type.

We returned to the skiff and motored to nearby Nootka Island. There we climbed up a large rock covered with red and yellow Indian paintbrush and bright white daisies. A pungent smell of wild onions filled the air. Our shoes dug into rich loam, uncovering charred wood and clamshells, evidence we were on a midden—an ancient garbage dump.

We looked out to sea across the maze of jagged rocks and islands that make up Nuchatlitz. I thought about what we had just seen and realized we would have never found the canoes or the burial cave on our own. And that's when I understood that it was because we entered under sail, through a channel where most boaters fear to even motor, that we had won acceptance at Nuchatlitz and had seen sights that few others were privileged to see.

Nuchatlitz Village

The Last Boat up the Inlet

On our first trip to Nuchatlitz I was nervous about visiting Nuchatlitz village—the home of the Nuchatlaht band of the Nuu-chah-nulth nation. Farther south we had heard rumours that yachts weren't welcome in Native villages. The village looked alien to me: it was a motley collection of small houses huddled together on a nearly treeless island of sand and cobble. And for such a small village there seemed to be a lot of people around. Some of them were standing around in small groups on the beach and I found that disturbing. What were they doing?

It seemed presumptuous to just go ashore uninvited. But we had worked so hard to get here I wasn't about to let my nervousness stop me. A burly-looking young man in a baseball cap met us at the dock. I thought, "Here it comes, he's going to tell us to leave."

Fog streams up Esperanza Inlet beyond the old Nuchatlitz Village site.

"You're just in time," he said, looking at Steve. "We're having a baseball game and we need an umpire we've never beat up before." We had arrived at the start of a Sunday afternoon baseball game between the Nuchatlaht band and the Queens Cove band.

While Steve played umpire, I explored the small village of six or eight homes. Grass-carpeted trails bordered by clover and yellow asters led along the shore and among the houses. I passed several women on the trails and they smiled at me; they didn't seem to think it odd for strangers to just drop in. Although several houses were vacant with boarded windows and peeling paint, others looked almost new and were well maintained. On one of the newer houses a large deer carcass hung over the porch. From just about everywhere on the island, the villagers looked across fields of daisies to a breathtaking view of rocky islets surrounded by blue sea.

I wandered back to the ball field and joined the spectators sitting on the grass and on wooden benches. Steve stood behind home plate, his eyes intent on the ball. I heard him yell "Ball 4!" as spectators cheered and hooted. I was relieved to hear that even the hoots sounded good-natured and that they weren't talking about beating up the umpire.

After the second game, the children pointed us toward a small blue house on the north side of the village where the basket weaver lived. We knocked on the worn wooden door, and a teenaged boy eating plums from a can let us in. Lillian Michaels, a frail old woman with a shock of white hair, sat in an easy chair weaving a basket. We would not have believed her gnarled hands could move, much less weave, if we hadn't seen them flying around the basket, deftly twisting the reeds in tight knots. She showed us the reeds that she was using—long white blades of grass, some dyed red, green, and black. When I asked her where she got them, she replied, "Boston."

The basket weaver, Lillian Michaels, obtained her reeds from Neah Bay, which she called "Boston."

"Boston! I was born in Boston," exclaimed Steve. The old woman smiled and nodded. I looked closely at the reeds, but I couldn't see what was so special about them that they had to be mailed all the way from New England.

That evening we told Dan Devault about the reeds from Boston. He laughed. "'Boston' is the Indian word for United States," he told us. The 1803 capture of the US fur trading ship *Boston* in Marvinas Bay put "Boston" permanently into the Nuu-chah-nulth vocabulary. The "Boston" reed was bear grass from the low country south of Neah Bay in Washington State. I had learned in high school history that northwest Natives used the name "Boston men" to refer to Yankees. But I hadn't imagined they would use that term today. Hearing it made the history seem closer.

On our second trip to Nuchatlitz, in 1987, we arrived at mid-week to find the ball field empty and the basket weaver away in Campbell River for cataract operations. We knocked on the door of the chief's house and he invited us in for tea. The chief, Alban Michaels, was a soft-spoken stocky man; his wife, Rose, a friendly but quiet woman. While his wife worked at the stove, the chief brought out a large blueprint and spread it before us on the kitchen table. It showed a village site in Espinosa Inlet with houses neatly arranged in a crescent. Indian and Northern Affairs Canada was building a new village for the Nuchatlaht.

Stunned to think the Nuchatlaht could leave this beautiful setting, I asked the chief if he wanted to move. He was quiet for a minute and then explained that every winter the women and children moved to Campbell River for the children's schooling and the men remained at Nuchatlitz alone. At Espinosa the children would be able to ride a school bus to Zeballos and live with both parents. Men would be able to drive to work.

Blackberries now grow in the windows of Lillian Michael's abandoned house.

Nuchatlitz would become a summer camp—a place for baseball and summer fishing.

By our third trip in 1991 only a few vacant houses remained. The rest had been loaded onto barges and moved to the new townsite. We never saw the Nuchatlaht at Nuchatlitz again. Our trips never coincided with theirs and the Devaults told us that as the years went by, they came to their old village less and less often. We felt sad to lose the opportunity to know them better, but our friendship with the Devaults and the other members of the white community on the island to the east of the reserve made up for it.

Laurie Jones, in *Nootka Sound Explored,* described Nuchatlitz in its early years as a tiny but thriving village with a trading post and store. In the 1800s, sealing schooners took Nuchatlaht men and their canoes to the Bering Sea where the men would hunt down seals in the open sea. In good years, the sealers earned $120 a day. When an international treaty stopped fur sealing in 1911, the Nuchatlaht turned to fishing salmon and then to pilchards. Of the 26 pilchard reduction plants on the west coast of Vancouver Island, five were in Esperanza Inlet. Nuchatlitz served this fishery with a store, fuel stop and fish buyers. A steamer made regular deliveries of supplies and mail and on the reserve a Catholic mission church operated a day school.

The pilchards disappeared in the 1940s and the Nuchatlaht turned back to salmon. But within a few years fish processing companies built ice plants in the larger towns away from Nuchatlitz. Fishing boats carrying ice didn't need to return to port every night and the Native fishermen with their small, simple boats could not compete with the white men in their new, larger boats. The store and fuel stop closed and the population dwindled. Eventually the school closed, too.

The Nuchatlaht band moved to Oclucje at the head of Espinosa Inlet.

In his 1972 book, *A Small and Charming World,* the Indian agent John Gibson told of arriving at Nuchatlitz in a seaplane during a snowstorm. He had come to take a seven-year-old girl away from her parents to live with a foster family in town where she could attend school. Gibson saw the chief as a struggling father and leader of a diminishing band on a small island, a people whose lifestyle was no longer significant. He wondered "In how many years will the last person leave the village and the last boat head away up the inlet towards the east?"

We can now answer Gibson's question. But each time we sailed past Espinosa Inlet we looked at the new village of Oclucje through binoculars and saw that it was growing. Blackberries were pushing through the windows of the abandoned houses at Nuchatlitz but the Nuchatlaht were returning to their new village from Campbell River and other towns on the east coast of Vancouver Island.

In 2001 we decided to see the new village for ourselves. The sun was shining and we had the whole day with nothing else to do. We sailed up the inlet in a glorious following breeze, past rocky cliffs and forested hillsides. But when we reached the top of the inlet, the waves made the small dock too perilous to land. The water was too deep to anchor so we settled for sailing along the shore and looking at the village through binoculars. I counted 15 houses, most new and larger than those at Nuchatlitz. And I saw a ball field, but no field of daisies.

Ocean villages like Nuchatlitz were once strictly summer villages, places to dig clams and pick berries before dismantling the longhouses and loading them into canoes for the return trip up inlet away from winter storms. When the fur traders arrived, many Nuu-chah-nulth bands abandoned their winter villages in favour of staying accessible to the fur traders and fish buyers year-round. In moving to Espinosa the Nuchatlaht band had returned to their winter village.

Nuchatlitz

Making a Living without Killing Fish or Chopping Down Trees

Dan Devault and his cousin Bob Devault have found a way to live on the west coast of Vancouver Island without killing fish or chopping down trees; they farm oysters in the protected waters of Nuchatlitz. Growing oysters sounds easy, like growing daisies in a garden, but it's not. Nuchatlitz isn't like Chesapeake Bay, where oysters just grow and can be harvested right off the bottom by watermen with tongs. It isn't even like Puget Sound where growers sow seed oysters on the beach and wait for them to grow. Nuchatlitz after all is on the west coast of Vancouver Island where everything is more difficult.

Bob, a congenial man in his fifties, lives on the backside of the same small unnamed island that Dan lives on. His house bristles with radio antennas, solar panels, wind generators—all the trappings of technology. Bob loves to read natural history books and he talks about the science of oysters as an expert.

Bob Devault uses his vessel, *Nootka Rose,* to deliver oysters to Tahsis. The logs to the right of the boat are oyster rafts.

"Our oyster farm is unique," Bob told me one Christmas when he stopped in Seattle on his way to visit his parents in California. It was one of the few times I've seen Bob when he wasn't preoccupied with some detail of oystering and he took the time to reflect on the adventure of farming oysters.

Most oyster farms are in estuaries where oysters grow on tidal flats in shallow water diluted with runoff from a nearby river or stream. Nuchatlitz has no river or stream but Bob explained that oysters don't need low salinity, they just tolerate it where other organisms cannot. Similarly, oysters don't really need to grow on tidal flats. Once they have matured, they grow quite nicely hanging on PVC tubing in the open water.

The farm's isolation and cold, deep water require self-sufficiency, innovation and hard work. Where other oyster farmers can hire labour or contract out part of their business, Dan and Bob must do everything themselves, or with the help of Fyffe and Else, their wives—"and the work never stops." They set the oyster larvae, build the oyster rafts, construct harvesting machines, harvest and bag the oysters and tow them to market.

Nuchatlitz's oysters are from Japan via Tillamook, Oregon. Japanese oysters won't breed in Nuchatlitz's cold waters, but they will grow. In Tillamook, workers pack tiny oyster larvae into coolers and deliver them to the airport where they are loaded onto a plane for a flight to Campbell River. Dan or Bob must drive across the mountains to fetch them at Campbell River, then turn around and drive them back to Tahsis where they load them into a boat for the final trip to Nuchatlitz. In Nuchatlitz, the Devaults release the larvae one million at a time into 1,500 gallon fibreglass vats filled with PVC tubes suspended in sea water heated to 26 degrees Celsius. I've looked at one of those vats filled with a million oysters and I could have sworn it held nothing but clean sea water.

Within days the larvae settle on the tubes, lining themselves up like parked cars on special grooved surfaces. Dan and Bob then move the PVC tubes into the harbour where they hang them from buoys. Two weeks later they move them from the buoys to the beach where they stack them in rafts. On the beach the alternating drying and submersion of the tidal cycle keeps other organisms from fouling the tubes and helps the young oysters prosper. I once went to the beach to look at the oysters while Dan was working among the rafts. At first I thought there was nothing on the rafts but specks of dirt and wondered why he was bothering with them. But when I looked closer I could see miniature oysters complete with purple stripes and fluted shells.

The oysters spend a year on the beach then two years back in the harbour before they are finally harvested at a length of five to seven inches.

Bob describes oyster growing as similar to growing carrots: not all that are planted will be harvested. Ten to 50 percent of the larvae will settle on the tubes, but only 50 percent of the tubes will have the right density to keep; the rest must be rejected, cleaned and reused. Of the 16 to 30 million larvae the farm purchases in a year, only 600,000 will reach maturity.

Dan Devault tending oyster rafts. Young oysters spend a year on the beach where the alternating drying and submersion of the tidal cycle keeps other organisms from fouling the tubes.

Like farm crops everywhere, Nuchatlitz oysters are subject to the vagaries of nature. Some years are better than others with oysters thriving when the conditions—salinity, temperature, food—are just right. Crabs, starfish and snails prey on the oysters and the Devaults are always plotting to rid Nuchatlitz of these predators. Dan saw us putting down a crab pot one afternoon and told us not to bother—there weren't any crabs left to catch. We left the trap in anyway and, much to Dan's chagrin, caught three big rock crabs.

Among nature's biggest threats to oyster farms is PSP, paralytic shellfish poisoning, commonly called red tide. PSP is a toxin created by a certain species of dinoflagellate, a type of single-celled alga, that concentrates in the oysters when they feed. The oysters aren't harmed but anyone who eats them risks serious illness or death. Blooms of the dinoflagellates that cause PSP come without warning and can last for weeks, during which time the oysters can't be harvested.

There's less chance of PSP in the winter and that's when the Devaults harvest their oysters. Whenever I'm tempted to envy the Devaults for their year-round life at Nuchatlitz, I just imagine harvesting oysters in the winter and I'm cured. The days are short and dark, the sky grey and lowering, the rain incessant and cold. It's the type of rain that mixes with the fog off the ocean and penetrates necks and sleeves of even the best foul-weather gear. Sometimes the wind blows gale force for days and the boom of surf on the outer rocks of Nuchatlitz and the roar of wind through the trees is constant. Other island residents, those very few who stay all winter, tell of being stormbound for days, afraid to walk in the woods for fear of falling trees. "But those Devaults just keep working," they say with amazement.

When a batch of oysters has been harvested, it usually falls to Bob to deliver them to Tahsis. The trip to town in Bob's boat, the *Nootka Rose*, with the oyster barge in tow, is long and slow. Bob discovered he could prop a book in front of him in the *Nootka Rose*'s wheelhouse and read underway. Once he got so engrossed in his reading he ran the barge into the side of the inlet. Fortunately, the barge just bounced off the steep rock sides without any damage.

Hard work has paid off. When we first visited Nuchatlitz in 1984 the oyster farm was little more than a few experimental oysters hanging from a buoy. In 1999, 15 years later, the farm produced 230 tons of oysters—enough to comfortably support two families. But as Bob says, the work never ends. When Bob and Dan aren't working on the oyster farm they are building their houses, repairing electric generators or working on their boats. There are no plumbers to call, contractors to hire or hardware stores to run to for help. Before they started their oyster farm, Bob and Dan each built a small house and a workshop.

With the exception of Indian Reserves and one privately owned island, the islands of Nuchatlitz are a provincial park.

Their workshops were bigger than their houses. Bob's was big enough to build the *Nootka Rose* inside. But they both got married and their houses became too small, so they each built a second house.

You would think that government agencies would be anxious to help businesses that have found a way to make a living without killing fish or cutting down trees, but that isn't always the case. One day the Devaults woke up to find they were running a business in the middle of a park. Park employees came out and surveyed the location of the oyster rafts and drew a map showing the boundaries of the oyster farm—and the farm is supposed to stay within those boundaries. "What if we want to expand?" asks Dan. And then there's the matter of the PSP testing: The Canadian government tests for PSP, but in remote areas where they find it difficult to regulate samples, they simply close large stretches of the coast to shellfishing in lieu of testing. Oyster growers have to scramble to find another way to test.

But the Devaults' biggest challenge may not be the oysters, or the weather, or even the government, but doing business in a modern world that can't imagine a life like theirs. Nuchatlitz lacks electricity, running water, sewers and adequate phone service. Nuchatlitz's only phone service is a radio connection to a land line in Zeballos. One afternoon at my house in Seattle, I answered the phone to hear Bob on the other end. I was so excited I started talking too fast, as I might do to any friend calling. But the radio telephone won't accommodate normal conversation and half my sentences got cut off. I had to speak slowly and pause after every sentence to wait for the phone to catch up. If friends who have visited them on their island have trouble communicating, imagine a seafood company executive from Vancouver trying to make a deal. And then there was the problem of answering machines—they don't work with radio telephones.

The solution, surprisingly, may come with more technology, not less. In 2003, the Devaults installed a satellite internet system. They can now send emails to the outside world—and to each other—and browse the web. Nuchatlitz may be remote, but it is no longer isolated.

Nuchatlitz

Stormbound

It rained all night the day we arrived in Nuchatlitz in 2000 and was still raining when we got up the next morning. The weather radio predicted more rain and storm warnings for the north part of Vancouver Island. We'd promised nine-year-old Evan Devault, Dan Devault's son, that we would take him north with us to Kyuquot Sound for a few days. But we weren't going anywhere until the weather turned.

Evan came down to the dock with his parents and sister, Janine. When I saw him carrying his pack and wearing his life jacket, I knew he had his heart set on the trip, his first in a "big" sailboat.

"There are storm warnings for the north coast," I told him.

"So? So?" He clutched his pack to his chest. His brown hair was plastered to his forehead and his jacket was already soaking from the rain.

"It wouldn't be much fun. It would be very rough," said Steve.

The setting sun lights up a cottage at Nuchatlitz.

"So? So?"

"Maybe tomorrow."

It rained all day a steady, relentless downpour that drummed on the cabin roof and soaked through the canvas dodger. Both Steve and I were restless at being cooped up, but I was glad we hadn't tried to go. It would have been crazy to take a nine-year-old out in a storm.

At mid-morning we walked up a short trail lined with rhododendrons and huckleberries to Dan and Fyffe's new house. We found Evan and Janine putting together a jigsaw puzzle on the dining room table while Fyffe baked banana bread. "You're just in time," she told us, taking a loaf out of the oven.

Fyffe, in neatly cut black hair, looks like she would be at home in a suburb. That day she was wearing jeans and a sweatshirt, but I have seen her wearing shorts and T-shirts on days I wear a jacket. She runs her house like my grandmother ran hers—baking cookies, canning fish, hanging laundry on an outside clothesline—and organizes the activities of her two children. Their house, a year-round residence for Dan, is a summer home for Fyffe and the children. The Devaults face the same problem the Nuchatlaht once faced—the need to separate so the children can attend school.

Dan had been building the house for several years. It still had a plywood floor and unfinished walls. That it was built at all was amazing to us, knowing that Dan had done it all himself. Houses are smaller on the west coast than in cities, they have to be when the owners build them themselves and when building materials are either brought in by boat or made on site. Dan and Fyffe had chosen to build a large open kitchen-dining-living area but to leave the bedrooms the size of large closets. We sat at their dining-room table talking and looking out past the rain to the ocean. I couldn't imagine a better place to be stormbound.

A maze of rocks and islands protects Nuchatlitz from the ocean waves.

That afternoon, we walked across the island in the rain on a moss-carpeted trail to visit Bob and Else who live on a narrow channel at the back of the island. On the way we looked into the small sawmill that Bob and Dan use to cut lumber for their houses and workshops. Sawdust littered the floor and a pungent smell of freshly cut cedar filled the air.

Else, a sturdy woman with short greying hair greeted us at the door. "We heard you were here," she said, then went to put the kettle on for tea. Originally from Seattle, Else met Bob in 1982. Finding herself newly single and daunted by the Seattle singles scene she had been reading personal ads. One afternoon she pulled a copy of *Mother Earth News* out of the trash in the advertisement department where she worked and read an ad placed by Bob. Living on an island appealed to her so she answered the ad.

Their house had a comfortable cluttered look with stacks of CDs and books on the desk and a collection of shells, stones and pine cones on the windowsill. A computer sat on the desk. We took up our conversation from where we had left it a year ago. Bob and Steve immediately got embroiled in a discussion of engines, drawing diagrams and making plans while Else and I talked about art and photography. Just as I was thinking we should head back, Bob invited us to a halibut dinner at one of their neighbours. He figured he could invite us since he had caught the halibut.

At the Taylor-Scotts we added our foul-weather gear to a large collection by the door and entered an unfinished room with large picture windows facing the channel. A hissing gas lantern hung from a hook in the ceiling, adding light and warmth to the afternoon gloom. About twenty people were milling around the room, sitting on a collection of miscellaneous plastic chairs and frying fish and potatoes on a camp stove. A comfortable buzz of conversation filled the room. While I was eating tender white chunks of halibut, Chris, a tall man in his sixties sat down next to me.

"I hear you're writing a book about the west coast. What will you put in it?" he asked.

I reminded him of the walk he had taken us on a few years before, across a small island and back at sunset. I might write about that, I told him. I described the twisted cedars, the sunset on the beach and the sea lion bones by the creek. He had set such a pace I had had to run to keep up. And all the time the light on the trees had been beautiful. I had wanted to stop and take a picture, but didn't have time.

"You should have said something."

"No, it was dark by the time we got back. You were right to keep going."

Fyffe walked by, offering a tray of chocolate brownies. We each took one. They were delicious, rich and dark.

"You should write about the food. Don't forget the food."

The trees across the channel were dark and featureless against the evening sky when the party broke up. In the dark entryway, we groped for boots and jackets. "I've got one of everything, but I'm not sure they're mine," confessed Else.

We rode back to the dock in Dan and Fyffe's skiff. The rain had tapered to an occasional drop. As Fyffe piloted the skiff through the rocks and out the back channel, I looked toward the west and saw the sky lightening, promising better weather the next day. Evan would get his sailing trip.

Zeballos

Island Time

The westerlies pushed us up Esperanza Inlet and around the corner into Zeballos Inlet, following the twists and turns of the channel as if the wind too planned a visit to town. The farther up the inlet we went, the stronger the wind blew until the water almost boiled with foam. It was one of those rare days on the west coast of Vancouver Island when the air was warm enough for shorts and T-shirts and I was enjoying the downwind ride. Then I remembered that the weather report promised the same conditions the next day when we would be going back. We would have to tack every inch of the way.

We turned the corner at Little Zeballos River and I promptly forgot my worries as an amazing vista opened ahead of us. Odd-shaped mountains with bulbous tops and sheer rock faces rose almost straight up from the water. Astonished, I stared in awe, for we had been to Zeballos twice before, but until that year, 2004, we had never seen the mountains; low clouds had hidden them from view.

In Zeballos Inlet westerlies almost always blow up inlet, following the inlet's twists and turns all the way to town.

A few minutes later, we rounded the next bend and could see the town of Zeballos and its neighbour, the Native village of Ehetsis, on either side of the Zeballos River. Both looked small and inconsequential beneath the tall mountains. We tied up at the public dock with tree-covered slopes towering above us.

To the west of the dock a small finger of land jutted out into the inlet, just wide enough to hold Mid-Island Ice Ltd., a fish-packing plant and the Zeballos General Store; which was our first destination. We hoped that Zeballos' direct road to Campbell River meant better supplies than Tahsis.

Our hopes disappeared the minute we walked into the store. I looked with dismay at yellowed celery, withered iceberg lettuce and dejected-looking nectarines. Even the shelves for dry goods looked bare. They didn't even have a simple comb to replace one Steve had broken. When we took our purchases to the checkout stand the owner said, "We'll have more food tomorrow afternoon. We've been so busy with the slow-pitch tournament here, we haven't had a chance to make a run for supplies."

I wasn't sure what a slow-pitch tournament was, other than that it had something to do with softball, but I recognized immediately that we had been hit with another bad luck schedule. We always seemed to be arriving a day too late or too early for the best shopping.

We delivered our meagre supplies to *Osprey* and set off to town. Zeballos is known for its quaint western buildings with false fronts, a hold-over from the days when it was a rough-and-tumble gold-mining town. Nowadays it depends on fish, lumber and tourism instead for its livelihood.

We saw the first of these false-fronted buildings in the parking lot to the dock: a new restroom building. So determined is Zeballos to preserve its mining heritage that bylaws require the wild-west motif on even the most mundane of new buildings. From the parking lot we followed the main road, passing more false-fronted buildings: a community centre, a fire station, a municipal hall, a post office and several vacant stores, many backing on to a small channel of the inlet.

Zeballos has one of the last remaining ice plants on the coast.

One of many false-fronted stores in Zeballos. Bylaws require the wild-west motif on all commercial buildings.

The owner of the general store had told us that the laundromat had closed but the Zeballos Hotel had coin-operated washers and dryers. So when we came to the hotel, a rambling two-storey structure with a wide veranda and a red metal roof, we decided to investigate. On opening the main door, I expected to see a standard hotel desk with a clerk behind it. Instead, a grizzled-looking miner sat at an old rolltop desk weighing out gold. Startled, I took a few seconds to realize he was a mannequin and not a real person. No one was around to ask about the laundry but a sign next to a door said, "Laundry, upstairs," so we opened the door and walked upstairs to a long bare corridor. Low ceilings and creaking floorboards told us we were in one of Zeballos's original buildings. We had heard that the ghost of Sussie Woo, one of Zeballos's first Chinese immigrant workers, haunts the hotel, but not even ghosts stirred in the afternoon quiet.

We found two silent washers and dryers occupying two small rooms. It didn't look as if we would have a lot of competition for the machines, so we decided to come back after dinner. I hoped to do the laundry that night so we could leave first thing in the morning before the wind came up.

Next door to the hotel was the library, one of the few buildings in town without a false front. But its square front and flat roof still managed to make it fit in with the wild-west theme. An open door lured us in. The dusty smell of old books greeted us. Like the hotel, the library appeared deserted. I was reading a pamphlet on Vancouver Island writers when a young woman carrying a computer printout came out of a small room off to the side to ask if she could help us. She was wearing a T-shirt that said, "Keep your hands off my planet."

"We're glad to see the library open," said Steve. "The first time we were here the library shared this building with a liquor store. The liquor store was out in front and the library was in a small room at the back. The liquor store was open six days a week while the library was open two days a week for two hours each."

She laughed. "I moved here from Vancouver only three months ago. I didn't know about the liquor store."

"We're off a boat on the dock," Steve told her. "If I wanted to check out a book here and return it to Ucluelet, could I do it?"

The Zeballos Public Library is staffed exclusively by volunteers.

"You're supposed to have an address here to check out books," she told us. Then she picked up a record book and waved it at us. "But here's what I would do. I would just put your name here and write "public dock, Zeballos," as the address. But the only books you could return in Ucluelet are the ones that say VIRL for Vancouver Island Regional Library. All the books with red dots are ours and have to be returned here. Most of them have been donated by people who live here." There was only one small shelf of VIRL books and many shelves with red-dot books.

"The Regional Library sends us books when they remember we are here, which isn't too often. It comes from having a name that begins with a Z."

I asked her what had brought her to Zeballos.

"I had a job in one of the lodges," she explained. "But they laid me off after only a month. It was supposed to be my big chance. I was going to work for a few months, then buy a car. I said, no way. I'm going to stay here on EI [Employment Insurance] at your cost."

"And now you're only working four hours a week," said Steve.

"No. Not even that. Those are just volunteer hours. Nobody gets paid here. But as long as I'm going to stay here and collect EI, I might as well do some good."

As we left, I asked her about donating books. "Could we just drop them in the book slot?"

"Sure, but I'll probably be here. I don't go along with those volunteer hours. A public library should be open for the public to use."

As we walked away from the library, I noticed a sign above the door of a building across the street. "Rosa Island General Store." We hadn't known there were two general stores here. The door was closed and locked although a sign said the store was open until six and it wasn't even five. We were peering through the window when we heard a voice say, "What you want? I open for you."

A stout woman in her sixties came around the corner and unlocked the door. We walked through a small empty café and into the store where we poked around the shelves, feeling conspicuous as the only customers under the eye of the owner. I bought some tomatoes and a package of lentils.

"I have more tomorrow," she said. "I work on slow-pitch tournament all week and no time to go for supplies." I asked her where she was from. "Hungary. I've been here three years, Canada 12."

I thought how odd it was that, in the space of an hour, we had met two people who viewed Zeballos as a land of opportunity. It was an astonishing idea in light of the fact that since the last mine had closed in 1969, Zeballos depended on fish, logging and tourism, just like every other small town on the West Coast.

Zeballos was named for Lieutenant Ciriaco de Cevallos, who explored the area in 1791 as part of Spain's Malaspina expedition. The Spaniards were looking for gold. Spanish archives record that they took three-quarters of a million dollars in gold from the coast. Unfortunately, the archives did not record exactly where they found it.

The first recorded discovery of gold near Zeballos was made by a fisherman from Kyuquot in 1908, but mining didn't begin in earnest until the 1930s during the Great Depression, when men who were unable to find work elsewhere came to Zeballos. They worked long hours in the rain, packed supplies on slippery trails up steep mountains, cut trees with hand axes and delivered heavy ore to steamships on rafts. They lived in isolated one-room shacks in the hills, often too poor to afford even candles to light the long winter nights. Then in 1937 the Privateer Mine shipped 4,800 pounds of ore worth $2,600. News of the strike lured corporate investors. Men rushed to Zeballos, some hoping to strike it rich, others just looking for a job. Just one short year later Zeballos was a real town, complete with hotels, bank, electricity, a school, a newspaper, a library, a hospital, taverns and a brothel. Zeballos enjoys the distinction of once having its streets literally paved with gold: the owners of one of the mines once scraped the surface of the road to remove residual gold.

But Zeballos's heyday lasted only a few years. By 1942 labour shortages and a low grade of ore made the mines unprofitable and they closed for the duration of the war. They reopened briefly in 1948, then closed again when the government fixed the price of gold at $35 an ounce. Zeballos's gold, although high-grade in places, was inconsistent. Only the Privateer Mine remained open, and only for exploration. Search for the next rich vein continues there to this day. An iron mine followed the gold mine in 1962. But that too closed, in 1969.

As we continued our walk through the town, we passed the Zeballos Museum, a small white house with a replica of a mine entrance next to it. We had toured the museum on our last trip here and enjoyed looking at the old photographs and the exhibit of mining equipment. I wasn't surprised to see the museum closed so late in the afternoon but I was dismayed to see that the list of hours on the door was even more complex, and almost as short, as the library hours.

But if the public buildings have limited hours, the restaurants and bars do not. Bob Hale, author of the *Wagonner Cruising Guide* described Zeballos as having many eateries but no fine dining. We picked the restaurant at the Iris Motor Lodge as the most appealing. We walked into a lively scene of groups gathered around pitchers of beer while calypso music played in the background. Posters of eagles and bears adorned the wall while above the kitchen on a high shelf sat a collection of brown-skinned baby dolls dressed as Natives, trappers and other northwest characters.

The waitress who came to take our order was very thin and very black. From her accent I realized we were talking to another recent immigrant to Zeballos. "What kind of beer do you have?" Steve asked her. Her answer, in a soft voice with a strong accent, was unintelligible over the roar of the crowd. She disappeared and returned with a Budweiser. Steve reacted in horror and pantomimed pushing it away. She finally showed him a menu and he ordered a bottle of Sleeman and the chicken curry. I ordered a glass of white wine and the chicken salad.

A man with a digital camera was standing in front of the table next to us saying, "I just want to send a message to the folks back home," he said to a man wearing a T-shirt that said "Lucky Logger Pub." Lucky Logger turned around to let the man with a digital camera take a picture of his back. We could see the words, "Try wiping your ass without felling a tree."

Digital Camera asked Lucky Logger where he was from.

"Campbell River."

"Ah, the capital of salmon fishing."

"Sometimes it is. But that's Zeballos now."

"Yeah, Zeballos is hot," said one of his tablemates.

I looked at my watch. Almost 8 o'clock and we were still waiting for our dinner. My plans to do the laundry after dinner were fast evaporating. "I think we just got caught by 'Island Time'," I told Steve, referring to the way the pace of life is so much slower on Vancouver Island than in a city. It is ironic that we sail up the coast, sometimes taking days to travel a distance the locals can travel in a few hours in their speedboats, yet we get impatient with an extra hour in a restaurant. When our food came, the curry was hot and steaming and the chicken salad crisp and flavourful. It was worth the wait.

The setting sun was turning the distant mountains golden as we left the restaurant. Not eager to return to the confines of our boat, we walked along the shore and out to the fish-packing plant. A fishboat was unloading live fish from a fish farm, sending them down in chutes to workers who caught the flapping fish and bled them in a few quick motions with a knife. We stood and watched, amazed by the rapidity with which the fish vanished into boxes.

On the way back to the dock, we stopped to talk to the owner of Zeballos General Store who was out walking her dog.

"How is the town doing?" Steve asked her.

"The town is at a crossroads," she told us. "It's been a hard year. We had two deaths, a murder and a suicide, and that tore the town up. And the fish-processing plant lost its major contract with the fish farm. Eight people lost their jobs."

"When logging was big, there used to be educated people here," she told us, "people who were committed to the town. The educated people left and the ones who stayed live in RV parks and go home to Campbell River on weekends. The town needs to do more for tourism, give tours of the old mines or something. The town is cute, but what can you do here? There used to be 2,500 people living here, working in the mine and logging and fishing," she said. (Now there are just over 200.)

"How does the town get along with the Native community?" Steve asked her.

"Good. It used to be bad. Everybody just grew up and realized they had to live together. We had a big community potluck. Lots of people from both villages came and got along fine. Outsiders don't understand that."

Her description of Zeballos at a crossroads was an understatement. According to Zeballos's internet newspaper, the *Zeballos Privateer*, the winter had indeed been one of turmoil. Drunken vandals had terrorized the town, throwing rocks through windows, breaking into houses, slashing tires and terrifying children. The townspeople rallied to fight the vandalism, posting notices and organizing citizen patrols. The vandals fought back, tearing the notices off telephone poles and throwing rocks at the patrols. Then a young girl was murdered. Reporters from across British Columbia descended upon the town. And in the ensuing bad publicity tour operators cancelled bus tours and more people lost their jobs.

Zeballos is now poised to recover. Meetings were held; plans were made; citizens rallied and organized the potluck dinner. The RCMP promised increased police presence. The school district promised to assign a youth worker to the town. There is even hope on the economic front: geologists from Simon Fraser University announced a study of the Privateer Mine and the owners of the Zeballos Iron Mine talked of reopening.

The next morning we stuffed our laundry into big net bags and lugged it down the street, planning to eat breakfast in the dining room at the Zeballos Hotel while the

The town of Zeballos encourages tourism with facilities like this picnic table on the shores of a channel behind the town.

laundry washed. But to our dismay, the dining room was shuttered and dark. Across the street the Rosa Island General Store was dark also, a sign on the door proclaiming "gone for supplies."

We put the laundry in the wash and walked down the street to the Iris Lodge. But the lodge too was closed, with another sign saying "gone for supplies."

Discouraged, we trudged back toward the hotel. Lucky Logger and his girlfriend were coming out of the front door. He was still wearing the Lucky Logger T-shirt.

"We ate at the Iris Lodge earlier," he said. "Then they closed. They ran out of food because of the slow-pitch tournament."

As we left the dock later that morning, having finished our laundry, mailed a bunch of postcards and bought a comb for Steve at a small used goods store that also sold odds and ends of new goods, I had a sudden longing to stay. A place where an entire community can rally around softball games and people had hope for the future against all odds was worth another day. I thought how pleasant it would be to wait for the museum to open, to hike to the Little Zeballos River and to sit at a picnic table beside the water doing nothing. Perhaps, it was time for us to adopt Island Time. But then I realized Island Time would have to wait for another day; we had promised to pick up ice and gasoline for a friend at Nuchatlitz and he expected us back that day.

At the fuel dock we had to wait our turn behind two fishboats and a sport fisherman, who took forever to buy just a few gallons of gas. When we finally left almost an hour later, the wind was blowing strong, but to my amazement, it was blowing in the opposite direction from the day before. The wind followed us out the Zeballos Inlet and into Esperanza Inlet, almost all the way to Nuchatlitz. In all our years of sailing on the west coast of Vancouver Island, we had never before seen outflow winds in the middle of a sunny day.

Kyuquot Sound

We anchored in 25 feet of water, well off the rocks of Rugged Point. The rain had ended. I looked with pleasure at the craggy rocks of Rugged Point, at the bold head of Kyuquot Hill on Union Island to the west and at the steep-sided hills to the east. The open water, with its expanded views raised my spirits. Now that we were here I could look up Kyuquot Sound into the mountains of Vancouver Island and watch the last rays of the sun turn the face of Union Island red.

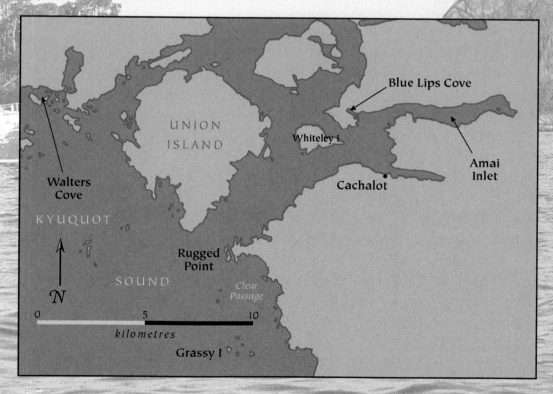

Blue Lips Cove

UNION ISLAND

Whiteley I

Walters Cove

KYUQUOT

Cachalot

Amai Inlet

N

Rugged Point

SOUND

Clear Passage

0   5   10

kilometres

Grassy I

Grassy Isle

The Jurassic Coast

Between Esperanza Inlet and Kyuquot Sound a string of small barrier islands creates a protected channel called Clear Passage. The islands have always intrigued me; several of them have flat tops that look like manicured lawns, as if they have been sculptured and clipped by a seagoing gardener. So green and smooth are they that I half expect to see golfers on their slopes and hear the cry of "Fore!" coming over the water. Not surprisingly, one of them is called "Grassy Isle."

On a sunny morning in 2001 we left Esperanza Inlet bound for Kyuquot Sound with two passengers on board, 12-year-old Janine Devault and her 10-year-old brother Evan, of Nuchatlitz. It was a windless day, the sea so smooth the air seemed to be filled with light from reflected sunlight. We hadn't planned on stopping at Grassy Isle but when we saw the green slopes, we changed our minds.

"Would you like to go to Grassy Isle?" I asked the children. Evan jumped up and down in excitement; his sister merely nodded her consent.

We anchored just south of Clark Island in a pocket of deep water between the island and a drying 15-foot rock. A few years earlier Steve and I had tried to anchor here in a light southerly wind but had given up when after three attempts the anchor refused to

Grassy Isle. What looks like a smooth lawn from a distance is actually impenetrable brush.

grab. We had promised ourselves we would come back on a quieter day. This was our chance. The anchor rumbled across the rocky bottom but grabbed as the chain stretched out ahead of us.

Despite the glassy sea, a low swell rolled through the anchorage so that the dinghy rose up and down beside us as the sailboat rolled back and forth. One at a time we jumped in, timing our jumps to catch an upward swing of the dinghy.

Grassy Isle itself has no landing place so when people talk of landing on Grassy Isle they usually mean an unnamed island just to the south. This unnamed island has a small sandy beach on its south shore. We landed on this beach in the low surf, all of us jumping out quickly to grab the dinghy before the sea sucked it out in the next wave. Broken white shells mixed with beach sand made the shallow water look turquoise in the sunshine. If I hadn't felt the cold water around my feet, I would have thought we were on a tropical beach.

White clam shells littering this beach on Grassy Isle give it a tropical look.

Now we could see that the grassy manicured slopes were an illusion. What had looked like lawns were actually fields of windswept shrubs growing in a thick impenetrable tangle. It would have been impossible to walk across the island, much less swing a golf club on its slopes.

Following the beach, we walked north around the island until we came to a field of barren black rocks stretching out toward the real Grassy Isle in a black moonscape. Flocks of oystercatchers with red beaks flew overhead and called to each other in thin high-pitched voices. That day, the island was peaceful, though stark. We could hear distant murmurs of surf from the ocean side. In a winter storm it would be a different place, with rocks being thrown helter-skelter by surf and salt spray flying across the land.

While the children ran ahead looking for glass net floats among the driftwood, Steve and I poked along the beach, turning over rocks, looking for fossils. Else Klevjer had told us that fossils could be picked up off the beach here like pebbles. I picked up a small black rock etched with white lines and threw it on the stony platform at my feet. The rock broke open and I was thrilled to see a mass of grey striped lumps: they

Top: Looking for fossils on the beach on Grassy Isle.

Above: Jurassic fossils in a sandstone rock. Fossils on Vancouver Island are more closely related to those found in India than to those found in neighbouring Alberta or Puget Sound.

were fossilized bivalves, ancient relatives of today's clams and mussels. "Fossils!" At my call, the children came running back.

The four of us started picking up rocks and hurling them at the beach, like angry ballplayers. Once we had found the first fossil, we saw them everywhere, loose on the beach and embedded among the rocks in the nearby bank. Janine made the best find: a large rock with its entire surface dimpled with the imprint of ancient clams. Hoping to find something exotic, an ammonite or a trilobite, I examined every fossil I could, but all I found were more bivalves, so many they looked like the remains of an ancient clam bake.

According to Rolf Ludvigsen and Graham Beard, authors of *West Coast Fossils*, the stretch of coastline between Esperanza Inlet and Kyuquot Sound is rich in fossils from the Jurassic period, a time 210 million years ago to 140 million years ago. When these fossils were created, the seas swarmed with strange creatures now long gone: ammonites—animals with spiral shells shaped like a ram's horn and related to today's squids and nautiluses; trilobites—segmented arthropods related to today's crab and lobsters but resembling huge sow bugs; and strange bony fishes, hexacorals, swimming reptiles and bivalve mollusks. On land dinosaurs tromped through the jungles where mammals, birds and flowering plants had just made their first appearance.

Strangely, fossils on Vancouver Island are more closely related to those found in India than to those found in neighbouring Alberta or Puget Sound. Vancouver Island's wandering habits explains why it is so different from its neighbours. Its travels began 400 million years ago in the ancient Pacific near the equator when a series of volcanic eruptions beneath the sea formed a cluster of islands that geologists refer to as Wrangellia. Wrangellia, which included the beginnings of Vancouver Island, the Queen Charlotte Islands and the nearby mainland, began travelling north at a rate of seven centimetres (one and a half inches) a year, pulled by currents of molten lava beneath the earth's crust—like packages on a giant conveyor belt. As it traveled, Wrangellia acquired layers of sediment and fossils alternating with layers of volcanic rock. By the early Jurassic period Wrangellia had passed the equator. By the late Jurassic, 170 million years ago, it had overtaken California. Then in the early Cretaceous period, 130 million years ago, Wrangellia collided with the ancient continent of Laurentia and the continent of North America was born. Scientists know about Vancouver Island's journey from

the presence of tropical and subtropical fossils and the direction of magnetic rocks in volcanic stones—directions that were set when the rocks were flowing lava.

With our pockets bulging with fossils, we continued on around the island, climbing over piles of bleak black rocks and jumbles of driftwood delivered by last year's winter storms. Near the southwest corner of the island we climbed up and over a small cliff and through a miniature canyon. I followed the children, who climbed like monkeys among the rocks. Yellow daisies and frail purple flowers grew in nooks and crannies. Patches of lichen spotted the black canyon walls with splotches of orange. It looked like a desert landscape and I felt as if we had wandered into some exotic land. When we emerged on the other side of the canyon, I was surprised to see the green-forested hills in the distance reminding me we were still on the west coast of Vancouver Island, not on Wrangellia.

Flowers grow in the nooks and crannies of rocks with only a bare amount of soil to nourish them.

Rugged Point

Navigating through Grief

When I first saw Rugged Point on the chart, I thought it was too open, too unprotected for a good anchorage. But after we had been there several times, I decided that openness was its best feature. I liked to look up Kyuquot Sound into the mountains of Vancouver Island and watch the last rays of the sun turn the face of Union Island red. But the time I most appreciated Rugged Point's openness was during a rainy week in 1987. One night we anchored in Dixie Cove, a small, completely enclosed bay at Hohoae Island, four miles up Kyuquot Sound. The weather report predicted southeasterly gales and we thought Dixie Cove would be a good place to wait out the storm.

After we anchored, Steve went fishing and I stayed in the boat to write some letters. But when I sat down with pen and paper, I couldn't think of anything to say. I got up and looked out the port lights. Dark trees crowded the shore, pressing out toward the water,

The sunset over Union Island is visible from the anchorage behind Rugged Point.

as if to escape the dense forest. The water was so calm that it reflected the dark greens of the trees and the grey skies overhead. As I looked out at the water, raindrops started falling, sending concentric circles across the dull surface. I started to feel sorry for myself, alone in this small cove, with nothing to do but watch the rain. Tears ran down my face and struck the paper I was holding.

Earlier that year my middle brother, Jeremy, had been distraught because he had been unable to find a job to support his wife and small daughter. A musician, who dreamed of being a composer, he had felt like a failure when he was unable to perform the most basic function of breadwinner. Then his marriage failed and he moved in with our parents. On a sunny afternoon, three days after Mother's Day, he sat down at my father's baby grand piano, played the opening of Beethoven's "Moonlight Sonata," then walked down to the basement and hung himself from a water pipe. By the time my father found him it was too late.

The death of a sibling by suicide is enough to send anyone into anguish, but three weeks later my mother surrendered to the leukemia she had been battling for months and I had a double grief to bear. I didn't know how to navigate through this grief. Although I hadn't been close to either of them, their deaths hit me like no other pain I had ever experienced. To the grief was added the

Volcanic rocks on Rugged Point. Wind and waves have carved the point into strange shapes.

horror of the suicide—the recriminations, the regrets, the analyses by well-meaning family members. I felt as if I was dragging myself around in a fog.

It was my Aunt Barbara, one of my mother's sisters, who gave me the key to getting through these new treacherous waters. She said to me one day, "I remember when Auntie's husband died. I went to see her to offer my condolences. I expected her to cry but instead she looked me sternly in the eye and said, 'Time heals all things.' I have found this to be true." As she talked, Aunt Barbara put her shoulders back in an imitation of her great-aunt Emily. I found myself doing the same.

Navigating through grief, I discovered, was like sailing to windward. You point the boat as close to your destination as the wind will let you, and keep tacking until you get there, no matter how long it takes. It requires faith—faith that grief will end, that the boat really is moving toward its destination, even though to those who don't understand sailing, it looks like you are heading somewhere else. So, when Steve said he wanted to keep the plans we had made to spend a whole month sailing on the west coast of Vancouver Island, I agreed. I didn't really want to be sailing, but then I didn't want to be home in Seattle either. I knew there was nowhere I could go to escape myself, that I just had to wait for time to do its healing.

The next day we left Dixie Cove for Rugged Point. We motored past Whiteley Island and into Kyuquot Channel where we raised sail—full main and 150 genoa. As we tacked towards Chatchannel Point, I saw that the sky had turned purple over Union

A hiking trail leads across the peninsula to one of the most beautiful sandy beaches on the coast.

Island. In a few minutes a gust hit us and *Osprey* heeled hard, burying the rail and sending water rushing across the deck. Rain came down in sheets, pelting the deck and stinging our faces. The wind blew straight up the channel from Rugged Point, right where we wanted to go.

"It's just a squall," yelled Steve over the roar of the wind. "We can wait it out. Just let out the sheets." I loosened the jib sheet and *Osprey* straightened slightly. But the wind only strengthened and the sails flapped and flogged in the wind. We had to do something.

"Let's put up the self-tender," yelled Steve, referring to the small self-tending jib that sat on the foredeck, already hanked-on to the stay under the 150 genoa and ready to go. I ran to the mast to let the jib halyard go and in a few seconds *Osprey* straightened as the sail came down. Steve hooked up the self-steering vane and came forward to help me gather up the sail, take it off the forestay and tie it up along the starboard bow. The water around us frothed from wind and rain, but the boat rode easily in the low seas. Except for the rain, working on the foredeck was easy. In a few minutes the smaller sail was up and I was cranking in the sheet while Steve went back to the wheel. Soon we were tacking briskly back and forth across the channel. Wind that had seemed frightening when we had too much sail now seemed just right.

As we approached Rugged Point, the rain turned to drizzle and the wind slackened. The self-tending jib, which had been drawing so nicely just a few minutes before, flopped on its boom above the foredeck. We reversed the process we had gone through just an hour earlier and put up the 150. I grumbled to myself that any normal skipper would just start the engine at this point, but I really didn't mind. I was glad the wind had died before we had to anchor.

We anchored in 25 feet of water, well off the rocks of Rugged Point. The rain had ended. I looked with pleasure at the craggy rocks of Rugged Point, at the bold head of Kyuquot Hill on Union Island to the west and at the steep-sided hills to the east. The open water, with its expanded views raised my spirits. It was as if my eyes, free to see greater distances, could see beyond my immediate troubles. Tomorrow we would be able to cross the narrow isthmus of Rugged Point and walk on a real ocean beach. And as I thought about all of this, I realized I hadn't felt sorry for myself since leaving Dixie Cove.

Amai Inlet

Blue Lips Cove

We were on our trip in 2001 and had just finished dinner when Steve turned the VHF radio to the weather station. I didn't pay much attention until Steve asked, "Did you hear that? Solander Island, northwest 40 knots!" I stopped to listen and heard, "Vancouver Island, north part, gale warning." Surprised, I got up and looked out the port light. In our anchorage behind Rugged Point the sea surface was still glassy calm. Although the wind always blows stronger at Solander Island, a rocky island off Brooks Peninsula to our north, the 40-knot difference made us wary. Our calm weather couldn't last.

Our two guests, Evan and Janine Devault, looked at us, wondering what the two adults were fussing about. The boat was quiet, we were anchored for the night; their only concern was who was going to get stuck doing the dishes.

As I watched through the port light, a gust travelled across the open sound from the north, darkening the water around us. Ripples soon turned to waves. The boat shifted on its anchor chain.

Amai Inlet as seen from the entrance to Blue Lips Cove.

I had thought we were safe in this anchorage. We had anchored here many times before and had encountered rough water only once, when a land breeze had come up during the night. Always before, the northwest wind had blown into the sound, leaving the anchorage sheltered. But this wind was more north than west and we were on a lee shore. This trip was Janine's first experience sailing and we didn't want it to be an unpleasant one. We got out the chart to look for another anchorage and saw that Amai Inlet was only four and a half miles away. We knew from experience that the little cove at its mouth would offer good protection in a storm. We had another two hours of light, enough time to get there.

In just a few short minutes we were underway. We put the dirty dishes into the sink for washing later, started the engine, raised the anchor and headed out into the open sound. We wanted to put the lee shore of Rugged Point behind us as fast as we could. As we headed out, I heard waves crashing on the beach and wind roaring through the trees.

In the open sound the wind was blowing 20-25 knots and building. Soon we were sailing at a brisk six knots, the boat heeling as it pushed steadily through the waves. The weather front that had brought the wind had also cleared the skies and the low slanted rays of the evening sun lit up the contours of the land, setting green hills and valleys in relief. I walked out on the side deck on the windward side and stood there, feeling the boat move steadily under my feet. The wind blowing from the land was warm on my arms and face. Evan came and joined me and we both held on to the shrouds and looked ahead. His face lit up with a slow smile as he looked up at me. "I like this," he said. I thought how wonderful it would be to be 10 years old again and not be afraid of the wind.

The wind slackened as we passed Whiteley Island then died to a mere flutter before we entered Amai Inlet. We drifted quietly, the boat moving forward with the momentum of past winds, before gliding to a stop in the quiet water. I felt as if we should whisper in the quiet air. We drifted quietly for a few minutes; then Steve started the engine and motored through the narrow channel into the small cove near the inlet's entrance. Ahead of us a half moon peeked above the hills in the darkening sky. When we rounded the corner, we saw another boat anchored in the cove. As we passed, the boat's crew raised wineglasses in salute. I realized they knew nothing of the gale building in the sound.

We had been to this cove twice before. On our second trip we brought with us a copy of Don Douglass's recently published *Exploring Vancouver Island's West Coast*. Douglass calls this cove, which is nameless on the chart, "Petroglyph Cove" for animal petroglyphs he claimed to have seen etched in the vertical cliff on the north side of the channel. But although we looked carefully underneath the overhanging rock where Douglass told us to look, we saw nothing that resembled our idea of petroglyphs. The only possible man-made markings were some faint swatches of red paint, looking suspiciously like bottom paint for a boat.

We dismissed the notion of petroglyphs in Amai Inlet as wishful thinking. But later I read *Since the Time of the Transformers: The Ancient Heritage of the Nuu-chah-nulth, Ditidaht, and Makah* by Alan McMillan and saw a picture of a pictograph of a thunderbird. I connected the picture immediately with the swatch of "bottom paint" in this cove. The description matched too: McMillan noted that pictographs, paintings in red ochre, are located along protected inner waterways (like Amai Inlet), while petroglyphs—rock carvings—are found on the exposed ocean coast. Now that we were here again, we decided to take another look.

The next morning it took us awhile to find the swatches of red paint; they were fainter than we remembered and amorphous in shape. We could not identify any animal

forms. But they certainly could have been pictographs, worn to unrecognizable shapes by the weather.

After finding the pictographs, we felt that "Petroglyph Cove" was not an appropriate name so we started calling it "Pictograph Cove." Then, in 2004 we learned a better name: "Blue Lips Cove." In Walters Cove that year we met Gary Liimatta, a former resident who was back for a visit. Gary grew up in Walters Cove and raised four children there before the loss of the salmon fishery pushed him away. He told us a story about Amai Inlet. His mother sent him to work for a prospector who lived at the head of the inlet and had a reputation of being a hard worker. One day Gary came across the prospector chopping wood. He appeared to be wearing an old pair of gloves that hung in tatters from his hands. "You need new gloves," he told him. The prospector stopped chopping and held up his hands. The tatters weren't gloves: they were skin. He had burned his hands on the stove but had just kept on working, not even stopping to bandage his hands. "Every young person should have an opportunity to work for someone who really knows what hard work is," Gary told us.

Gary knew about the cove. "We called it 'Blue Lips Cove'," he told us. When I asked him why he said, "Because when they went in there it was cold and their lips turned blue."

Kyuquot residents named this snug little Bay in Amai Inlet "Blue Lips Cove" because it was so cold when they went in there that their lips turned blue.

167

Cachalot

A Losing Race

A chance remark by Bob Devault of Nuchatlitz in 1999 spurred us to go to Cachalot. We had been telling Bob about our friend Babe Gunn, the sculptor in Bamfield, when he mused, "I wonder if she did the whale at Cachalot?" "What whale?" we asked. And that's how we learned that on the shores of a deserted inlet in one of the West Coast's least populated sounds, was a statue of a whale.

Whales and whaling were already on our minds. We were on our way home from the Queen Charlotte Islands (Haida Gwaii) where we had visited the site of the former Rose Harbour Whaling Station. We had inspected the remnants of large boilers and walked on the beach among giant rusting tanks where Chinese workers had once cooked whalebones.

The year 1999 was also the year that the Makah killed a grey whale near Cape Flattery in Washington State, an event that upset many people, including some Makahs.

Cachalot. The Pacific Whaling Company operated a whaling factory here from 1918 through 1926.

The Makah killing one whale didn't bother me. I thought if a whale hunt would help the Makah regain their sense of pride and not endanger the whale species, then they should be allowed to do it. What bothered me was industrial whaling, the type they did at Rose Harbour which had caused the near extinction of several species.

We didn't have time to visit Cachalot that year, but during the winter I acquired a copy of the book *A Window on Whaling*, by Joan Goddard. From it I learned that Cachalot had once been a major whaling station similar to Rose Harbour. The name Cachalot, despite its local pronunciation, does not refer to a place where you can catch a lot of fish. It is French for sperm whale and is correctly pronounced "ca-sha-lo."

Modern shore-based whaling stations in British Columbia were self-contained villages with bunkhouses, cookhouses, machine shops and large factory buildings. The station at Cachalot employed 200 people in its heyday. From these stations 90-foot-long steam-driven boats imported from Norway steamed out to sea to hunt blue whales, humpbacks, fin, sei, sperm whale, and the few remaining right whales. From the whaling grounds, they towed the whales three to five at a time back to the whaling stations. There, crews of Japanese, Chinese and Native workers hauled the whales up floating ramps to the sheds, flensed them of their blubber and cooked them in large vats. Meanwhile, the boats steamed away in search of more whales.

But it was the whale statue as much as the station site itself that intrigued me. I called Babe Gunn to ask her if she was the whale's sculptor. She was not; no one seemed to know who the sculptor was. No one seemed to know what the statue was made of, either. Bob had said it might be cement, but one of our neighbours in Seattle had seen it and he thought it was wood. Few boats visit this isolated inlet and no one we talked to knew more than that the statue commemorated the site of the Cachalot Whale Station.

We had to see it for ourselves. We left from Nuchatlitz the next summer with nine-year-old Evan Devault on board. It was to be Evan's first trip on a big sailboat. Evan had never seen the whale either, but he was sure it was concrete.

"How do you know?" I asked him.

"I've got a picture," he said.

"But I thought you had never seen it?"

"Well, the picture was taken before I was born."

We left in the early morning and motored north across windless seas and under grey skies, threading our way through the islands of clear passage and up the coast to Kyuquot Sound. A southeast gale had blown through the day before and had left an uncomfortable chop. Evan curled up in a corner of the cockpit and went to sleep—the best defence against seasickness. I stayed awake, hanging on to the steel frame of the dodger as the boat rolled.

I was relieved when we passed the craggy rocks of Rugged Point and entered the calm waters of Kyuquot Sound. We followed the shoreline as it curved to the right past Whiteley Island to the entrance to Cachalot Inlet. Dark green hillsides rose steeply above us where patches of mist swirled among the trees. The Norwegian crew of the Cachalot whaling boats must have felt at home in these fjords.

As we approached the site of the former whaling station, the three of us stared intently at the beach, looking for the whale. Steve finally spotted it through the binoculars, just east of Cachalot Creek. If we hadn't known it was there, we would never have seen it. From a distance it looked like a rock or a log.

We anchored just east of the old pilings in 25 feet of water and took the dinghy ashore. Leaning pilings and crumbling rock pier were the only traces we could see of the whaling station. The wharf, the houses and the large factory building with ramps were gone. Steve and Evan poked among the trees looking for machinery, while I searched

We found whale bones and pottery shards near the old dock.

the beach for artifacts. The tide was out, exposing a broad cobble beach. Steve found a few pieces of rusting iron and I found a china shard—a piece of a bowl decorated with delicate pink and green flowers. Near the pilings Steve and Evan found two-foot-long sections of worm-eaten whalebones.

Shore-based whaling began in British Columbia in 1905 with the establishment of the first whaling station at Sechart in Barkley Sound by the Pacific Whaling Company. Kyuquot Station followed two years later (renamed Cachalot in 1918). Naden and Rose Harbour stations on the Queen Charlotte Islands were built in 1910. During this time the American Pacific Whaling Company also built a station at Bay City in Grays Harbor and Norwegian whalers built two stations in Alaska.

Several events spurred the development of shore-based whaling in the Northwest. Populations of sperm, right and bowhead whales had dwindled and traditional sailing whale ships were on their way out. Yankee whalers and Norwegian capitalists developed new technology consisting of grenade-tipped harpoons that allowed whales to be hunted more efficiently. Whale oil also became more profitable with the development of hydrogenation to convert it to a solid. Whale oil was in demand for margarine and for the production of candles, soap and cosmetics as well as the traditional uses of lubrication and lamp oil. By cooking every part of the whale, the factories extracted far more oil from the whales than the old whaling ships had ever done, earning more profit for the owners. They even ground up the bones for fertilizer.

Another reason for the resurgence of whaling was the loss of the sealing industry. Fur seals were becoming scarce and new laws and treaties threatened to end pelagic sealing. The owners and captains of the sealing schooners who had carried Nuu-chah-nulth seal hunters and their canoes to sealing grounds in the North Pacific were looking for new work.

For a picture of life at the Cachalot Whaling Station, we can turn to Joan Goddard's description of life at Rose Harbour Whaling Station. Even at these modern whaling stations, whaling was a dangerous and unpleasant life. Workers could slip and fall into vats of boiling whale oil. Medical help was days away. A rank odour of dead flesh and burning whale oil permeated the stations. It was so strong that the mail boat refused to tie up to the dock, insisting the residents row out for their mail. The ship's captain claimed the putrid air discoloured the ships' paint. William Hagelund, author of *Whalers No More,* a book about life on the whaling ships, described the smell at low tide at Rose Harbour in 1941 as revolting, "oozing up from the slime and mud under the station and out of the old timbers."

We could smell no trace of these odours at Cachalot, only a faint scent of rotting seaweed normal to low tide. We left the pier and walked along a cobble beach to where the whale statue reared out of a sea of thimbleberry bushes. It was about 15 feet long with the small jaw and square head of a sperm whale. Steve knocked on its snout with his fist and the whale answered with a hollow metallic sound. From the sound and the rough texture of the surface, we concluded it was ferroconcrete.

An anonymous sculptor placed this ferroconcrete whale at Cachalot in memory of the whales butchered there.

The Cachalot Whaling Station enjoyed only a few good years of whaling. The "modern" shore-based whalers hunted so efficiently they nearly drove the whales to extinction. At the same time, competition from petroleum and vegetable oil drove down the price. Desperate for profit, whaling companies searched farther afield and brought in more of the disappearing whales, which became more scarce. It was a losing race and in 1917 dwindling whale population forced Sechart Whaling Station in Barkley Sound to close. The Cachalot Whaling Station hung on longer, producing canned whale meat as a beef substitute during World War I, then finally closing in 1926. A total of 4,765 whales had been processed there.

Cachalot's facilities reopened a year later as a pilchard reduction plant to take advantage of the sudden appearance of vast schools of pilchards on the coast, and then closed for good in the 1940s when the pilchards, too, dwindled in number.

There was one more attempt to make whaling profitable on Vancouver Island. In 1948 the Gibson Brothers of Tahsis opened a new whaling station at Coal Harbour in Quatsino Sound. The owners hoped to take advantage of rising beef and pork prices, but packers flooded the market with horsemeat and consequently whale meat never caught on in Canada or the United States. Coal Harbour closed, ending whaling in British Columbia.

While Steve and Evan explored the woods, I stayed by the whale. I closed my eyes and tried to imagine the whaling station as it once was: boats coming and going to the docks, workers hauling whales up the ramps, vats of boiling oil burbling out odours. But the only sounds were birdsongs and the only smell that of seaweed at low tide. The whale's eyes watched over a quiet scene of empty water and tall spruce. I thought of the New England whaling town of New Bedford, Massachusetts, where a museum full of scrimshaw, tools and mannequins dressed in whaling clothes commemorates the men who hunted the whales. Here at Cachalot, the whales have the memorial and the men are forgotten.

Although the whale statue is distinctly European in style, the idea of a statue memorializing dead whales is common among northwest First Nations.

Abandoned whaling machinery rusts in the forest behind the whale statue.

The Nuu-chah-nulth, and other northwest First Nations, believed that a whale or a fish would willingly give up its life for a hunter that showed respect. By placing the whale sculpture at Cachalot the sculptor has restored some of that respect. Cachalot differs from New England whaling towns in another way: the physical structures are almost gone, swallowed up by the forest. While I like to see the scars of history heal, I worry that their disappearance also erases the lessons history teaches us. By marking the spot where buildings and docks once stood, the whale statue reminds us of Cachalot's history.

Whaling history has taken a new twist on Vancouver Island. For the second time in British Columbia's history, whales are big business. Whales have been making a comeback since the establishment of the International Whaling Commission in 1946. Today's whalers depart from Ucluelet, Tofino and Tahsis in high-speed inflatable boats sitting in neat rows and wearing matching red and yellow float suits. In less than an hour they are on the whaling grounds with grey whales, killer whales and humpbacks. But today's whalers shoot with cameras, not harpoons; their captains seek tourist dollars, not blubber.

Canada has become one of the top three whale-watching countries in the world, the other two being Spain and the US. According to a study by the International Fund for Animal Welfare, total income from whale-watching worldwide grew to over $1 billion in 1998, nearly double the estimated $504 million in 1994. West Coast towns are reaping the benefits of this new boom in tourist dollars spent on tours, travel, hotels and souvenirs. These whalers have found a way to make a living without killing fish or chopping down trees, and certainly whale-watching increases people's appreciation for nature. But some experts fear they are too much of a good thing—that the increasing numbers of watchers and their boats are harassing the whales and endangering their health.

We left Cachalot that afternoon in a freshening breeze, raising the sails as we passed Whiteley Island. It was Evan's first chance to sail on the *Osprey* and he did such a great job cranking in the jib sheets that we promised to take him on another sail the next year. We anchored that night at Rugged Point so Steve and Evan could go fishing, but they came back an hour later saying they had been skunked—not even a bite.

The whale's sculptor remains a mysterious figure. The next year we visited Walters Cove, also called Kyuquot, the only town in Kyuquot Sound, and I asked a number of people there if they remembered the sculptor's name. No one did. They each referred me to someone else who in turn referred me to someone else until I ran out of referrals. However, I did find someone who remembered the sculpture's arrival. I tracked down Susan Plensky through e-mail over the winter. She told me that one day in the 1970s the artist, with the whale in a trailer, arrived unannounced at Fair Harbour where Susan and her husband Skip were living in a float camp. The sculptor didn't have a clue of how to get it to Cachalot and had to ask for help to find a boat to deliver it. Susan remembers that the statue was built in memory of the dead whales. Perhaps the sculptor didn't want to be known. Part of me hopes I never do find out who he is.

Walters Cove

The Uchuck III

Cumulus clouds raced overhead, casting shadows on the water as we left Kyuquot Sound in 2001. We were heading for Walters Cove where Evan and Janine were to catch the *Uchuck III* home to Nuchatlitz. It would be upwind sailing all the way through narrow, rockbound Nicolaye Channel. And although the strong wind would give us rough water leaving Kyuquot Sound, we would be able to use the self-tending jib, which would make tacking in the narrow channels easy. As we left the Sound and turned northwest toward Nicolaye Channel, *Osprey* pounded into the waves and spray flew over the dodger. "Can we go below?" asked Janine. She had figured out quickly that when the self-tending jib is up we wouldn't need her or Evan to help tack.

Just south of Amos Island, a nasty-looking group of rocks confused us. Because of the angle we approached, we couldn't see our way through. Steve thought we should leave the rocks to starboard; I thought we should leave them to port. I anxiously pointed to the patch on the chart that I thought corresponded to the rocks. Steve pointed to another patch. Whichever patch they were, we were coming up on them fast. Then we saw the light on Amos Island and realized we needed to go between the rocks and Amos Island, which meant we had to leave them to port. If we had left them to starboard, we could have got around them, but not without risking hidden rocks. The narrow passage

The entrance to Walters Cove is famous on the West Coast for its narrow and winding channel.

required short, quick tacks. Every time we tacked, the boat heeled sharply. After one of those tacks, I looked into the cabin to see how Evan and Janine were doing. Janine looked up from a clutter of cards and books and asked, "Are we there yet?"

Once past Amos Island we were in the lee of the Mission Group Islands. The channel widened, the seas flattened and the wind no longer blew so strongly. We had time to get out the chart and prepare for the entrance to Walters Cove, famous on the West Coast for its narrow and winding channel through a maze of rocks and islands. Steve, of course, wanted to sail through the entrance.

"The *Uchuck* comes through this channel all the time and she's a lot bigger than we are," he said.

"Yes," I agreed. "But she doesn't sail in." But I knew I wouldn't win that argument. Fortunately, the wind would be behind us, making the entrance less difficult.

Evan and Janine came on deck as we slalomed through the channel, leaving red buoys to starboard, green buoys to port. Steve let out the mainsail as we headed downwind and I tended the jib. Just as it looked like we would sail smack into an island, a green buoy appeared. We left it to port to pass between two small islands and into an outer harbour formed by a circle of more small islands. We were now in civilization. *Osprey* drifted along while Evan and Janine, who had been here before with their parents, pointed out the houses of friends.

We made our final entrance into the protected inner harbour through a narrow channel marked by a black beacon on Walters Island. I reflected that despite Walters Cove's reputation for a tricky entrance, there were so many markers that if we had absolute faith in red-right-returning and followed that rule religiously, we almost didn't need a chart. And sailing hadn't been as bad as I had feared; the wind had slowed as we entered the islands. Inside the harbour the wind died to a whisper. We motored to the dock and tied to the float on the north side of the public pier. From there we had a good view of the town and everything going on in it.

Steve and I had visited Kyuquot a number of times, but had rarely stayed for more than a few hours. Our first visit there, in 1987, had discouraged us. Fishboats had been rafted three deep at the dock and a generator to a fish-processing plant clattered and roared. We had hurried through our shopping and left the dock, thinking we could anchor away from the noise. But when we went to drop the anchor, we heard a yell, "Don't anchor there, there's a water pipe!" In fact, so many underwater power lines, water pipes and phone lines criss-crossed the cove that anchoring seemed almost impossible. A young man in a skiff finally came out to show us a safe spot. After that trip, we made only quick daytime stops for groceries and then sailed on to the Bunsby Islands or back to Rugged Point. Now the fish-processing plant was gone, there was space at the dock and the town was quiet. Like other small towns on Vancouver Island's west coast, Kyuquot was struggling for its life in the face of declining fish runs and reduced logging.

About 300 people live in Walters Cove—about half live in Houpsitas, the Nuu-chah-nulth village on the Vancouver Island side of the cove; the other half, of mostly Scandinavian descent, live scattered on Walters Island and a number of small neighbouring islands. There's a Red Cross Outpost Hospital with two resident nurses on Okime Island, a school for both Native and white children on the reserve and a general store and restaurant on Walters Island. Bed and breakfasts are scattered all around the cove. Abandoned fuel tanks above the town speak of the time when Kyuquot was a centre of commerce for an active fishing community. The nearest road is at Fair Harbour, almost 12 miles away through the winding channels of Kyuquot Sound. The only way to get to Walters Cove is by private boat, seaplane or on the coastal freighter, the *Uchuck III*.

We had come to Kyuquot to meet the *Uchuck III*, which was to be Evan and Janine's transportation home to Nuchatlitz the next morning. And we had promised the children they could have hamburgers at Miss Charlie's, the town's only restaurant. "Miss Charlie" is the name of a pet seal, Walters Cove's most famous resident. The Kayra family, who own the store and the restaurant, had rescued Miss Charlie as a pup (first named Charlie) after her mother was shot. That was more than 35 years ago and Miss Charlie is still around.

The first thing we always do when we come to a town is look for the garbage dumpster. Here we found it on the dock under a sign warning, "No dumping, by order of the harbourmaster." A second smaller sign said, "Please do not overload the dumpster." We had to squeeze our bag of garbage in to get it to fit. It was too early for dinner so we decided to take a walk. We strolled past the general store and onto the boardwalk that leads along the harbourfront. Evan was glad to get off the boat and he raced ahead of us, then back, his feet thumping on the wooden planks.

Although the town had come into hard times, pleasant well-maintained cottages lined the boardwalk. One of the cottages, no more than a small house by Seattle standards, sported the sign, "Kyuquot Beach Resort."

We soon came to the end of the boardwalk and walked out onto the beach and around the corner toward the open water of Nicolaye Channel. There we came to a rocky ledge that jutted out into the narrow channel between Walters Island and Vancouver Island. In the centre of the ledge was a solitary rock stack—a lone column left standing after eons of waves and rain had eroded away the softer rock around it. Its presence startled me. Rock stacks were a geological formation I associated with the open coast, not something I expected to see in a quiet little town with a protected harbour.

Miss Charlie's Restaurant has closed. It's now for rent as a lodge.

Above: A stack stands on a rocky ledge between Walters Island and Vancouver Island.

Opposite top: View from the Native village of Houpsitas. About 300 people live in Walters Cove, about half in Houpsitas.

Opposite bottom: The coastal steamer *Uchuck III* delivers gasoline, groceries and tourists, and takes away the garbage.

While Steve and I walked around the base of the stack and looked up at its thatch of bushes, Evan and Janine tried to climb it. But even Evan, who climbs rocks like a monkey, found it too steep. Looking at the stack and watching the water surge back and forth against the rock shelf, I had a different perspective on Kyuquot. It wasn't just a sleepy little town, but a place where nature wore away at the world and left only the toughest behind. I had a vision of the town in the winter, besieged by storms, isolated by driving rain, its residents standing proud against the elements.

The evening sun was turning the stack golden as we left for the restaurant. We walked back on the boardwalk and up onto a porch hung with colourful flower baskets. The scene inside looked like preparations for a party. Workers scurried around carrying pots and pans. "It's good you came early," one of them told us. "When the *Uchuck* arrives we'll have 32 hungry tourists all clamouring for their dinners."

Varnished pine floors, white painted wood-panelled walls, a gaily-coloured plastic parrot and a giant rubber plant all gave Miss Charlie's a tropical feel. French doors led out to a deck, where we settled down at a table to admire the view. I ordered chicken, Steve ordered halibut and Evan and Janine ordered hamburgers.

"Hamburgers!" Steve said to them, teasingly. "That's dead cow!"

"Why eat fish at a restaurant?" asked Janine, looking at Steve's halibut with scorn. "We get that at home." She might have added, "and on the *Osprey*," which was why I had ordered chicken.

The evening was as perfect as an evening can get on the West Coast. The sun sparkled off the blue water and bounced off the green trees across the cove. It was almost warm enough to wear T-shirts. As we finished dinner we saw the bow and derricks of the *Uchuck* emerge from the forest at the harbour entrance. It tied up at the town dock and put out a gangplank. Suddenly Kyuquot burst into activity. We paid our bill and hurried down to join the excitement.

The *Uchuck III*, affectionately known to locals as the "*Upchuck*," is a converted minesweeper imported from the US in 1948. The derricks are from the *Princess Mary*, the engine room telegraph and steering from the *Princess Victoria* and the cargo winches from the *Princess Alberni*. One-hundred-thirty-six feet long, and 24 feet wide, the *Uchuck III* can carry 100 passengers and 8,000 cubic feet of cargo. (On open ocean runs, it is limited to fewer passengers.) It has been plying the waters of the west coast of Vancouver Island since 1955 and serving Kyuquot and Nootka Sounds since 1982. Freight service to logging camps, fish farms and isolated communities like Kyuquot is the *Uchuck*'s bread and butter, supplemented by tourism. In the summer the *Uchuck III* offers day trips to Friendly Cove and Tahsis and two-day trips to Kyuquot. Kayakers

take the *Uchuck III* to remote paddling areas where the ship's derricks lower them and their kayaks into the water on straps—paddles poised and ready to go.

Part of the attraction of the *Uchuck* to tourists is watching a working freighter unload freight in out-of-the-way places—a scene long gone from urban waterfronts. A fleet of skiffs carrying empty gasoline drums converged on the *Uchuck*'s starboard side while crewmembers prepared to exchange them for full drums. On the port side, men unloaded boxes of vegetables and bags of potatoes to eager hands on the dock. Tourists milled around among the handcarts as townsmen with clipboards directed them to

guesthouses on Walters Island and Houpsitas. In the midst of all this a young boy jumped up and down on the metal lid of the dumpster in a vain attempt to pack in all the garbage before the crane lifted it aboard. I thought guiltily of the way we had squeezed our garbage into it.

All evening the activity continued. We sat in the *Osprey*'s cockpit and watched tourists stroll by. For the last few nights, Steve had been reading bedtime stories to the children from a book called *Politically Correct Bedtime Stories*. He saw no need to change just because our cockpit was now a fishbowl. As he was reading a version of Cinderella in which all the women at the ball throw off their corsets and shoes and dance barefoot in shifts, a tourist carrying a camera stopped and listened. "That doesn't sound like the Cinderella I read to my kids," he said. That night from our bunks we heard the rumble of handcarts on the dock well into the night as the *Uchuck* unloaded.

We awoke to a morning of grey sky and fine mist. Just before 8:00 a.m., we delivered Evan and Janine to

A young fisherman shows off his catch on the dock at Walters Cove.

the *Uchuck* where the cook had agreed to keep an eye on them. On the way to the kitchen, we passed through the main cabin where passengers were sitting at small tables decorated with navigation charts.

"These kids can be your tour guides," said Steve to several passengers. "They're from Nuchatlitz."

We stood on the dock and watched the *Uchuck* disappear into the morning mist. Later, as we cleaned up breakfast I kept expecting to hear Evan chattering away or see Janine reading a book. It seemed awfully quiet. I couldn't decide whether to be sad they were gone or relieved to have the boat to ourselves again. I thought how well the last few days had gone. I had been apprehensive about three days with the kids, afraid they would be bored with old fogies like us while we would be overwhelmed by their energy. Instead, they had settled right in, making *Osprey* their home. And I was still amazed that their parents entrusted the children to our care— two near strangers who showed up unannounced every summer in a green sailboat.

The whole town seemed quiet now that the *Uchuck* had left. *Osprey* was the only boat at the dock. In Miss Charlie's two or three people sipped coffee, surrounded by empty tables. On the boardwalk, a solitary dog sniffed at the flowers. But in the general store, workers were busy emptying boxes and shelving food. When we looked in to ask when they would open, a tired-looking worker stopped shelving for a minute and told us, "We didn't finish unloading until 2:00 a.m. last night. And the frozen French fries for the restaurant were at the bottom underneath everything else so the customers at Miss Charlie's didn't get fries with their hamburgers."

The best time to shop at the Kyuquot General Store is the day after the *Uchuck* arrives. If we hadn't come here to drop off Evan and Janine, we would have come here just to shop. When the store finally opened, I felt as if I had been admitted to an event. Shelves full of neatly stacked boxes and bags filled the small space. I cruised the aisles looking for anything that I might want or use. We needed flour, cornmeal and eggs and I soon found all of those. But the real finds were a quart box of blueberries, red ripe tomatoes, almost crisp lettuce and fresh broccoli. And the freezer yielded two big bags of ice. The *Uchuck* had done well for us. We were ready to head north.

Checleset Bay

Checleset Bay is on the most remote part of Vancouver Island's west coast, and it was here that I saw my first sea otter. I came out on deck in the early morning calm and there he was, about 50 feet from the boat, floating on his back with his paws clasped on his chest and his feet and tail in the air. We watched each other for a while, until he rolled over and dove. When he surfaced a few minutes later, his head was just a distant dark spot on the calm water.

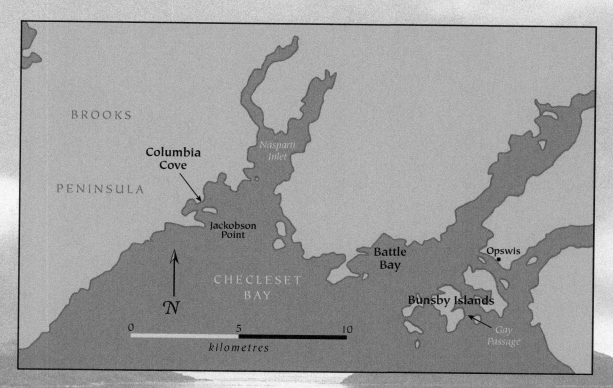

BROOKS

Columbia Cove

PENINSULA

Nasparti Inlet

Jackobson Point

Battle Bay

Opswis

CHECLESET BAY

N

Bunsby Islands

Gay Passage

0   5   10
kilometres

Bunsby Islands

Searching for Bunsby

The noise came like a gunshot—a sharp "crack." I looked up from the winch where I was pulling in the jib sheet. Metal clanged on metal. Something hard hit the deck. I didn't know what had happened, but something was seriously wrong. Then Steve yelled, "We've lost a shroud! Get the sails down." I ran to the mast to drop the sails as Steve swung the boat into the wind. The starboard forward shroud lay on the deck, snapped at the end where it attached to the mast.

We had been sailing to windward from Walters Cove to the Bunsby Islands. We had planned to spend a night in the Bunsbys then head north into Nasparti Inlet and to Columbia Cove, farther than we'd ever been before. But we couldn't sail with a broken shroud—to do so risked breaking the mast. In fact, we were fortunate the mast hadn't gone when the shroud broke. We faced the prospect of completing our trip wholly dependent on our 23-year-old diesel.

The Bunsbys are a favourite anchorage for boats circumnavigating Vancouver Island.

CHECLESET BAY: BUNSBY ISLANDS

"We're going back to Walters Cove," announced Steve as soon as the sails were down and the engine on. And then, "Damn, it's Saturday." I looked at the injured shroud lying on the deck and wondered what the point of going back to Walters Cove was. Surely, they wouldn't have the tools or the parts in that little town to fix it.

Normally when something goes wrong on the boat, when some part breaks or doesn't work as claimed, Steve gets irate and starts cursing designers, manufacturers and sellers. "Those bloody bastards," he'll say. "Don't they ever use what they build?" These opinions he delivers in a voice loud enough to be heard across whatever cove we're anchored in. If there are other boats around, I want to run below and hide. But I've learned that the decibel level of Steve's voice is unrelated either to the consequences of the breakage or the importance of whatever broke, but rather to the amount of stupidity Steve sees in the engineer who designed it. Cheap materials or shoddy workmanship especially anger him. "For just pennies more, they could have done it right," he'll say. "Those bastards." But eventually he calms down and figures out how to fix it or to substitute something else for whatever broke.

So when Steve was quiet on the way back to Walters Cove, I knew that didn't mean everything was okay. In fact, I had a pretty good idea it meant that things weren't okay, that the shroud was going to be very difficult if not impossible to fix.

"Classic lines with a modern rig," was the builder's claim when he advertised our Annapolis 44 sloop in 1978. Modern rig meant rod rigging instead of wire; it was stiffer with less wind-resistance—better for racing, but difficult or impossible to repair at sea or on remote coasts. Ordinary wire rigging can be swaged onto fittings with tools that are small enough and inexpensive enough to carry on a sailboat. Extra shrouds and stays of wire rigging can be coiled and carried on board or sent express in a small airplane. Rod rigging like ours, on the other hand, can't be fixed on board. Riggers have to forge small balls onto the ends to fit into special fittings on the mast and into special turnbuckles on the deck. New rod rigging can't be shipped. Its coils are eight feet in diameter—too big for a small plane or an ordinary truck of the kind used to transport goods across Vancouver Island. And a boat with rod rigging can't just convert to wire rigging. The fittings aren't right. Our turnbuckles, for example, were sleek stainless steel affairs—elegant, but useless for wire rigging. And here we were in Checleset Bay on the most remote part of Vancouver Island's west coast.

"Maybe that old Finn on the *Export* will have an idea," said Steve, referring to the skipper of a red fishboat that had been tied to the dock when we had left. I felt foolish to be coming into a place we'd left just an hour earlier. After Steve's talk about getting there fast and talking to the old Finn, I expected him to go to the store or to hunt down the Finn as soon as we arrived, but instead, he headed for the phone. "It's only 11 o'clock," said Steve. "Peter might still be there—if he works on Saturday." Steve's hurry to get back to Walters Cove had nothing to do with the hours of the Kyuquot General Store. He had been rushing to call a rigging shop in Seattle.

Steve was back in three minutes. "No luck, closed on Saturday. Damn! Well, let's go see what we can find in the store. Perhaps they've got some cable we can use." The store had no cable but did have a large galvanized turnbuckle, made in China. It looked decidedly unyachty, but we bought it. "No telling if we'll be able to find another one anywhere else," said Steve. Steve is not one for discussing plans when he repairs

Our starboard shroud had broken at the fitting and could only be fixed by a professional rigger.

something and I have learned that my questions and suggestions usually just make him angry. But by now I had figured out that Steve was trying to find a way to rig a new wire shroud using ordinary cable in place of the rod. There were just two problems: we didn't have cable and we didn't have wire fittings.

We wandered back down to the dock where the old Finn stuck his head out from *Export*'s wheelhouse window to talk to us. When Steve described our problem, his grizzled face looked serious as he considered the options. "I don't have any cable," he told us. "But Dave over there might know where you can find some." He pointed toward a small house and dock on the beach. "He repairs engines and he keeps a lot of odds and ends around."

Dave didn't answer our knock, so we picked our way past several rusty outboards to the dock. Dave wasn't there either and his dock didn't look very promising, littered with bits of rusty chain, trolling poles and someone's discarded stereo. There was no point in sticking around over the weekend, we decided. The Bunsbys were only five miles away; our engine would get us there and back easily. Unfortunately, our plans to explore Nasparti Inlet would have to wait.

It felt strange to be motoring in a good sailing breeze, as if we were students cheating on a test. "I suppose we could sail on a port tack," mused Steve. But taking down the sails every time we came about didn't make much sense. We anchored in the small cove just west of Gay Passage where we could see across the narrow isthmus of the island toward the sea. The Bunsbys are rugged islands with lots of small coves and islets, a favourite place for kayakers to camp. We knew we wouldn't be bored.

The tale of how Captain Richards of the British Survey vessel HMS *Hecate* named the Bunsby Islands for a character in Charles Dickens's novel *Dombey and Son* in 1862 appears in every cruising guide and magazine article about Checleset Bay. But no one ever says who Bunsby was or why Richards chose a character from one of Dickens's more obscure books. The only reason ever given for this odd choice of names is that Dickens's grandson was on board the *Hecate*.

Motoring through Gay Passage, Bunsby Islands. The Bunsby Islands were named for a character in the novel *Dombey and Son* by Charles Dickens. Gay Passage also bears the name of a character in the book.

I had inherited a complete set of Dickens from my grandmother, so one winter I got out the leather-bound volume of *Dombey and Son.* When the name Bunsby didn't leap out at once from the pages, I resorted to reading the whole book, finally finding the first reference to Bunsby on page 221. Bunsby, it turned out, was only a minor character in the book, but he was a seaman—the captain of a brig named *Cautious Clara.*

When I finished the book, I got out the chart of Checleset Bay. On the westernmost island of the Bunsby group is Cautious Point. Further out in Checleset Bay is Clara Islet. To the north were the Cuttle Islets, named after Captain Cuttle, another of the novel's minor characters. Gay Passage, I realized, had been named for Walter Gay, the book's hero, a self-reliant young orphan being raised by a poor uncle. Walters Cove and Walters Island also bore his name. As I looked at the chart, I couldn't get rid of the ridiculous notion that Dickens's characters were real. Seeing their names on that official paper made them more substantial. I even caught myself wondering who Clara was and why she was so cautious.

As all heroes do, Walter Gay faced a grave crisis. His uncle Solomon was in debt to Walter's employer, the rich and unfeeling Mr. Dombey. Dombey proposed to send Walter to the West Indies, far away from the uncle who depended on him and far from Dombey's young daughter, Florence, whom Walter loved. Walter goes to his uncle's friend Captain Cuttle for advice. Cuttle chews on his iron hook, which he wore as a replacement for his right hand, and cogitates.

> "There's a friend of mine," murmured the captain, in an absent manner, "but he's at present coasting round to Whitby, that would deliver such an opinion on this subject, or any other that could be named, as would give Parliament six and beat'em. Been knocked overboard, that man," said the captain, "twice, and none the worse for it. Was beat in his apprenticeship, for three weeks (off and on), about the head with a ring bolt. And yet a clearer-minded man don't walk."

In spite of his respect for Captain Cuttle, Walter could not help inwardly rejoicing at the absence of this sage, and devoutly hoping that his limpid intellect might not be brought to bear on his difficulties until they were quite settled.

> "If you was to talk and show that man the buoy at the Nore," said Captain Cuttle, in the same tone, "and ask him his opinion of it, Wal'r, he'd give you an opinion that was no more like that buoy than your uncle's buttons are. There ain't a man that walks—certainly not on *two* legs—that can come near him. Not near him!"
>
> "What's his name, Captain Cuttle?" inquired Walter, determined to be interested in the Captain's friend.
>
> "His name's Bunsby," said the captain. "But Lord, it might be any thing for the matter of that, with such a mind as his!"

Captain Bunsby couldn't solve Walter's problem. To solve them Walter had to go to sea, be shipwrecked and then be rescued before returning home to marry Florence and living happily ever after. I could see why Captain Richards chose these characters' names to grace the rocks and islands of Checleset Bay. To sail on the west coast of Vancouver Island, you need to be self-sufficient like Walter, but sometimes you also need to be rescued.

Fixing the broken shroud required a fishing boat turnbuckle from the Walters Cove General Store and aircraft cable fetched by a friend from Campbell River.

Steve finally reached the Seattle rigger on Monday and he agreed to make a special rod-wire connector in the form of a mini-rod with an eye on one end to attach the wire and a ball on the other end to fit in the special rod fitting on the mast. He promised to mail it to us in Tahsis. In Nuchatlitz, where we stopped for a few days on our way to Tahsis, we met a woman named Sylvia who lived in Tahsis. Sylvia planned to drive to Campbell River to meet someone at the airport the next day. Steve gave her a list of supplies: 80 feet of 5/16 aircraft cable, plus wire clips and thimbles.

Cable and parts were waiting for us two days later when we arrived at the Westview Marina. The next morning we walked to the post office to inquire about the fitting from Seattle. The postal clerk hadn't seen it, but she remembered somebody saying something about a package that had been sent by mistake to the hardware store. If she hadn't been willing to help with a few phone calls, we never would have found it.

I hoisted Steve up the mast to install the connector. From the deck I heard him mutter, "Those bastards, they should come out here and do this themselves." To attach the connector, he had to first unscrew the fitting that held the remnants of the old rod, a process that loosened the port shroud as well as the starboard shroud. He then attached the mini-rod. To screw the fitting back in he had to hold the mini-rod 90 degrees from the mast while simultaneously screwing the fitting into the mast and keeping the port shroud from falling out—all while dangling 60 feet above the deck in a bosun's chair. It was difficult with the three-foot mini-rod; it would have been impossible with a full-length rod. The only way to replace a full-sized rod was to remove the mast and install the shroud on the ground.

To make the cable shroud strong enough to sail, we had to loop the cable up then back down again, making it two cables thick. I was afraid the loose end coming out of the galvanized turnbuckle would rip the sail, so I took a scrap of sailcloth from my sewing kit and made a sleeve to protect it. The new shroud looked definitely jury-rigged, more like something you might find on an old boat than a modern sailing yacht. But it got us home. The next winter we replaced all of *Osprey*'s rod shrouds with wire.

Bunsby Islands

A Keystone Species

In 1987 I saw my first sea otter here in the Bunsby Islands. We were anchored in the small cove on the west side of Gay Passage not too far from a low reef of rocks and kelp. I came out on deck in the early morning calm and there was an otter, about 50 feet from the boat, floating on his back in that characteristic otter pose with his paws clasped on his chest and his feet and tail in the air. We watched each other for a while, until he rolled over and dove. When he surfaced a few minutes later, his head was just a distant dark spot on the calm water.

Otters are unique among mammals because they rely on their fur, instead of on a layer of blubber, for warmth and floatation. They have the densest fur of any mammal—about 100,000 hairs per square centimetre or 645,000 per square inch compared to about 9,000 per square centimetre on a dog. An individual otter pelt can have as many as 800 million hairs. All those hairs can hold a lot of air, which is what keeps otters floating. I have seen otters floating high on their backs or standing up like bottles bobbing in the water. They keep air in their fur with constant grooming, like birds preening their

Much of the area surrounding the Bunsby Islands is an ecological reserve.

feathers. New-born sea otters are extra buoyant. They can't dive until they are at least two months old.

This dense, fine fur was once the most valuable fur in North America, more valuable even than beaver or seal.

Before the arrival of the fur traders in the late 1700s, the Nuu-chah-nulth hunted sea otters sparingly. Solitary hunters would track the otters with harpoons and arrows, bringing back only one or two at a time for the chiefs to use for cloaks or to decorate ceremonial masks. The death of an otter for fur was a gift from the otter to the chief. But when the fur traders arrived, otters became a trading commodity and the Nuu-chah-nulth changed their techniques. They would wait until the sea was glassy calm, then go out in force, 10 to 12 men at a time, two to three to a canoe, and spread themselves out over a large area. When a hunter spotted an otter, he would signal with his paddle. The canoes would then converge on the otter at once, unleashing a rain of arrows.

This new efficient manner of hunting almost caused the otter's extinction. By 1793, only five years after Captain Cook's men bought their first otter pelt, the Spanish naturalist, José Moziño, noted that the Natives of Nootka Sound had killed so many otters they had destroyed the basis of trade. Friendly Cove, once known for its otter furs, became only a port for water and supplies, a staging ground for expeditions to other fur trading areas such as Checleset Bay or the Queen Charlotte Islands. By the early 1800s, sea otters were so rare the otter boom was over; by the mid-1800s, sea otters were nearly extinct in Canada.

As the sea otters disappeared, the ecology of the coast changed. Otters are what biologists call a "keystone species," meaning their presence profoundly affects the environment for the rest of the plants and animals. When the first explorers arrived in the Northwest, they found huge kelp beds running parallel to shore. Even in stormy weather, the Nuu-chah-nulth could paddle their canoes in a narrow band of sheltered water between these great beds and the beach. Otters lived among the kelp eating abalones crabs and their favourite food, red sea urchin. When the otters disappeared, the sea urchin population, previously kept in check by the otters, exploded. The sea urchins ate the kelp and the kelp beds disappeared. With the loss of the kelp went habitat and spawning grounds for fish, crab and other sea creatures.

Otters were the first of many species on the west coast of Vancouver Island to face near extinction from hunting or fishing. It's fitting, therefore, that they were also one

Sea otters off Chief Rock outside Walters Cove. Otters gather in large groups called "rafts."

of the first to make a comeback. It is also fitting that the comeback began here in Checleset Bay, where the last indigenous otter on the west coast of Vancouver Island died, shot by a hunter in 1929. The otter's return began in 1969 with the transplanting of 29 otters rescued from a nuclear test in Kamchatka. Sixty more Alaskan sea otters were released in 1970 and 1972. The population grew so fast that by 1984 biologists counted 345 otters: 196 in the Bunsbys and 149 at Bajo Reef off Nootka Island. In 2001 biologists estimated that there were 2,000 otters on Vancouver Island's west coast. With the return of the otters came the return of the kelp beds. When we sail into an anchorage like the Bunsbys or Nuchatlitz, I am thankful for the otters, for kelp now marks submerged rocks, which before we could not see.

An immature eagle perches on a rock near Gay Passage.

We never go far along this coast without seeing an otter. From a distance, I can recognize them as two dark bumps, a head and tail, sticking up above the water surface. But although seeing a single otter has become routine, seeing an otter "raft," a cluster of otters, still thrills me. We saw our first otter raft in 1999 at Chief Rock, just north of Walters Cove on a quiet sunny day. We were motoring from Battle Bay to Walters Cove when I saw what looked like either a large patch of lumpy kelp or a low rock covered with brown seaweed. I looked through the binoculars and saw the kelp move. It was a living, swimming, squirming mass of otters. Otters were everywhere around Chief Rock, sleeping in the kelp, diving around the buoy, or just clinging together in groups. Since then we have noticed that there is always a raft at Chief Rock.

One day I commented to a resident of Walters Cove about how common otters had become. She replied that they had become almost a nuisance. Since the otters had become abundant, abalone, crab and puffins had become scarce. Recently, the Nuu-chah-nulth have requested permission to hunt them for ceremonial purposes.

Despite their numbers, sea otters are shy and difficult to photograph. So, when we anchored in the Bunsby Islands in 2001 where otters are supposed to be abundant, I thought it would be a good opportunity to photograph one. I decided that the inflatable kayak would be the best way to get close enough to get a good picture. I waited for the morning fog to lift then paddled south toward the collection of rocks and reefs at the head of the bay, my camera around my neck. A light breeze blew off the ocean and a low swell sloshed among the rocks, sending strands of brown kelp swirling. The kelp grabbed at my paddles as I navigated through the rocks and I had to push my way out of the kelp patches. I expected to find otters among the kelp, but the only warm-blooded animals I saw were several scruffy-looking young eagles preening themselves on the rocks. I circled the small island on the eastern side of the anchorage and paddled down Gay Passage toward the cove.

Just as I had given up on finding an otter and was heading back to *Osprey*, I saw a flick of brown fur near the rocks in Gay Passage. I stopped paddling and sat motionless, the kayak barely drifting in the light breeze. A few seconds later the otter surfaced, looked around and then dove again. I got my camera ready, then paddled carefully forward, taking short strokes so as not to splash. For the next 15 minutes, the otter played with me. When he dove, I paddled. But each time he surfaced, he had swum exactly the distance I had paddled. In my camera viewfinder, the otter was only a small brown patch. Finally, frustrated, I aimed the camera and snapped. The otter dove. When he surfaced, he was a long way away. I understood why the Nuu-chah-nulth had hunted the otter in packs.

Columbia Cove

Safety in Numbers

View from Columbia Cove. A forest fire that took place more than 200 years ago may explain the many dead trees on the Brooks Peninsula.

At the base of the Brooks Peninsula, near the entrance to Nasparti Inlet, is a small cove that is a favourite of sailboats circumnavigating Vancouver Island. Although the cove is nameless on the chart, yachtsmen call it Columbia Cove and local fishermen call it Peddlars Cove. We had heard so much about Columbia Cove that we had always wanted to see it, but coming from the south, we had never had time to get that far north on our usual vacations. So when we had two whole months on the coast in 2001, we decided to make it our northernmost stop.

The day we planned to go there, the weather radio predicted southeast gales. A small cove on the edge of the Brooks Peninsula, the windiest and most remote land in this area, didn't sound like a good place to be in gales. But our anchorage in the Bunsby Islands was open to the southeast so we couldn't stay there. And when we looked at the chart, we saw that Columbia Cove would be doubly protected—first by Jackobson Point sticking out like a finger from the Brooks Peninsula and second by a small island behind the point.

We left the Bunsby Islands and headed across Checleset Bay. Not a breath of wind stirred the water, which stretched out before us like a silvery blanket under grey clouds. We motored past the Acous Peninsula and its rocky archipelago, around the bare grey rocks of the O'Leary Islets and toward the cloud-covered wall of the Brooks Peninsula. For once, we were glad for calms. The broken shroud had turned our sailboat into a motorboat. Knowing we couldn't use the sails made me feel uneasy. I didn't like being so dependent on our 23-year-old engine. I thought of the other boaters we often sailed with in Puget Sound and wished they were here to call on if we needed help.

On the rocks just inside Jackobson Point the rusty red hulk of a Coast Guard cutter confronted us, its bow torn off to show dangling wires and rusting machinery. The sight of it shocked me. It was like seeing someone with their guts hanging out and was a reminder of man's fragility on this coast. Farther down the small inlet we saw the bow itself. I thought about the amount of force needed to rip a bow from the rest of a hull and felt a prickling of unease about this anchorage.

The wreck of a Coast Guard cutter provides a cautionary tale to boaters anchoring in Columbia Cove.

Continuing past the cutter's bow, we rounded the small island into the cove where three sailboats tied to Parks Service buoys rode on water so still their hulls and rigging reflected perfect copies below. The sight of them comforted me; we weren't the only ones who thought the cove would be safe in a storm. I let go the anchor and watched it fall through the clear water until it came to rest among white clamshells on a sandy bottom. An eerie quiet reigned, as if the clouds had dampened the sound as well as the light.

The *Columbia Rediviva* of Boston under Captain Robert Gray anchored three times in this cove, the first time a quiet June evening in 1791. With the ship's boat the sailors towed *Columbia* into the cove and anchored in three-fathoms, putting one anchor off their bow, a second on the rocks ashore and tying a stern hawser to the trees. They named the cove Columbia's Cove. From here *Columbia*'s men traded with the Natives and explored Checleset Bay, which they called Bullfinch's Sound.

Columbia anchored here a second time in May 1792. This time there were fewer men on board because a number of the crew had gone north on the sloop *Adventure*. (See Chapter 3 for the story of the building of *Adventure*.) The Natives remembered them from their previous visit and asked where the other men were. Although *Columbia*'s officers tried to hide the true size of their crew, saying the men were below sleeping, the Natives weren't fooled. That night several large canoes came into the cove and stopped by the rocks near the ship's anchor. The crew prepared to defend themselves. One of the larger canoes, with 25 men on board, pulled out ahead. The sailors ordered them to stop, but the canoe kept coming. On Captain Gray's orders, the men fired. The canoe drifted ashore as the dying groans of the Natives echoed through the woods. Whether firing on the canoe was necessary is debatable. Fifth mate John Boit wrote in his diary that the Natives might have only been after their anchor.

The *Columbia* left the next day, after nailing a sign saying "Beware" on a tree. They returned for the third time a month later for a prearranged rendezvous with *Adventure*. It must have been a crowded harbour that night, for with *Columbia* came the ship *Margaret*, also of Boston. *Columbia* and *Margaret* had met off the Queen Charlottes and agreed to travel together. There was safety in numbers for, despite the earlier incident, the Natives seemed cheerful and no further incidents occurred.

John Hoskins of *Columbia* described the land above the cove as "high and mountainous, well covered with trees to summit, on some of the hills many of the trees are dead, and on others are a few barren spots; which gives an uncomfortable appearance."

The dead trees are still there, their bleached trunks standing out against the green forest. They may even be the same trees. I e-mailed a photograph of the dead trees on the hillside to Richard Hebda of the Royal British Columbia Museum in Victoria who wrote me that they looked like the results of a forest fire. According to Hebda, the cool wet climate and nutrient-poor soil of Brooks Peninsula slows decomposition and hinders new growth so much that the trees could be from a fire that occurred more than 200 years ago. Margaret Sharcott partially corroborates the forest fire theory in her 1960 book, *A Place of Many Winds.* She relates a local story that a forest fire killed these trees long ago.

Brooks Peninsula is what geologists call an "ice age refugium." Twenty thousand years ago when glaciers covered most of Vancouver Island, Brooks Peninsula remained ice-free. Plant species wiped out in glaciated areas are still found here. Designation of the Brooks Peninsula as a Provincial Park helps preserve those rare species. It also gives boaters like us the chance to enjoy the wilderness. We had heard so many boaters go into raptures about the beach on the ocean side of Jackobson Point that we were eager to see it. We decided to take advantage of the quiet before the storm to look for the trail across the point that leads to the beach. We found it in the southwest corner of the cove marked by a provincial park sign. Landing our dinghy near a creek mouth, where it wouldn't be stranded by the outgoing tide, we followed the trail into the forest.

The trail crossed the peninsula on a flat stretch of land, twisting and turning around trees and climbing over deadfalls. It was a short walk and soon we heard surf murmuring on the beach. We climbed over a log, pushed aside some salal and stepped onto a beachcomber's paradise: a broad sandy beach with a river at one end and a rocky

Fishing floats mark the trail back to Columbia Cove.

outcropping at the other. We spent the next hour walking the beach and poking among the sand for treasures. Net floats were everywhere: large round black floats, small flat yellow floats and miscellaneous white floats. Scattered among the net floats were enough hard hats to outfit a construction site and enough running shoes to outfit a track crew, if every team member had only one foot. In just one small area, we found eight shoes—six left feet and two right feet with no matches. Somewhere out in the ocean a shipping container had broken loose and scattered its cargo of shoes along the coast. But the best find was a child's brightly coloured water rifle. With these treasures Steve set about creating a beach guard—a net float wearing a hard hat, waving a red fisherman's glove and guarding the beach with the water rifle.

Steve put together a beach guard with our beachcombing treasures—a hard hat, a fishing float, a glove and a water rifle.

Leaving the beach guard on watch, we returned to the trail conveniently marked by previous beachcombers with white and orange net floats. When we reached the cove the tide had dropped, but we had chosen our dinghy landing well and needed to carry the dinghy only a short distance. When we motored around the point to the anchorage, we saw that a fifth sailboat, *Courtship*, had anchored between *Osprey* and the other boats and we were alarmed to see *Osprey* had swung within a few feet of a sandbank. There was little room to move in the small cove so we put out a second anchor to keep us off the shallows, leaving the first to keep us off the island. The sea surface was still glassy under grey sky. We grabbed our fishing poles and headed toward Jackobson Point in the dinghy. A half-hour later we returned with a legal ling cod.

The storm came in the night, with a rattle of rain on the cabin roof and the roar of wind in the trees. In the morning, we looked out to see a strong sea running outside the harbour while in the anchorage the boats drifted in quiet water. We watched as *Courtship* headed out to the sea. "They'll be back," Steve predicted and, half an hour later, they were. We spent the day on board listening to the rain on the cabin roof. In the late evening, the wind died and the rain turned to a light mist. We climbed into a very wet dinghy and motored toward a white cutter named *Loncia*, just visible in the fading light. Three inflatable dinghies trailed from her stern. We asked permission to come aboard and added our dinghy to the collection.

Down below, the warm glow of a kerosene lantern illuminated gleaming teak bulkheads. Three couples sat around a varnished table, charts and cruising guides spread before them, a bottle of red wine and a plate of chocolate brownies off to the side. The laughter was comfortable as they recalled their last week of sailing and planned their next. They had been "buddy boating" for a week, but acted as if they had been friends for life, teasing each other and sharing memories. All three couples were circumnavigating Vancouver Island. They had met in Bull Harbour, crossed the Nahwitti Bar together and rounded Cape Scott in sight of each other. Jack and Lucy in *Wy'East* were from Portland, Tom and Louann in *Liberty* were from Bainbridge Island in Puget Sound, as were Jill and Brent in *Loncia*.

We had seen buddy boats before, travelling in groups of three or four around Vancouver Island, but this was the first time we had shared in their camaraderie. Because we were so often heading north while the buddy boats headed south, and because we had to move quickly once we did head south, we rarely saw the same boat more than once. We hadn't minded because our solitary travels pushed us to make friends with the residents. But here in Columbia Cove, where there were no residents, we were glad of the other boaters' company.

The morning after a storm brings quiet waters.

By the time we left *Loncia,* the mist had changed to rain and the wind once more ruffled the water. It rained all that night and into the next afternoon. Restless from forced inactivity we climbed into our wet dinghy and went to knock on *Courtship's* hull. Two youngish faces looked out at us from beneath the dodger. They introduced themselves as Tim and Susan and soon the four of us were parading through the woods in bright yellow and orange slickers. At the end of the trail we found Steve's beach guard watching over a changed world. The surf that had murmured so pleasantly two days before now roared so loud that we had to yell to make ourselves heard. The wind threw sharp rain into our faces. Angry waves bit gouges into the soft sand and piled great masses of tangled kelp at our feet. Near one of these tangles, Steve found a small glass net float, recently thrown ashore by the waves.

We went to sleep that night with the rain still drumming on the cabin roof. But when we awoke in the morning, the rain had stopped and the wind had died. I opened the hatch and looked out to see *Courtship* leaving the harbour while crews on the other boats uncovered sails in preparation for leaving. We hurried to join them. Half an hour later a string of five boats stretched south across Checleset Bay toward Walters Cove.

Historical note: The historian Frederic Howay connected the incident of the attack on the Native canoes to a story told by Spaniards who were stationed at Friendly Cove at the time. In the Spaniards' story, Natives arrived by canoe at Friendly Cove asking for help against a vessel that had attacked their village, killing seven, wounding others and seizing their otter skins. Their description of the captain matched that of John Gray. The ship's crew and the Natives had been unable to agree on a price for the skins. Recently, John Scofield, in the book *Hail Columbia,* argued that this was probably a second incident that took place at a cove the *Columbia's* men called St. Patrick's, whose location has never been definitively identified. He noted a three-day blank in Boit's log during which this second incident could have occurred. Scofield believed St. Patrick's was probably in Esperanza Inlet. However, this seems unlikely since the *Columbia* travelled south from St. Patrick's to reach Columbia Cove, which is north of Esperanza. It seems more likely that the attack described by the Natives was in fact at or near Columbia Cove as suggested by Howay or somewhere north, perhaps in Quatsino Sound or Klaskino Inlet. Boit's log describes St. Patrick's Harbour as being a "complete snug cove" with a depth of 15 fathoms. When the *Columbia* left St Patrick's, Woody Point (Brooks Peninsula) was in sight. There are coves in both Klaskino and Klaskish Inlets that meet that description.

Battle Bay

Keeping the Ghosts Away

On a quiet morning in 1993, we crossed from the Bunsby Islands to Battle Bay, entering between the Skirmish Islets to starboard and Acous Peninsula to port, then threading our way among rugged black rocks to anchor off a pebble beach. Crescent-shaped Battle Bay stretched before us in a broad jagged curve. We had come to visit the former winter home of the Che:k:tles7et'h', the northernmost band of the Nuu-chah-nulth. The Che:k:tles7et'h' were once a powerful people whose territory reached from Malksope Inlet in the south to the Brooks Peninsula in the north. Their descendants now live with the Ka:'yu:'k't'h' in Houpsitas in Walters Cove.

It took us awhile to find the village site. We knew only that it was to the west of Battle Bay. We hadn't yet learned to recognize a Native village site by looking for a midden or a canoe skid, or even the more obvious way of checking for Native reserves on the chart. We walked along the rocky shore, climbing over rocks and wading through tide pools,

Battle Bay may have been named for battles that took place between the Che:k:tles7et'h' band and Haida from the Queen Charlotte Islands (Haida Gwaii).

We found this wolf carving in the salal. The Nuu-chah-nulth believe that the return of a carving to nature is part of a natural cycle and shouldn't be disturbed.

The corner post of a longhouse can be seen behind this pole.

searching the shore for evidence of past habitation. Just as we were about to turn around and give up, we came to a pocket-sized beach of coarse sand and pebbles—a break in the rocky shore. On a low bank above this beach, a plain wooden pole peeked out from the trees. My discouragement forgotten, I climbed up the bank and into the forest, Steve close behind me. At the top of the bank in the shadow of large spruce trees stood a frontal pole to a longhouse, with weathered carvings of a beaver, a killer whale and a solitary head, all topped by a thatch of salal.

I had seen totem poles in museums, many of them more finely carved than this. But none of them gave me the same thrill as finding this pole in the forest. I was fulfilling a childhood dream. Ever since my mother had read me bedtime stories from Emily Carr's book *Klee Wyck,* I had dreamed of exploring forgotten Native villages. Emily Carr's stories and pictures had stayed with me for years—paintings in both words and oil of fantastic carvings, deserted villages, dark foreboding forests and glimpses of a dying culture.

Behind the pole was an enormous beam angled toward the sky, near which we found five longer beams hidden among the salal. The poles were the remains of an old longhouse, the communal house occupied by a hereditary chief or *ha iih,* his family, his slaves and commoners under his protection. A solitary carving of a wolf lay on the ground. Perhaps it had once sat on top of the single bare pole.

Margaret Sharcott, author of *A Place of Many Winds*, describes visiting this site in the early 1950s with her fisherman husband. Even then the village was deserted, its houses fallen and flat. Among the house beams, the Sharcotts found boards with mill marks and common nails—signs the houses had been built after the arrival of the fur traders. But it must not have been too long after: by the late 1800s missionaries had persuaded most of the Nuu-chah-nulth to desert their traditional communal homes for smaller houses occupied by only one family.

Assuming we had seen everything there was to see at the village site, we left in our dinghy to explore the Battle River. We entered the river between a rocky promontory to the west and a sandbar to the east. The river wound through a marsh and past tall cedars and spruce until it came to a small pool formed by a log jam. Steve stopped the engine and we drifted, listening to birdcalls and enjoying the peace of a sunny afternoon.

As we turned for the downstream journey, I leaned over the side and looked into the water. In the shadowy depths, I could see a long thin shape hovering beneath us, maintaining its position with slow deliberate movement of body and tail. A distinctive snout and rows of bumps down its sides identified it as a sturgeon. I hung on to a branch to keep in place and we stayed quiet, watching this graceful sinuous fish for several minutes. Then I let go of the branch and we drifted downstream and back to Battle Bay and *Osprey*.

According to Margaret Sharcott, one explanation for the name Battle Bay attributes it to a battle with the Haida from the Queen Charlottes. The Haida came from the north in enormous dugout canoes that carried as many as 90 warriors each. Hugging the shore among the rocks to remain undetected they swooped down with battle cries upon the Che:k:tles7et'h'. Women, children and elders hid among the rocks and trees of the Skirmish Islands. Few Che:k:tles7et'h' who did not hide survived the battle with the ferocious Haida.

In 1999 we followed the path of the Haida war canoes into Battle Bay, sailing south from the Queen Charlotte Islands and down the west coast of Vancouver Island. On a calm sunny day, we rounded Brooks Peninsula, passing the O'Leary Islets with their herd of sea lions and approaching Acous Peninsula from Ououkinsh Inlet. When we entered the bay, we saw that another boat was

The totem pole fell between 1993, when we first visited, and 1999.

ahead of us, anchored close to shore. When I looked out over the Skirmish Islets toward the Bunsby Islands and the mountains beyond, I felt as if I had arrived home. Even the other boat was a welcome sight. What I saw here was as beautiful as anything we had seen in the Inside Passage and the Charlottes. Only the massive clear-cuts in the distant hills marred its beauty.

We returned to the small beach where we had found the frontal pole six years earlier, locating it by the single bare pole among the trees. As we stepped out of the dinghy onto the smooth beach, Steve pointed out two lines of rocks on either side of us. We had landed on an ancient canoe skid, a rock-free channel created by the Nuu-chah-nulth by pushing rocks to either side. In the forest, we found the frontal pole on its back, cracked and broken. We could tell it had fallen only recently because it was still free of blackberries and salal. A short distance away the wolf lurked in the undergrowth, its nostrils flared and its teeth bared against a shaft of sunlight filtering through the trees. Already covered in moss and lichens, in a few years it would be hidden forever.

We had spent the last month visiting abandoned Haida villages. The Haida watchmen who guarded them had taught us well. Among the tall spruce we identified four longhouses in addition to the one we had found before. The decaying humps of roof beams and the depressions for excavated living areas gave them away. Near one of these houses we found a carved figure lying on its face while huckleberries and spruce grew from its back. Deep indentations carved into the wood hinted at a powerful figure, perhaps a bear.

We left the beach and motored out to the islets off Acous Peninsula, winding through rocks and around islets until I was no longer sure where we were. A small rocky island surrounded by jagged black rocks looked like an intriguing place to explore so we beached the dinghy. While I poked around the beach, taking pictures of the Bunsby Islands framed by black rocks, Steve explored the interior. I was surprised when I heard Steve yell, "There's a boat in here." I found him standing in the woods next to a white fibreglass runabout, complete with Mercury outboard, a fishing pole and empty pop cans rolling on the floor.

At first, we thought the boat had been abandoned and had drifted ashore, but then I walked around it and saw a grave covered by loose gravel and marked with a wooden sign. We had stumbled on the modern equivalent of a burial canoe. The Nuu-chah-nulth buried the dead's prized possessions with them. In the 19th century they decorated their graves with sewing machines and other valuable personal belongings. This boat and its fishing gear had been someone's prized possessions. A few feet away two skulls, barely visible beneath a layer of moss, watched over the gravesite from atop a more traditional burial canoe. I took pictures, knowing I could never use them; the Nuu-chah-nulth held their gravesites to be sacred and I would not want to disrespect that sacredness. If we had known this was a gravesite and had asked permission to come here, it would have been denied.

On the back of the island we found an ancient spruce tree hung with long tendrils of moss swinging lightly in the breeze. The island was from another era, an Emily Carr sketch in real life. But no shiver went up my back. This was no haunted island, just a small, green jewel of an island surrounded by dramatic black rocks and blue sea.

That evening while *Osprey* rocked gently in the low swell, we watched the moon rise over the land, a silver streak reflecting in the dark water below. I thought about our summer, a rare trip beyond our normal cruising ground. In the Queen Charlotte Islands we had travelled with ghosts: Haida warriors paddled past us in ghostly canoes; long-dead prospectors laden with equipment walked ahead of us on old mining trails; and ghostly fishing fleets moored at docks long gone. A land that had once supported 10,000 people of the Haida nation was now empty. In the park where officials limit the number of visitors at any one time to preserve the ecology and cultural sites, we had longed to see another boat to break the silence.

Here in Battle Bay, in a similar abandoned village, there were no ghosts—only beauty and a sense of peace. The Nuu-chah-nulth feared the dead, believing that they could come back and take the living away with them. To keep the ghosts away they hustled the dead into wooden burial boxes or canoes as soon as they died, removing them from their houses through holes in the side walls created especially for this purpose, then closing them back up immediately. They believed that by taking the dead through the side of the house instead of a door, they discouraged the dead's return.

Perhaps the Che:k:tles7et'h' had kept away the ghosts with these precautions. Or perhaps the other boat in the anchorage and the knowledge that the town of Walters Cove was just around the corner chased away the ghosts for me. The west coast of Vancouver Island is a living, working, changing community of people—of Nuu-chah-nulth, fishermen, oyster farmers, artists, loggers, storekeepers and maamałni like us: a place whose interest for us is not just nature and history, but the future.

The next morning we raised our anchor under gathering clouds and left Battle Bay, heading south toward civilization.

The Battle Bay area provides ample beaches and islands for beachcoming. This island is off the Acous Peninsula.

The Voyage Home

This was downwind sailing as it should be: the course holding steady; the autopilot doing the steering; the sun warming our backs; the only sound the swish and gurgle of water running by the hull. If only we could see where we were going. We were headed for a small cove entered through a narrow channel between Wolf Island and Lamb Island. It would be our last gunkhole of the trip: we might as well do it in style.

Sometime close to the end of the northbound leg of each of our voyages, an unbidden thought of my vegetable garden surprises me. I wonder if the housesitter remembered to water the tomatoes or if the cucumbers are still growing. Later I think of a report on my desk at work. Then I know the end of our voyage is near. If it is August, Steve or I will comment on how the sun sets earlier each evening or one of us will notice that the wind blows more frequently from the southeast. We pay more attention to the weather radio.

Still, we are reluctant to break the rhythm of our cruising: the pattern of mornings in quiet coves, afternoons under sail, evenings spent sitting in the cockpit and watching the dusk deepen around us. We postpone our return as long as we can, plotting our itinerary on paper and counting the days. "Three days from Bamfield to home," we tell each other. "We have to leave Bamfield on Friday. So we should leave Nuchatlitz on Tuesday, Wednesday at the latest." Or, "Just one more day, then we'll have to head south."

We plan our trip home to travel as far as possible each day, putting miles behind us in the open ocean. We'll sail from Checleset Bay to Nuchatlitz in a day, then Nuchatlitz to Hot Springs in another and finally Hot Springs to Barkley Sound—all distances we might have taken as much as a week to travel going north. We assume we'll have the northwesterlies behind us, but plan an extra day or two in our trip just in case.

Rugged Point to Nuchatlitz

Still to Windward

When I saw the anchor disappear into the murky water of Nuchatlitz harbour, my knees suddenly went weak. I sat down on the hatch cover in the rain, turning away from Steve so he couldn't see my tears—tears of fatigue and relief. There had been times that afternoon that I wasn't sure we would make it.

In the anchorage behind Rugged Point that morning the weather hadn't seemed that bad. A light mist fell and a light southeasterly ruffled the water. The weather report predicted southeast gales, but later in the day. We were behind schedule on our trip south and needed to move on. Plus, if we didn't leave that day, we wouldn't have time to spend with our friends in Nuchatlitz.

We planned to sail south through Clear Passage, where the barrier islands would protect us from the worst of the seas. But once we cleared Rugged Point, we could barely see Grogan Rock at Clear Passage's north entrance, and the wind blew stronger than we expected. We were afraid the southeasterlies would break across the southern entrance, so, instead of staying in the semi-protected nearshore waters, we headed out to sea; it might be rougher out there, but it would be safer.

Sailing south against the wind on a cloudy day. We learned the hard way that we couldn't always count on northwest winds for our trip home.

The mist turned to rain; it came down in a cold relentless downpour that made me think of November in Seattle. The wind rose and we shortened sail, first taking a reef in the main, then changing the 120 jib for the self-tender. Shortly after noon, we put in a second reef. I stood at the wheel while Steve handled the mainsail, rain seeping down my collar and spray flying over the dodger into my face. I could just barely see through the salt spray on my glasses.

As the day wore on and *Osprey* tacked back and forth, first heading out to sea, then back toward the rocks, then out to sea again, I felt as if we would never get there. The longer the wind blew, the higher the waves became. *Osprey* would plunge into a trough, only to rise a few seconds later on a crest. Even on the crests, we could see very little; the land had become a grey featureless mass, barely visible through the rain. The wind howled through the rigging and the boat heeled in the wind, rolling with the swells and jerking as waves crashed against the bow. Every now and then the bell on the bulkhead in the cabin would let out a loud "clang," as the boat's motion sent the clapper swinging.

The author on a stormy day. As August wears on, we wear our foul weather gear more often. *Photo: Steve Hulsizer*

I wanted to complain, but to whom? It wasn't fair: this was supposed to be summer. And we were supposed to be sailing downwind, not struggling to windward.

Every half-hour I went below to plot our position while Steve stayed at the wheel. I was glad to escape the rain. Each time I checked on the cat who was curled in a tight ball on his bunk above the quarter berth. Once or twice he gave a plaintive mew that made me feel guilty. I knew he would so much rather be at home on the front porch, but then at that moment, so would I.

As I plotted the course on the chart, I was reassured. A steady line of triangles zig-zagged south on the chart. I listened to the wind and the sound of the boat rushing through the water. I would rather have been just about anywhere else, but I made a resolution not to complain, not even to myself. I looked at the anemometer—42 knots—and made another resolution: I wouldn't look again. What was the point? When a few minutes later Steve called down and asked, "What's the wind speed?" I replied. "I don't know. I stopped looking at it when it passed 42." He didn't object.

As we approached Gillam Channel at the entrance to Esperanza Inlet, I stayed below to plot our course. We had to pass Low Rock and Middle Reef before we could enter the channel. From up on deck all we could see were waves; we couldn't see the buoys marking the entrance. But down below on the radar, they showed clearly.

As we turned into Gillam Channel, the wind came from behind, and *Osprey* surged ahead, almost surfing on the swells rolling into the channel. To starboard, breakers crashed on Blind Reef. I could see its black mussel-covered surface alternately bared by the waves and covered with white foam. Amazingly, several small recreational fishboats bobbed in the waves not far from the reef. We sailed past the Nuchatlitz light and rounded Rosa Island to drop our sails in its lee before motoring through the channel. It was the only time we have ever motored through the channel instead of sailing when there was wind. In the anchorage the rain still fell, but the wind was down and the waves were gone. The trip hadn't been the downwind ride we had hoped for, but we had made it nevertheless.

Catala Island to Hot Springs Cove

Downwind at Last

"Be careful what you wish for—you just might get it" would have been good advice for us in 1984, the first year we sailed north of Clayoquot Sound in *Velella*. The northwesterlies blew strong that year and we struggled to get north against them, postponing the open ocean passage around Estevan Point until the winds moderated and then spending more time than we had planned in the protected waters of Nootka Sound and Esperanza Inlet. "Let's just hope the wind doesn't change direction," we told each other. "If it does, we'll never get home on time."

The wind not only stayed from the north, it grew in force as the days went by until "gale warnings" became the most commonly repeated term on Tofino Coast Guard Radio. When we finally reached our northernmost destination, Catala Island at the entrance to Esperanza Inlet, we dallied some more. We even made one false start south, only to turn back when our dinghy swamped. The night before we finally left, we shared an anchorage with a fleet of salmon trollers. They liked the wind even less than we did because it was keeping them from fishing. That they were staying at anchor when we were planning on sailing made me nervous.

Despite its name, Rolling Roadstead behind Catala Island can be a peaceful anchorage.

The morning we left, the weather radio still predicted gales but we couldn't wait any longer: we had to start home or risk arriving late to our jobs. I listened to the weather radio with dread and thought about the day ahead. I wished we had left three days earlier; I wished we hadn't come so far north; I even wished we had gone to the San Juan Islands where the wind doesn't blow so hard. Our route would take us around Estevan Point, whose low, featureless land mass, treacherous rocks and shallow water extending far out to sea make it one of the most dangerous areas on the coast.

Earlier that year, before leaving Seattle for the west coast of Vancouver Island, we had carefully gone over our charts to make sure we had one for every sound and inlet we planned to visit. We had checked off Barkley Sound, Clayoquot Sound, Nootka Sound and Esperanza Inlet. We thought we were covered and, technically, we were; we had a chart for every mile of coast. But what we hadn't realized until we left Clayoquot Sound was that we had no single chart showing the entire passage around Hesquiat Peninsula and Estevan Point, which meant we couldn't draw a line from our departure point to a safe distance off the point. (This was in the days before inexpensive loran and GPS.) For that we needed the ocean chart in addition to the inlet charts. The lack of an ocean chart had merely been an annoyance sailing north; sailing south, the lack was to be a serious danger. But we laid our course out on the several charts the night before as best we could, and we knew that the most important thing was to stay offshore from Estevan Point. Visibility was good, the sky was clear—we figured we would be okay.

At first, the trip didn't seem too bad: the sun shone and the seas were blue, if a bit rough. We sailed down the coast of Nootka Island with views of jagged mountains in the distance. Ahead, we could see a smudge on the horizon—the long low land of Hesquiat Peninsula.

We passed Bajo Reef at seven knots, *Velella* surging ahead in the waves, sailing wing-on-wing. The up-and-down motion of the downwind run made my stomach queasy, so I stayed out on deck where I could see the horizon. As the morning wore on, the wind increased and the seas grew until *Velella* seemed to be almost flying from one wave to another, making a steady seven to eight knots, climbing a wave, then plunging down its far side in a surge of hissing, boiling white water. The wind vane could no longer steer the boat and Steve took over the tiller. "At this rate, we'll be there in no time," said Steve. I just hung on to the dodger and prayed he was right.

Around noon we took a second reef in the main, hoping to quiet the boat's motion. Now all of Steve's energies were focussed on keeping *Velella* sailing downwind without broaching. An hour later we took the main down altogether, leaving only the jib up. Our speed kept steady at seven to eight knots.

Up, up, up we would climb, until we crested the wave and could see for miles across the heaving seas, then down, down, down the other side into the troughs where water surrounded us. The waves looked 30 feet high, but I suppose they must have been no more than 12 feet high, but were very steep. The boat moved constantly, back and forth, up and down, so that we had to hang on tightly to anything we could find just to move from one side of the boat to the other. Going below to use the head or to make lunch was a nightmare of motion and sound. Every few minutes the wind caught the jib on the wrong side and the

Shallow water off Estevan Point can create mountainous seas.

sail collapsed in a whoosh, then snapped with a bang as the wind filled it again. I thought it would surely tear.

We were almost to Estevan Point when I looked astern and saw a mountainous wave rearing above us. *Velella*'s stern rose and for a minute I thought we would be okay, that we would just surf down the other side. But then a gust hit the sail, the boat broached and a second wave hit full force. *Velella* heeled and a surge of water swept across the cockpit in an angry roaring mass. I had to hold on to the dodger to keep from getting swept overboard.

Before I realized what had happened *Velella* righted, shuddered and surged ahead. In the cockpit water gurgled and swirled down the oversized drains. I leaned over and looked into the cabin. Books, charts and miscellaneous gear we thought we had stowed away so well floated in the cabin on several inches of water.

"Don't just sit there," Steve yelled. "Pump, goddamn it, pump!"

Steve's yell woke me from my shock and I grabbed the pump handle from its holder, stuck it in the pump and started working it up and down, frantically moving it as fast as I could. Steve, meanwhile, was hanging on to the tiller, doing his best to keep *Velella* steering downwind with the waves behind. I pumped until my arm ached, then pumped some more. The automatic bilge pump was working too, but it couldn't pump fast enough. We couldn't risk taking another wave when we already had so much water on board; more water would drown the engine or, worse, affect our sailing ability. We were in danger of swamping and being swept ashore on the rocks. Finally, I saw that the floorboards were dry and I let the automatic bilge pump finish. When I put the handle away, I realized my seasickness was gone—chased away by adrenalin.

To our port, the stately white tower of Estevan light, the tallest lighthouse on the West Coast, stood out against the dark green of the forest. I could see its distinctive skeleton-like supports so clearly that I knew we had sailed too close to Estevan's treacherous shores. In the shallow waters around the point the seas had grown steeper and more confused.

Velella still raced along, climbing the waves and surfing down their backsides. But the farther we went the lower the waves became until finally we were in the lee of Matlahaw Point in almost quiet water. Far ahead I could see the small white light at the entrance to Hot Springs Cove. The seas began to build again as we left Matlahaw's lee, but now they were just ocean waves, not the mountains we had seen off Estevan. As we passed Barney Rocks and turned into the cove I gave a sigh of relief. It was five o'clock, so there was still time to walk to the Hot Springs that evening. We had been sailing almost 10 hours and I was exhausted. We had been in greater danger than anytime in our sailing history, including the ocean crossings to and from Hawaii. Salt matted my hair and stung my eyes. A soak in the hot springs had never sounded so good.

Bamfield to Becher Bay

The Last Gunkhole

The fog crept into the inlet as I was putting away the inflatable kayak after dinner. I had postponed this task until the last possible minute. I didn't want to say goodbye to our summer and putting away the kayak seemed so final. I had just unscrewed the black plastic valves and was rolling up the kayak to squeeze the air out when I looked up at the hillside above the town of West Bamfield and saw smoke curling among

A low, thick fog bank blocked our vision ahead but not the sun above.

the treetops. I stopped to watch it for a minute, wondering where it was coming from. Then I saw it creep down the hillside, enveloping the trees. Not smoke—fog. Soon it reached the rooftops of the houses along the shore. By the time I had heaved the kayak into the cockpit seat locker, the fog was streaming across the water.

My heart sank as I saw the shore disappear from sight. We had a long trip ahead of us the next day, 80 miles from Bamfield to Becher Bay at the east end of the Strait of Juan de Fuca. I knew from experience that the fog would stay all night and could last all day in the Strait. It was August after all, the month West Coasters call "Fogust." Although we had radar, a depth sounder, GPS, a foghorn and a VHF radio, and would be out of the shipping channel all the way, the prospect of not being able to see where we were going made me feel uneasy.

We left at seven o'clock the next morning, the fog still so thick we could see only the dim outlines of docks along the shore. There was not a breath of wind and what little we could see of the sea surface was glassy smooth.

The only thing we saw as we were motoring out Trevor Passage was the whistle buoy off Seapool Rocks—and we caught only a glimpse of that before it, too, disappeared behind us in the fog. I followed our progress on the chart—past Execution Rock to port and Helby, Diana and Edward King Islands to starboard. I felt cheated that I couldn't catch one more glimpse of Barkley Sound before leaving.

While Steve watched the radar below, I stayed at the wheel. The fog misted my glasses and covered my face with a damp film as I stared intently into the grey. It's hard to focus in the fog because there is nothing to focus on, so I was never sure whether the waves up ahead were a few yards or a quarter of a mile away.

As we neared the mouth of the inlet, I felt the rise and fall of the ocean swells and heard the deep diaphone of Cape Beale lighthouse, then the occasional short blasts of sport fishing boats among the rocks. We continued, turning southeast when our GPS told us we were out far enough, setting course for the mouth of the Strait of Juan de Fuca.

"Keep your eye out for two boats to starboard," Steve called to me from his position on the radar. A minute later the pale outlines of two catamaran sailboats suddenly emerged from the fog, then just as quickly disappeared again as they passed us. I noticed that neither of them had radar. By 9:30 a.m. we were passing Pachena Point. I heard the mournful call of the horn, but could only imagine the white lighthouse and keeper's houses with their red roofs. The two catamarans were still ahead, two green glowing marks on the radar.

We had turned on our foghorn as we left Bamfield Inlet and our Whistleminder™, an electronic timer, sounded the horn every two minutes. At first I had wondered how I would stand its incessant clamour. But now I stopped and wondered, "Is the foghorn working?" I had gotten so used to hearing it every two minutes that I had screened it out.

Somewhere past Pachena Point a light headwind started rippling the water—not enough to sail but enough to lower the temperature by several degrees. The fog, the wind, the cold, the gloom all depressed me. I wanted to go below and curl up on the bunk and read a good book, but instead I had to keep staring into nothing.

In fog like this we plot our position on the chart with the GPS every 15 minutes, drawing little triangles to show our progress. The triangles made our journey seem real. If I couldn't have seen them marching down the chart, I wouldn't have known we had left Barkley Sound.

In the late morning, we skirted Swiftsure Bank. I looked at the chart and saw the words, "Fishing Vessels—Navire en train de pecheur." We had seen salmon seiners working this area on less foggy trips and I remembered another foggy trip we made— without radar. We had come upon a seiner unexpectedly, its grey aluminum hull rearing out of the fog just a short distance away then disappearing almost immediately like a ghost boat come to haunt us. Now with radar we could stay far enough away from other boats that all we ever saw of them was green dots on the radar screen.

The radar now showed a fast-moving boat heading north—right for one of the two catamarans. I heard Steve calling on channel 16. "To the catamaran off Vancouver Island, catamaran off Vancouver Island—this is Osprey" he called, then repeated his call more urgently. No answer.

We were helpless to do anything as one catamaran and the fast-moving boat approached each other in the fog. Steve saw the two green dots almost merge, then separate quickly as the catamaran veered to starboard. How close they came, we don't really know, but it must have been almost paint-scraping.

I went below to make lunch. While I chopped onion and grated ginger for Top Ramen, the boat rolled in the swell and I had to brace myself against the counter as I worked. The sound of the horn at Carmanah Point told me we were approaching the mouth of the Strait.

Around 1:00 p.m. the headwind died and the westerlies began to fill in from behind. We raised the main and 120 jib and turned off the engine. In the silence I heard the cry of a seagull and the slap of water against the hull. I realized how much the thrum-thrum-thrum of the engine had been irritating me. Steve punched the button on the Whistleminder™ labelled "Fog, under sail." Now instead of one long blast every two minutes we heard one long and two short.

The wind rose as the afternoon wore on until soon we were flying along at seven knots, the surface of the water dark with ripples. Now we could see blue sky above us and feel the sun on our faces. My mood lightened as I anticipated the fog clearing soon. But although the sky above was clear, the fog ahead and to the sides was as thick as ever. We raced on, still seeing nothing. Slowly it dawned on me that we were sailing through a low, thick fog bank that blocked our vision ahead but not the sun above. It was a strange feeling, hurtling into nothing in full sunlight. Port San Juan was now behind us although we never saw its wide mouth, cut like a notch into the straight line of Vancouver Island.

By 4:00 p.m. the anemometer registered 30 knots of wind, too much for our full main and 120 jib combination. The afternoon westerlies had settled in. It might be cold and foggy in the Strait, but inland the August sun heated up the land, creating a low-pressure system that wind from the ocean raced in to fill.

We took two reefs in the mainsail but left the 120 jib up. The wind had shifted and we needed to jibe to keep on course. I turned the wheel to port while Steve pulled in the mainsheet to bring the main over. But as the boom started to swing, the topping lift (the line that hangs down from the top of the mast to the back of the boom and keeps the boom from crashing into the cockpit when we let the mainsail down) caught behind the port spreader. We put the boat back on the starboard tack and tried everything we could think of to get the line free—letting the sail all the way out, loosening the topping lift further, heading into the wind—but nothing could dislodge it. Finally, Steve took out his jackknife and cut it. We would have to be careful letting the main down but other than that, the loss of the topping lift was really not a problem; it wasn't essential gear for sailing.

The lighthouse on Sheringham Point stands out in the evening light.

By 5:00 p.m. we were far enough in the Strait that the ocean swells had shrunk to low rolling waves. With two reefs in the main and the 120 jib on the other side, *Osprey* forged ahead, rolling over the waves in a steady surge. This was downwind sailing as it should be: the course holding steady; the autopilot doing the steering; the sun warming our backs; the only sound the swish and gurgle of water running by the hull. If only we could see where we were going. The chart told me we were passing Sheringham Point and I remembered coming by here one year on a clear day and thinking how civilized the light looked, surrounded by neatly clipped lawns.

With the boat sailing smoothly, I had time to think back on our trip. I remembered an ad for the magazine *Good Old Boat*: "You are where you've been," it said. I suppose it referred to a boat. And certainly, *Osprey* shows the effects of all of our trips to the west coast of Vancouver Island, even with all the paint and new sails we seem to be constantly buying for it. But it could refer to people as well. I looked at Steve's hair, turned almost blond from the sun, and knew mine was the same. And although we both looked tanned, we had "West Coast tans": hands and faces tanned, the rest of us white. I thought of the people we know on the coast. If I have acquired only some of their characteristics, I would be pleased. They are self-reliant, optimistic, hardy and friendly toward strangers. I reflected that we had certainly learned to be self-reliant: we had to be to sail where there were few services to help us if our boat broke down. And it did seem to carry through to life at home, where we are always surprised to hear our neighbours talk of hiring someone to finish a floor or fix the plumbing. We just do it ourselves. And as for optimism, the steps ordinary people took to stop clear-cutting on Vancouver Island give me hope for Puget Sound.

It certainly takes optimism to keep on sailing through the fog. At six o'clock, just as I had resigned myself to entering Becher Bay in the fog, we sailed into clear air. One moment we couldn't see a thing; the next we were looking at the distant pale peaks of the Olympic Mountains to starboard and the green slopes of Vancouver Island to port. Ahead, two white triangles of sail stood out against the green land: the two catamarans. Still we raced on. At 7:00 p.m. we passed the entrance to Sooke where the catamarans turned off. Sooke Inlet is the most popular anchorage for boats returning from Barkley Sound, perhaps because of its public dock and pub. But after going in there a couple of times we got impatient at the time it took to wind our way past the sandspit to town. Then we looked at the chart and noticed Becher Bay, a semi-protected bay just five miles farther. We stopped at Becher Bay the next year and discovered that because the anchorage was so close to open water, it didn't take much longer to get there than to Sooke Inlet.

Beechey Head at the bay's west entrance was just ahead of us now, its high rounded hills sloping down to the sea. As we rounded Beechey Head, we turned *Osprey* onto a broad reach, the fastest point of sail for a boat of its type.

"Gusts!" I said to Steve, pointing ahead at dark streaks on the water. The wind snatched the word out of my mouth as the first gust hit and the boat heeled so far to starboard that water poured into the cockpit. The wind coming over Beechey Head from Sooke Basin to the north was falling off the cliffs like a willywaw and hitting the boat from above.

Becher Bay. Arbutus trees and dry grass told us we had left the rain-forest of Barkley Sound for the rain shadow of lower Vancouver Island.

"Let the sails out!" yelled Steve. I reached for the jib sheet and let it loose from the winch as he freed the mainsheet from its cam cleat. Now the sails flapped furiously.

"Get the chart," Steve ordered. "I need to see what the entrance looks like again." I climbed down the ladder, holding tight to the handrails as the boat heeled. We were sailing so fast and heeling so hard, the boat felt as if it were being dragged along on its side. I glanced at the anemometer above the chart table—37 knots of wind—then looked at the chart. We were headed for a small cove entered through a narrow channel between Wolf Island and Lamb Island. The channel was deep and free of rocks right up to the shore. I couldn't

The sailboat *Perpetua* anchored behind Wolf and Lamb Islands in Becher Bay.

think of any reason not to sail in, even in this wind. It would be our last gunkhole of the trip: we might as well do it in style.

The wind eased as we got farther into the bay. Soon we were skimming along at eight knots, heading for the narrow channel. As we entered the channel, Wolf Island blocked the wind. *Osprey* stood up straight and glided through on its momentum. Behind the island waited a shallow little cove with a shore of arbutus trees and patches of golden grass. The rainforest of Barkley Sound had given way to the rain shadow of lower Vancouver Island. We anchored next to a white wooden ketch. From there we could see out the Strait, where the sky was turning pink in the sunset. I felt a deep sense of relief not to be sailing in the fog anymore, combined with sorrow that this year's trip was almost over. We had been under way for over 12 hours and it was wonderful to be anchored in a snug and beautiful bay.

In the morning I went out on deck to sponge the dew off the dodger windows. Sunlight streamed into the cove, bouncing off the quiet water and filling the air with light. I saw that life jackets aired on the lifelines of the ketch next to us and a green awning protected its cockpit. The boat's name, *Perpetua*, made me think of perpetual summer.

A few minutes later a man came out on *Perpetua*'s deck and climbed into a small white lapstrake dinghy. He rowed over to talk to me.

"Where did you come from?" he asked. "Barkley Sound," I answered. "We got as far north as Esperanza Inlet this year. Now we're heading home to Seattle. Where are you heading?"

He looked over at *Perpetua* glowing in the sun and framed by red-barked arbutus trees. "I think we'll stay here for awhile," he told me.

"I wish we could too," I said. "But we'll be back next year."

Sources

Chapter One: The Voyage Out

Arima, Eugene. "Thoughts on the Nuu-chah-nulth Canoe." *Nuu-chah-nulth Voices, Histories, Objects and Journeys.* Alan L. Hoover, ed. Victoria: Royal British Columbia Museum, 2000.

Beals, Herbert K. *Juan Pérez on the Northwest Coast. Six Documents of his Expedition in 1774.* Portland: Oregon Historical Society Press, 1989.

Cook, James and James King. *Captain Cook's third and last voyage to the Pacific Ocean: in the Years 1776, 1777, 1778, 1779 and 1780.* London: n.p., 1785?

Drucker, Philip. *Indians of the Northwest Coast.* Garden City, NY: Natural History Press, 1963.

Fish, Harriett. *Tracks, Trails, and Tales in Clallam County, State of Washington.* Port Angeles, WA: privately published, 1983.

Graham, Donald. *Keepers of the Light: A History of British Columbia's Lighthouses and their Keepers.* Madeira Park, BC: Harbour Publishing, 1985.

Hill, Beth. *The Remarkable World of Frances Barkley: 1769-1845.* Sidney, BC: Gray's Publishing, 1978.

Marshall, Don B. *Who Discovered the Straits of Juan de Fuca? The Strange Tale of Apostolos Valerianos.* N.p.: Ye Galleon Press, 1991.

Meany, Edmond S. (1907). *Vancouver's Discovery of Puget Sound; portraits and biographies of the men honored in the naming of geographic features of northwestern America.* Portland, Oregon: Binfords and Mort, 1957.

Nicholson, George. *Vancouver Island's West Coast, 1762–1962.* Victoria, BC: n.p., 1965.

Sproat, Gilbert Malcolm. "Boatmanship." *Indians of the North Pacific Coast.* Tom McFeat, ed. Seattle: University of Washington Press. 1967.

Sullivan, Robert. *A Whale Hunt.* New York: Scribner, 2000.

Swan, James Gilchrist. *The Indians of Cape Flattery, at the entrance to the Strait of Juan de Fuca, Washington Territory.* Washington DC: Smithsonian Institution, 1870.

Wagner, Henry Raup. *Spanish Explorations in the Strait of Juan de Fuca.* Santa Ana, CA: Fine Arts Press, 1933.

Walbran, Captain John T. *British Columbia Coast Names: Their Origin and History.* Vancouver: Douglas & McIntyre, 1971. Originally published by the Government Printing Bureau, Ottawa, 1909.

Chapter Two: Barkley Sound

Note on the sources for Effingham Island: There are two versions of Melvin Swartout's visit to Village Island: the version written by Swartout himself under the pseudonym Charles Haicks, and an account by Alfred Carmichael, a friend of the Swartouts who accompanied them to the island. One of the peculiarities of these two versions is that in writing his fictionalized account, Swartout chose to write it speaking as Alfred Carmichael, to whom he gave the fictional name of Charles Haicks.

Carmichael, Alfred. *To Village Island and Back.* Victoria: BC Provincial Archives. MS- 2305. N.d.

Efrat, Barbara S. and W.J. Langlos. "Contemporary Accounts of Nootkan Culture." *Nutka: The History and Survival of Nootkan Culture.* Sound Heritage. Volume VII, Number 2, 1978.

Golla, Susan. "Legendary History of the Tseshaht: A Working Translation." *Nuu-chah-nulth Voices, Histories, Objects, and Journeys.* Alan L. Hoover, ed. Victoria: Royal British Columbia Museum, 2000.

Haicks, Charles. (Pseudonym). *On the West Coast of Vancouver Island.* Unpublished manuscript by Melvin Swartout. Victoria: BC Provincial Archives. N.d.

Hedgpeth, Joel ed. *The Outer Shores.* Eureka, CA: Mad River Press, 1978.

Hill, Beth. *The Remarkable World of Frances Barkley: 1769-1845.* Sidney, BC: Gray's Publishing, 1978.

McMillan, Alan D. *Since the Time of the Transformers: The Ancient Heritage of the Nuu-chah-nulth, Ditidaht, and Makah*. Vancouver: UBC Press, 1999.

Meares, John. *Voyages made in the years 1788 and 1789 from China to the N.W. coast of America....* London: n.p.: 1791.

Ricketts, Edward F. and Jack Calvin. *Between Pacific Tides*. Revised by Joel Hedgpeth. Berkeley: Standford University Press, 1960.

Scott, R. Bruce. *Barkley Sound: A History of the Pacific Rim National Park area*. Victoria: n.p., 1972.

Scott, R. Bruce. *Bamfield Years: Recollections*. Victoria: Sono Nis Press, 1986.

Thomson, Richard E. *Oceanography of the British Columbia Coast*. Canadian Special Publication of Fisheries and Aquatic Sciences 56. Ottawa: Department of Fisheries and Oceans, 1981.

Walbank, Jean Buck. *Benson Island*. Mission, BC: Digital Communications, Inc., 1991.

Chapter Three: Clayoquot Sound, Southeastern Portion

Ecotrust Canada. *Seeing the Ocean Through the Trees: A conservation-based Development Strategy for Clayoquot Sound*. Vancouer, BC: Ecotrust Canada, 1997.

George, Paul and Adrian Dorst. *Meares Island: Protecting a Natural Paradise*. Tofino, BC: Friends of Clayoquot Sound and Western Canada Wilderness Committee, 1985.

Gibson, Kenneth. "My discovery of historical 'Fort Defiance', winter quarters of Captain Robert Gray, 1791–1792." BC Archives MS-2212, 1985.

Guppy, Anthony. *The Tofino Kid: From India to this Wild West Coast*. Nanaimo, BC: Priority Printing, Ltd., 2000.

Guppy, Walter. *Clayoquot Soundings: A history of Clayoquot Sound, 1880s–1980s*. Tofino, BC: Grassroots Publication, 1997.

Hayes, Edmund. "Gray's Adventure Cove." *Oregon Historical Society Quarterly* Vol. 68, 1967.

Howay, Frederic. *Voyages of the Columbia to the Northwest Coast, 1787–1790 and 1790–1793*. Oregon Historical Society Press in Co-operation with the Massachusetts Historical Society, 1990. Reprint of Massachusetts Historical Society edition, 1941.

Magnusson, Warren and Karena Shaw, eds. *A Political Space: Reading the Global Through Clayoqout Sound*. Minneapolis: University of Minnesota Press, 2003.

Morison, Samuel Eliot. "Columbia's Winter Quarter of 1791–1792 Located." *Oregon Historical Quarterly* Vol. 39, no.1, 1938.

Chapter Four: Clayoquot Sound, Northwestern Portion

BC Salmon Marketing Council website. 2002. http://www.bcsalmon.ca/

Cameron, Anne. *Daughters of Copper Woman*. Madeira Park: Harbour Publishing, 1981.

George, Chief Earl Maquinna. *Living on the Edge: Nuu-chah-nulth History from an Ahousaht Chief's Perspective*. Winlaw, BC: Sono Nis Press, 2003.

Glavin, Terry. *Dead Reckoning: Confronting the Crisis in Pacific Fisheries*. Greystone Books, 1996.

Glavin, Terry. *The Last Great Sea: A Voyage Through the Human and Natural History of the North Pacific Ocean*. Vancovuer/Toronto: Greystone Books, Douglas and McIntyre Publishing Group, 2000.

Guppy, Walter. *Clayoquot Soundings. A History of Clayoquot Sound, 1880s–1980s*. Tofino, BC: Grassroots Publication, 1997.

Lichatowich, Jim. *Salmon Without Rivers: A History of the Pacific Salmon Crisis*. Washington, D.C.: Island Press, 1999.

Nicholson, George. *Vancouver Island's West Coast, 1762–1962*. Victoria: n.p. 1965.

Ricketts, Edward F. *Scientists Report on Sardine Supply: Investigator Blames Industry, Nature for Shortage*. *Monterey Peninsula Herald*. 13th Annual Sardine Edition, p. 1,3. April 2, 1948. (available at http://www.geocities.com/Yosemite/Gorge/5604/ed_ricketts1948sardine.htm)

Sam, Stanley M., Sr. *Ahousaht Wild Side Heritage Trail Guidebook.* Vancouver: Western Canada Wilderness Committee, 1997.

Sharcott, Margaret. *Troller's Holiday.* London: Peter Davies, 1957.

The disappearance and return of the Pilchards to Barclay Sound as predicted in 1946 by a Nuu-Chah-Nulth elder. April 10, 1998. http://www.portaec.net/library/ocean/plchards.html

Chapter Six: Nootka Sound

Armstrong, Jane. "Whale 1, scientists 0—Orca Luna's capture and relocation prevented." *Globe and Mail.* June 26th, 2004.

Beals, H.K. *Juan Pérez on the Northwest Coast: Six Documents of this Expedition in 1774.* Portland: Oregon Historical Society Press, 1989.

Cook, James. *Voyages of Discovery.* John Barrow, comp. Academy Chicago Publishers, 1993.

Coyle, Brendan. *War on our Doorsteps: The Unknown Campaign on North America's West Coast.* Surrey, BC: Heritage House, 2002.

Graham, Donald. *Keepers of the Light: A History of British Columbia's Lighthouses and their Keepers.* Madeira Park, BC: Harbour Publishing, 1985.

Howay, Frederic. *Voyages of the* Columbia *to the Northwest Coast, 1787–1790 and 1790–1793.* Oregon Historical Society Press in Cooperation with the Massachusetts Historical Society. 1990. Reprint of Massachusetts Historical Society edition, 1941.

Jewitt, John R. *White Slaves of Maquinna: John R. Jewitt's Narrative of Capture and Confinement at Nootka.* Heritage House, 2000. Based on Jewitt's Narrative, originally published in 1815.

Meany, Edmond S. *Vancouver's Discovery of Puget Sound.* Portland: Binford & Mort, 1957.

Meares, John. *Voyages made in the years 1788 and 1789 from China to the N.W. Coast of America....* London: n.p., 1791.

Mowachaht–Muchalaht First Nations. Yuquot Agenda Paper. In *Nuu-chah-nulth Voices, Histories, Objects, and Journeys.* Edited by Alan L. Hoover. Victoria: Royal British Columbia Museum, 2000.

Nicholson, George. *Vancouver Island's West Coast, 1762–1962.* Victoria: n.p., 1965.

Pethick, Derek. *First Approaches to the Northwest Coast.* University of Washington Press, 1979.

Pethick, Derek. *The Nootka Connection: Europe and the Northwest Coast 1790–1795.* Vancouver: Douglas & MacIntyre, 1980.

Reunite Luna website. http://www.reuniteluna.com

Webster, Peter. "The Contact Period as Recorded by Indian Oral Traditions." Barbara S. Efrat and W.J. Langlois, eds. *Nutka. Captain Cook and the Spanish Explorers on the Coast.* Sound Heritage. Volume VII, Number 1, 1978.

Wiwchar, Dave. Mowachaht/Muchalaht keep Tsu-xiit free. West Coast Vancouver Island Aquatic Management Board. http://www.stcoastaquatic.ca/article_mowachaht_free_Luna0704.htm July 2, 2004.

Chapter Seven: Esperanza Inlet

Gibson, Gordon. *Bull of the Woods: The Gordon Gibson Story.* Vancouver: Douglas & McIntyre, 2000.

Gibson, John Frederic. *A Small and Charming World.* Toronto: William Collins Sons, 1972.

Johnson, Louise. *Not Without Hope.* Matsqui, BC: Maple Lane Publishing, 1992.

Jones, Laurie. *Nootka Sound Explored: A Westcoast History.* Campbell River, BC: Ptarmigan Press, 1991.

Murray, Peter. *The Vagabond Fleet: A Chronicle of the North Pacific Sealing Schooner Trade.* Victoria: Sono Nis Press, 1988.

Paterson, T.W. *British Columbia Ghost Town Series: Vancouver Island.* Langley, BC: Sunfire Publications, 1983.

Sharcott, Margaret. *Troller's Holiday.* London: Peter Davies, Ltd., 1957.

Watmough, Don. *Pacific Yachting's Cruising Guide to British Columbia Vol. IV, West Coast of Vancouver Island, Cape Scott to Sooke including Barkley Sound.* N.p.: MacLean–Hunter, Special Interest Publications. 1984.

Zeballos Privateer. www.zeballos.com\privateer

Chapter Eight: Kyuquot Sound

Douglass, Don. *Exploring Vancouver Island's West Coast.* Bishop, CA: Fine Edge Productions, 1994.

Goddard, Joan. *A Window on Whaling in British Columbia.* Victoria: Jonah Publications, 1997.

Hagelund, William A. *Whalers No More.* Madeira Park, BC: Harbour Publishing, 1986.

Jones, Laurie. *Nootka Sound Explored: A Westcoast History.* Campbell River, BC: Ptarmigan Press, 1991.

Ludvigsen, Rolf and Graham Beard. *West Coast Fossils: A Guide to the Ancient Life of Vancouver Island.* Vancouver: Whitecap Books, 1994.

McMillan, Alan D. *Since the Time of the Transformers: The Ancient Heritage of the Nuu-chah-nulth, Ditidaht, and Makah.* Vancouver: UBC Press, 1999.

Morris, Rob. *Coasters: The Uchuck III, Lady Rose, Frances Barkley and Tyee Princess.* Victoria, BC: Horsday & Schubart, 1993.

Sharcott, Margaret. *Troller's Holiday.* London: P. Daves, 1957.

Chapter Nine: Checleset Bay

Arima, Eugene Y. *The West Coast People: The Nootka of Vancouver Island and Cape Flattery.* Victoria: British Columbia Provincial Museum, 1983.

Black, Martha. *HuupuKwanum Tupaat: Out of the Mist: Treasures of the Nuu-chah-nulth Chiefs.* Victoria: Royal British Columbia Museum, 1999.

Dickens, Charles. *Dombey and Son.* Portsmouth, NH: Mandarin Paperbacks, 1991. Originally published in 1848 in Great Britain.

Drucker, Philip. "The Northern and Central Nootkan Tribes." *Bureau of American Ethnology Bulletin* 144. Washington: Smithsonian, 1951.

Hebda, Richard J. and James C. Haggarty. *Brooks Peninsula, An Ice Age Refugium on Vancouver Island.* Occasional Paper No. 5. Ministry of Environment, Lands and Parks. Victoria: 1997.

Howay, Frederic. *Voyage of the "Columbia" to the Northwest Coast, 1787–1790 and 1790–1793.* Oregon Historical Society in Co-operation with the Massachusetts Historical Society. 1990. Reprint of Massachusetts Historical Society edition, 1941.

Kenyon, Karl W. *The Sea Otter in the Eastern Pacific Ocean.* New York: Dover Publications, 1975.

Koppel, Tom. "Forests of the Sea." *Canadian Geographic.* March 1997. Vol. 117, p.68.

Obee, Bruce. "Sea Otters Return." *Canadian Geographic.* December 1984/January 1985. Vol. 104, Number 6, pp. 40–43.

Scofield, John. *Hail Columbia: Robert Gray, John Kendrick, and the Pacific Fur Trade.* Oregon Historical Society: 1993.

Sharcott, Margaret. *A Place of Many Winds.* Toronto: British Book Service, 1960.

Index